THE MANDARINS OF WESTERN EUROPE

THE MANDARINS OF WESTERN EUROPE

The Political Role of Top Civil Servants

Edited by

MATTEI DOGAN

Centre National de la Recherche Scientifique

Sage Publications

Halsted Press Division
JOHN WILEY & SONS
New York—London—Sydney—Toronto

Distributed by Halsted Press, a Division of
John Wiley & Sons, Inc., New York

Printed in the United States of America

Library of Congress Cataloging in Publication Data
Main entry under title:

The Mandarins of Western Europe.

    1. Government executives—Europe—Addresses, essays, lectures.
I. Dogan, Mattei.
JN94.A69E94   301.5'92'094   75-8734
ISBN 0-470-21749-9

FIRST PRINTING

CONTENTS

Foreword

This volume is published under the sponsorship of the Research Committee on Political Elites of the International Political Science Association.

The Committee's task is twofold: to encourage cross-national comparisons of political elite studies, and to facilitate international exchanges of ideas and discussion of research findings. In addition to the undersigned, the board of the Committee includes Klaus von Beyme (University of Tubingen), Jean Laponce (University of British Columbia), Joseph LaPalombara (Yale University) and Mogens Pedersen (University of Odense).

Political elites is a generic term which covers a very wide range of active participants in political processes: ministers, parliamentarians, party leaders, charismatic figures, top civil servants, military decision makers, union leaders, representatives of major interest groups, political journalists, mass-media specialists, policy experts, local notables, community spokesmen, and campaign coordinators. Analysis is unavoidably complex, given such a great variety. In each political system, career lines differ in distinctive ways which make cross-national comparisons difficult.

As a Research Committee of the International Political Science Association, we are commissioned to give priority to *comparative* analyses of various kinds of political elites. One of the difficulties of comparative analysis is securing agreement among scholars about concepts. Another is stating which evidence is persuasive. A third is to discover what level of analysis must be achieved before meaningful analysis occurs. The best strategy for resolving these difficulties is communication and interaction among scholars, particularly by organizing conferences and sponsoring projects.

We seek to avoid two pitfalls: extremely abstract models and endless description. Our approach is practical and collaborative. It is impractical for each scholar to try to understand the intricacies of the full range of political systems in which he is interested. It is practical to exchange knowledge with colleagues since this saves time and effort, especially when history is accelerating.

Our approach is also collaborative. Our belief is that when a scholar participates in a panel or contributes to a symposium having a clearly defined topic, he is inevitably engaged in the collaborative effort of a team which has a common frame of reference and a set of working hypotheses generally considered worth investigating. In this way, nation-based studies acquire truly comparative dimensions, and parallel investigations do converge!

Mattei Dogan
CNRS

Dwaine Marvick
UCLA

Acknowledgments

I discussed with Alfred Diamant, Indiana University, the framework of this volume and the main hypotheses that, during the first stage of the project, were submitted to some prospective contributors. His friendly help is warmly acknowledged.

Seven of the fifteen contributions to this volume were originally written in French. They were translated into English by Noal Mellott, Research Assistant at the Centre National de la Recherche Scientifique, who has also competently helped in editing the manuscript. Many thanks to him.

—MD

The Political Power of the Western Mandarins: Introduction

MATTEI DOGAN

This volume focuses on civil servants at the highest level in the central public administration, a level where the separation between politics and administration becomes artificial or, better said, where political power and administrative action merge.

These top civil servants, located near political decision making centers, are not numerous. Depending on the size of the country, they number only in the hundreds or perhaps up to a few thousand. Everywhere, they represent less than one percent of total personnel in the public administration. For instance, in England where there are about half a million civil servants, basically the "administrative class," about 2,800 persons, concerns us here. In France, between two and three thousand high civil servants are in charge of "planning, supervizing and controlling positions"[1] at the very top of the state apparatus: the hundred Directors in the ministries, most of the State Counsellors, Treasury Inspectors, Chief Auditors, members of the ministerial cabinets, managers of nationalized enterprises, and planners in economic agencies, to which we must add most of the prefects and a certain number of top military officers and ambassadors.

At the top level, a civil servant must have both political sensitivity and technical skills. He has to weigh the political implications of technico-administrative decisions. However competent he may be in his field, if he is mistaken about the political opportuneness of a given decision, he will finally be considered, from a political point of view, as incompetent. He stands out from other high-level civil servants who perform strictly technical or administrative duties.

According to this definition, an expert or technician who does not participate in decision making processes of a political nature, even if he holds a very

[3]

important position, does not enter into this study. The Dutch engineers responsible for the upkeep of the dikes or the officials in charge of navigation at the port of London do not exercise duties with political overtones.

The top civil servant who plays an important political role has a hybrid personality: half-political, half-administrative. Like Janus the Roman god, he has two faces. He is a kin to the mandarins of old Imperial China.

The Western mandarin, as was his Chinese counterpart, is most often recruited through competition well before he receives an important adminis-trative post. There is nothing surprising about the fact that so many European mandarins have training in law,[2] since a law or rule is necessary in order to formulate a political decision in administrative terms. In other words, juridicial language must express the decision. Like their Chinese ancestors, these modern mandarins are cultivated and talented men. Very seldom are they technicians with purely scientific backgrounds.

If through some miracle a group of mandarins from the Imperial Court could come to Paris, how would they behave in the French Republic? Certainly they would have to adjust to modern technology and democratic procedures, but otherwise they could act like genuine French mandarins except for losing their sumptuous silk robes. The very word mandarin, in Sanscrit *mantrin,* meant *Conseiller d'Etat.*

One way to portray the mandarins is to compare them with politicians. The two differ mainly in that the first are appointed whereas the latter are elected. Also, politicians stand in the limelight and have a reputation as talkers; mandarins are silent, behind the scenes. In return, the mandarins control the flow of information. They have graduated from the most selective schools, while politicians come from the school of life. The latter are periodically renewed whereas the former have tenure, if not in their positions at least in the civil service. Politicians are obviously partisan, this is their job; mandarins supposedly lack party ties. But there are many variants to these ideal types of the mandarin and the politician.

Many writers admit, explicitly or implicitly, that modern mandarins have a hybrid character. "How does one separate," asks E. Suleiman, "the technical from the political at a level where the technician's task is essentially to prepare decisions for the minister?"[3] Or as J. LaPalombara says, "The bureaucracy, particularly in its upper reaches, will always be deeply involved in the political process. Indeed, it is impossible, even in the most structurally differentiated political system, to conceive of a complete separation of functions."[4] For R. Putnam, the assumption of such a separation "is false for the realities of modern government."[5] B. Chapman affirms, "Since the whole object of posts of confidence is to help the minister span the worlds of politics and administration, holders of these posts must belong to both worlds."[6] This is clearly the case in Sweden according to T. Anton: "By tradition and function, the Swedish bureaucrat is an important political figure in his own right. . . . Political bureaucracies administer large and complex programs. . . . Their leaders have come to play an increasingly prominent role in national policy making. The bureaucracy is thus inherently political which means that, strictly speaking, it is silly to talk about an 'administrative' elite!"[7] For J. Christoph, the mandarins' skills are "in part political. . . . It takes some immersion in the political world to detect when a comparatively minor decision carries a potentially explosive political charge."[8] He goes on to distinguish five political roles in the British high bureaucracy: policy formulation, policy implementation, mutual political protection, advancing clientele claims, and conflict management.

As we see, these two functions—the political and the administrative—are merging at the top of the hierarchies in nearly every Western European country.

How may we explain the growing political influence that top civil servants have in European democracies? I see two principal explanations: the increasing scope of the modern state and the decline of parliament.

1. EXPANDING SCOPE OF STATE BUREAUCRACY

Everywhere in Europe, government budgets have undergone profound modifications in size and nature. A new conception has replaced the strictly financial budget. This new, interventionist conception uses the budget as an instrument for government control in the nation's economic and social life. At the beginning of the century, the state's budget included only administrative expenses for services of general interest and those receipts necessary to cover them. The government limited itself to having an army, police, diplomatic force, and judiciary. This was the period of the *Etat-Gendarme.* The currency, based on the gold standard, was stable. Public spending made up less than one-tenth of the GNP.

Since the end of the First World War and especially since the Second, the government has increasingly intervened in economic, social, and cultural domains. Accordingly, the budget has been redrawn along new lines. Having assumed functions as organizer, producer, and protector, the state invests, subsidizes, nationalizes, and redistributes. Currencies have become less stable. Public expenses have been growing at an accelerating rate since 1945. During the 1962-1964 period, government revenues accounted for more than a third of the GNP in France, West Germany, Britain, Norway, and Austria; nearly a third in the Netherlands and Italy; and more than a fourth in Belgium, Denmark and Finland.[9] In order to place a ceiling upon expenses, Germany decided that the increase in budgetary expenditures must not be greater than that in the GNP; France has followed this example.

This increase in the size of national budgets corresponds to a profound change in their nature. For instance, in France during the sixties, more than half of public expenditures went toward economic and social ends; purely administrative charges represented no more than a third of the total. Budgetary allocations for capital investments, which made up 5% of the 1938 budget, rose to 40% in 1949 and have stabilized at approximately 20% since 1960. On the other hand, expenditures involving the redistribution of income to certain social categories have increased each year. All other European countries have experienced the same budgetary tendencies.

The importance of the budget in relation to the GNP measures only one part of a government's economic and social role. Nationalized enterprises also enter the picture. Government is the biggest employer in France, with one-sixth of manpower engaged in industry. Moreover it is the major investor, having made 20% of total investments during the sixties. The state monopolizes the production of coal, electricity, gas, potassium fertilizers, and atomic energy. It owns the railroads and airlines, and more than two-thirds of river and maritime fleets. It controls the major automobile and airplane manufacturers and the largest banks (and therefore nearly three-quarters of bank deposits). It is also the largest insurance firm. It controls a majority share in the arms and electronics industries and also in highway projects. More than five hundred public enterprises make the government the major industrialist in France.[10]

Likewise in England, the government owns between one-fourth and one-fifth of the economy.[11] The nationalized sector comprises key industries. In Italy the *Ministero delle Partecepazioni Statali* exercises a determining influence over economic life.[12] The public sector is less impressive, though still important, in Scandinavia, where exists a heavier fiscal system for the redistribution of income, which means that government intervention is no smaller than in France or England.

The extent of nationalization, together with the redistribution of national income, most markedly and necessarily brings about an important transfer of power to the managers of public enterprises and to the directors of social, economic, and financial agencies in the government. This applies to all European countries; but state intervention in the economy has comparatively little effect on the political role of top civil servants in Switzerland, Greece, Spain, and Ireland.

Besides drawing up the budget and directing public enterprises, the government also has the responsibility for planning, forecasting, and programming the economy. This enlarges even further its prerogatives and its technocratic mission.

Undoubtedly, the government's role has considerably expanded during the last generation. Governments increasingly manage or control national economies in European countries. The state's evolution fits neither Liberal nor classical Marxist schemes. This metamorphosis requires another explanation. On whose shoulders do these new responsibilities fall? On those of parliamentarians elected by universal suffrage?

2. DECLINE OF PARLIAMENT AND RISE OF THE MANDARINS

Everywhere in Europe, parliaments have been declining in power. Legislative functions have been partly transferred to the executive branch, as seen by the importance of delegated powers which allow the public administration to set regulations. These regulations make possible the implementation of laws in matters that rightfully belong to parliamentary bodies. Laws promulgated as guidelines or decrees issued by the executive also point to this delegation of law making authority. Even bills passed by parliament are generally prepared and proposed by the government—in actual fact, by top administrative officials. Parliament has less initiative than the government. Not only is this true as regards the number of bills proposed but also with respect to the probability of any bill being passed when proposed by the government rather than parliament. As A. Grosser stresses, "Everywhere the legislative initiative has passed into the hands of the administrations. The legislatures sometimes amend, rarely reject, usually ratify. The members continue, indeed, to call themselves collectively 'the legislative power' on the law books, but in most cases they merely participate in a procedure of registration."[13]

This transfer of power is emphasized by several contributors to the present volume. About England, J. Christoph writes, "Parliament lays down a framework of policy and statutorily empowers the minister to work out the details. . . . This delegated legislative power is in turn subdelegated by the minister to his top civil servants."[14] Subdelegation comes about because, except for special cases, MPs have no direct connections with high civil servants: "With neither direct access to civil servants nor their own expert staffs, MPs can serve only fitfully as informed critics of policy and administration."[15] R. Ruffieux notes that "the civil service's role in ordinary legislative processes is longstanding. . . . Every year the Swiss Federal Administration prepares legislative texts, the budget and the management report; and high officials can amply exercise their powers of initiative, arbitration and even decision making."[16] About Denmark, E. Damgaard comments, "Many tasks labelled legislative in character have become executive in locus."[17] Likewise in Austria: "More than 90% of all draft bills are introduced by the cabinet. . . . The bureaucracy is indeed in charge of legislative work in the ministries. . . . It is often the bureaucracy itself which takes the first steps to draft bills and to start a legislative process."[18]

In France, the National Assembly no longer controls the organization of its own agenda. The 1958 Constitution imperatively limits parliament to meeting a few months during the year. Furthermore, it reduces the power of amendment that parliamentary committees and even the Assembly used to have. A government bill can become law without even being formally voted on by the parliament! To do this, the government can stake its future on the proposed bill; and if a vote of no confidence does not defeat the government, the text is adopted!

The referendum, conceived as a means for popular participation, has also taken traditional power away from legislatures: in Italy, the law on divorce was carried by referendum; in Britain, the question of Common Market membership was also submitted to popular vote. Legislation by referendum in Switzerland is well known; a recent example concerned immigration. R. Ruffieux shows how civil servants enter this process. French referendums have a different meaning because of their presidential origins; they pass over the heads of parliamentarians into the domain of public debate. In this case, opinion makers and mass media specialists exercise more influence than the mandarins.

Previously we asked who assumes the new functions created by the state's expanding scope. We will now examine the three most important aspects in the development of the government's economic role. Has parliament lost power here as in the case of law making?

THE NATIONAL BUDGET

The main purpose of legislative bodies has traditionally been the adoption of the budget, but they have gradually given up this prerogative. Nowadays the job of preparing the budget falls on the executive which, in turn, leans on bureaucrats, especially officials in the Treasury. In England, the Chancellor of the Exchequer informs other cabinet members about principal features of the budget shortly before his speech to the House of Commons. Since the government holds a majority in that chamber, discussion of the proposed budget lasts only a few days during the plenary session.

France's present constitution limits parliamentary participation in drawing up the budget. Deputies do not have the right to propose amendments which would increase public expenditures or decrease revenues. "Parliament is now only a registry office in financial matters. . . . After several weeks of discussion, less than one-thousandth of the proposed budget is changed. . . . A simple fact: What can parliament do when facing the budget? Nothing. What can the government do? Everything."[19]

After noting that the Norwegian "parliament appears not to act as a serious check on the influence of civil servants in the national budget process," J. Higley, K. Brofoss and K. Groholt stress that "the national budget is a clear example of the substantial latitude and influence enjoyed by the civil service elite."[20] Their conclusion undoubtedly applies to many other European countries. Quite significantly, several constitutions specify the length of parliament's budgetary session: in West Germany, Belgium, and the Netherlands, three months; in Italy, five months; and in France, seventy days.

Thus has an essential legislative prerogative—budget control—been transferred to the executive branch and ultimately to the higher reaches of the public administration.

PUBLIC ENTERPRISES

The nationalization of principal industries has deprived many men of their power and influence. According to some theories, these capitalists are the real "power elite." Who has inherited their power? Nationalized enterprises have enjoyed a certain autonomy and, except in England, the managers are mainly chosen from among senior civil servants, not politicians or businessmen.

Former French Prime Minister Michel Debré declares: "Nationalization has not increased the authority of politicians at all, but rather that of civil servants who have taken the place of private entrepreneurs. . . . The nationalized enterprises tend to become the private hunting grounds of certain administrative corps."[21] A report prepared by the National Assembly's Finance Committee has stated that "too many directorships in public enterprises are, at present, considered as the natural outlets open to high civil servants."[22] French public enterprises have been, wisely it is thought, spared constant parliamentary scrutiny. D. Derivry discusses this point.

On the other side of the Channel, the House of Commons has created a Select Committee on Nationalized Industries which examines the activities of public corporations.[23] This committee's impact, though positive, remains limited; and the high civil service still assumes a major share of the responsibility for coordinating the economic and financial activities of essential companies.

ECONOMIC PLANNING

Planning of this kind does not fit well with parliamentary procedures. The rigidity of law contrasts with the flexibility which planning requires. Parliaments lack the necessary technical means for really controlling a national economic plan. Even if the government presents parliament with several options, MPs cannot propose another global plan as an alternative. They must take position on a general option. L. Nizard emphasizes the lateness of parliamentary involvement in the decision making process: the agencies which closely participate in drawing up the plan have more influence than the body which must approve it. He goes on to note that the coherence of the plan is not compatible with the partial nature of legislative amendments.[24]

Here again, the transfer of power has, in the final analysis, favored high civil servants more than ministers. Of course, the cabinet plays an important role in the initial and final phases, but the planners themselves write up alternatives and devise criteria for making the most rational choice.

The influence of the civil service varies from one country to another, depending on the particular political context. We will now look at specific factors in each country.

3. SPECIFIC FACTORS FAVORING THE MANDARINS' POLITICAL POWER

In addition to these two general factors—the higher bureaucracy's enlarged scope, and the decline of parliament—a certain number of specific factors have likewise favored growth in the political influence of top civil servants. These factors come into play in some countries but not in others. We will only make an inventory of them, indicating the countries affected.

a) *Administrative Centralization.* Obviously reinforces the positions of higher administrative officials. France is the most typical example.

b) *Ministerial Instability.* A high turnover in the cabinet strengthens civil officials who remain in office, to the detriment of politicians who only pass through. This was so during the French Third and Fourth Republics, and has been true in Italy and Finland since 1946. As evidence, consider this statement by a senior mandarin, the former *Commissaire au Plan* Etienne Hirsch: "During thirteen years, I have personally had to deal with twenty-six governments. This means that the government was not the same during elaboration of the plan, then for discussion in parliament and finally for implementation. A large part of the time was spent explaining to some minister, facing parliamentary debate or threatened with a crisis, what was good to prepare for the following four years. Many times, I had the impression that the minister was wondering if I was truly aware of the situation in which he found himself." [25]

The stability of civil officeholders has sometimes been exaggerated as much as governmental instability. A comparative study of changes in the French and British cabinets between 1945 and 1957 has shown that, in France, the governmental core of the most influential politicians was as stable as that across the Channel.[26] As J. Lautman rightly affirms, the careers of French senior civil servants are as changeable as the fates of politicians: "Administrative continuity comes from the memory of the bureaux [their accumulated knowledge and experience] more than from personel stability."[27] In Italy, continual cabinet shufflings are weakening Italian democracy and, as Putnam's study suggests, inhibiting top civil servants from taking initiatives. So cabinet instability has not had the same effects on both sides of the Alps.

c) *Incompatibility between Ministerial Posts and Parliamentary Seats.* The Dutch and French constitutions do not allow the same person to simultaneously hold positions in parliament and in the government. Such provisions promote the selection of top civil servants as ministers. In the Netherlands between 1848 and 1958, 24% of the ministers came from the high civil service and 20% from the army.[28] Under the French Fifth Republic, more than half the ministers have been chosen from among top civil servants, who have thus become full-fledged politicians.[29] During several political crises in Finland, a government of senior civil servants was formed.

d) *Ministers' Personal Staffs.* The institutionalization of the so-called ministerial cabinets in France, Belgium, and other countries places some civil servants in quasi-political positions. When transferring from the State Council,

Treasury Inspectorate, or some service in the ministry into a ministerial cabinet, the senior official changes roles so much that he even reverses his attitudes about political decision making processes. E. Suleiman has made an enlightening analysis of this change of attitudes in terms of the theory of social roles.[30]

e) *Prefectoral System.* In France, Italy, and Spain, this system delegates extended powers to higher civil servants who, though not located in the central administration, assume an essential political role in the territorial administration.[31] The federal systems in Switzerland and West Germany and the strong municipalities in Belgium, Britain, and the Netherlands have just the opposite effect.

f) *Party System.* In one-party systems, as in Spain and the Communist countries of Eastern Europe, top civil servants mostly fulfill functions of policy implementation rather than policy formulation, because of the unique party's power. J. Wiatr's remarks about Poland can be extrapolated to other Communist countries in that part of Europe.

In multiparty systems with strong parties, as in Austria, Norway, Denmark, and the Netherlands, political leaders tend to control the political arena more easily than in nations with weak parties—e.g., France and Switzerland. For twenty years in West Germany (1949-1969) and also in Italy (1946-1968), a single or dominant party has ruled unchallenged. In some circumstances parliament merely ratified decisions already reached by party leaders, who were holding powerful ministerial portfolios. Influential civil servants, more so than party activists, surrounded these men.

A careful reading of this book will not enable one to rank European countries according to the importance of the top civil servants' political functions. Too many factors intervene, and they do not have one-dimensional effects; sometimes they act in opposite directions. We are at a loss to tell whether civil servants have more influence in Norway or Denmark, and we wonder whether a panel of Norwegian and Danish experts could reach agreement. Comparing two countries as different as Switzerland and Denmark, or Finland and Ireland, presents even more difficulties. Understandably, contributors to the present volume have emphasized what best characterizes the countries they have studied.

Nevertheless, it is obvious that the hallways of the French Fifth Republic have become the paradise of modern mandarins. Second to France is that very "European" country, Japan, with similar features: a strongly centralized administration, weak parties, and a legalistic tradition. "Japan is one of the world's most highly institutionalized bureaucracies, which is reputed to be the nucleus of Japanese political power; at the same time, input channels of popular control, such as the political parties, are less adequately institutionalized."[32] Among Western pluralistic democracies, Swedish civil servants, mainly because of the many administrative boards which run parallel to the ministries, have high visibility. In the British two-party system, the "administrative class" of officials is more essential than its counterpart in the West German two-and-a-half party system.

The higher civil service necessarily reflects certain characteristics of any given society's political system. From multiple perspectives, the diversity among European countries entails a variation in the political roles of public administrators. In order to clarify this dependence, contributors to the present volume have often gone beyond the high administration to discuss the entire political system.

4. INCOMPATIBILITY BETWEEN POWER AND PARTISANSHIP

Until now, we have tried to evaluate top civil servants' influence within the political system without treating the separate question of their degree of politicization. How much are these mandarins engaged in politics, more specifically in political parties? We are not referring to publicly prominent individuals, but rather to the mandarins as a whole. The essential point for analysis concerns the relationship between power and politicization. We shall look at particular countries.

Undoubtedly, Belgian top civil servants are strongly politicized. L. Moulin defines several criteria: their recruitment from or by political parties, their introduction of political preoccupations into the performance of their duties, and their custom of passing on official information to their parties. L. Moulin and H. van Hassel agree about the politicization of civil servants in both Walloon and Flemish areas. Belgium certainly has the most intense politicization in Western Europe.

In one-party systems, such as the Communist regimes of Eastern Europe, the party occupies the center of power. Parliamentary and administrative bodies revolve around this unique center. Only trusted party activists receive important, appointive or elective, offices; party membership alone does not suffice. Higher administrative positions are political by nature, so they are necessarily filled by and from the party rather than the administration. In short, the Eastern variety of mandarins, which J. Wiatr describes, are politicians holding positions functionally equivalent to higher civil positions in the West.

In both Belgium and Poland, top administrators, because of their high politicization, do not have the power and influence of their counterparts elsewhere. The opposite situation exists in France and Sweden, where civil service power goes along with a relative lack of partisanship. Though powerful, most top civil servants do not personally or openly participate in party politics, although there are notable exceptions. A comparison of the last three French republics reveals the inverse relationship between power and politicization. Whereas such politicization has diminished in each republic since the Third, the mandarins' power has increased, partly because they have become less partisan and thus more capable of working with successive governments. Likewise in

Sweden, high administrative power has been developing in the absence of partisanship. A third case exists in Switzerland and the Netherlands, where top civil servants are neither extremely powerful nor strongly politicized. So, in some countries civil servants are very powerful but not politicized (France, Sweden); in others, not really powerful but very politicized (Belgium, Italy, Poland); in still others, neither powerful nor politicized (Netherlands, Switzerland). I see no case in contemporary Europe where top bureaucrats are simultaneously very powerful and highly politicized, although I would hesitate for a moment about Austria.

Since Metternich's complaint that Austria was administered and not governed, "the preeminence of top civil servants has been slow to vanish."[33] R. Kneucker considers Austria to still be an "administrative state."[34] Discussing proportionality, *Proporz*, K. Steiner states that party affiliations favor promotion to high offices in the public bureaucracy.[35] G. Smith affirms the same: "High civil servants still occasionally receive ministerial appointments, and promotion often depends on being in the 'right' party."[36] R. Kneucker remarks that politicization is expected at the highest levels.[37] He also states that "ministers, on the basis of debates or discussions with their respective political parties, often prefer to select civil servants from their parties."[38] Once appointed, such officials have tenure. As a consequence, "incoming ministers must take over the present team of tenured top officials and create conditions for good cooperation."[39] Hence, Austria seems to have moderately powerful and moderately politicized top civil officials. Working relationships between administrative and political personnel do not conflict.

The incompatibility between the mandarins' political power and their extreme politicization calls for explanation. The top grades of public administration can be highly politicized only where powerful and well-organized political parties control the totality of the political system, including the

Contemporary Mandarins		Political Power	
		weak	strong
Politicization Partisanship	low	Switzerland Netherlands	France Sweden
		Austria	
	high	Belgium Italy Poland	

administrative hierarchy. In this case, the mandarins are, by necessity, more influenced than influential since political leaders keep as much power as possible for themselves. We can thus formulate the following generalization: in those countries where top civil servants are strongly politicized, in the sense of partisanship, they cannot play a truly essential role in decision making processes.

As for the four "fragmented democracies," Belgium, Austria, Switzerland, and the Netherlands, as A. Lijphart calls them, religious or linguistic cleavages reinforce party alignments. A ranking of top civil servants according to their politicization will place Belgium at the top and Switzerland at the bottom. Nevertheless these two countries resemble each other in so many ways that we may wonder why they are at opposite ends. This shows the complexity of the problem area this book studies. The depth of cleavages in Belgium may provide an explanation. On this, A. Molitor writes, "The Belgian educational system has created two major ideological families which very frequently confront each other. . . . Nine-tenths of Belgian citizens are formally labelled, and it is very difficult for them to leave the web they have been born into."[40] A fabric has been woven that enwraps the Belgian "from cradle to grave," as H. Van Hassel says.[41] This fabric has a closer mesh at the top of the society.

In Holland also, religious cleavages run deep. However, as A. Lijphart convincingly argues, a consensus at the top characterizes the country.[42] S. Eldersveld, S. Hubée-Boonzaijer and J. Kooiman fully confirm this: Dutch senior civil servants "clearly recognize the role of parliamentary party leaders in policy-making and generally feel that they do a good job."[43] This harmony does not resound in neighboring Belgium.

Another difficult case is Italy, where two very distinct public bureaucracies exist: the state's central administration (the traditional ministries), and the quasi-public administration of all sorts of agencies. R. Putnam studies bureaucrats in the first; S. Passigli deals with the second. Both of these two bureaucracies are marked by strong politicization, the agencies more than the central administration, since directors in the ministries try to resist the colonization of their domains by political parties.[44] To quote R. Putnam, "It is only sensible to be antipolitical in contemporary Italy."[45] Having tenure, the directors can do this. The differences in bureaucratic mentalities in Italy, West Germany, and Great Britain, empirically established by R. Putnam, come from national context, particularly from dominant party factionalism, as well as from generational gaps. Public officals in the agencies which S. Passigli studies are more similar to their German, English, Dutch, Swedish, or French counterparts.

A personification of the incompatibility between power and partisanship at the highest administrative levels is the commander of the *Carabinieri*, who is one of the most powerful men in Italy. By tradition, he is apolitical. Democratic periods during the last century produced only one example of the political involvement of one of these men.

Yet another factor in the politicization of high public administrators is elite circulation. If they cannot easily transfer from elective to appointive offices, the possibility of politicization is reduced. On the contrary, bridging the political and administrative hierarchies encourages partisanship among top civil servants. It also allows politicians to hope for administrative careers. A "royal career" in France simultaneously combines positions in both hierarchies, as Valéry Giscard d'Estaing, Jacques Chaban-Delmas, Michel Debré, Jacques Chirac, Maurice Couve de Murville, Léon Blum and dozens of others have done.[46] *These Princes Who Govern Us* [47] —to quote the title of a book by Michel Debré—are hybrids *par excellence.*

In contrast, Denmark has "virtually no movement from top positions in the central administration into government or parliament."[48] The same is true in England, but not in Germany, according to N. Johnson: "Britain has a tiny national political elite based in London whose members have grown up in a world sharply distinct from that of the bureaucracy. Movement from bureaucracy into politics is deliberately made as unattractive as possible. The German situation is the opposite of this. The political elite is dispersed and conglomerate, entry into it is often from the administration, and movement between bureaucracy and politics is easy. The result is bureaucratized politics and politicized bureaucracy."[49] As for Norway, J. Higley, K. Brofoss, and K. Groholt write that "for a number of persons, political and civil service careers merge in such a way as to suggest the existence of a 'state elite' whose members spend their working lives in the public sector."[50] Instead of two elites, we have only one in such a situation.

One country has institutionalized elite rotation: Yugoslavia. R. Lukic gives a clear explanation of the workings of this circulatory system. His contribution is probably the only study on this topic in Western European languages. This institutionalized circulation differentiates Yugoslavia from other Communist regimes, and its effects make Yugoslavia more "Western" than "Eastern." As another consequence, higher civil servants in Yugoslavia have much more influence than similar officials in Poland.

In pluralistic democracies, popular political participation has been increasing since the adoption of universal suffrage. At the same time, political parties have succeeded in mobilizing citizens to take more active interest in political matters. This may lead us to suppose that the voice of the people has muted top civil servants. We then encounter a paradox, one which quickly disappears. Why? First, the more people participate, the more groups make demands, and the more services must be created; therefore, the greater the need for an enlarged bureaucracy (even if lower and middle levels swell, the size of the top level does not necessarily change). Second, the greater the amount of participation, the more intense the political struggle, so also the greater the need for a go-between or for arbitrating bodies which maintain contacts with and among competing groups. Third, the larger the number of politically active people, the greater the need to delegate tasks of execution to a small body. Finally, the greater the participation, the greater the need for organization; the greater the need for organization, the greater the influence of administrative specialists. These conditions tend to preclude the possibility of top civil servants being highly politicized in a partisan sense, but these same conditions make them more aware of political inputs and outputs in decision making processes.

5. TYPES OF MANDARINS

We have been describing the mandarins as though they constitute a homogeneous elite with interchangeable members. In fact, a great variety exists among them, even if they do share the attributes already mentioned.

F. Ridley has proposed an interesting distinction between "specialists" and "generalists";[51] however, this seems less significant for the present study inasmuch as most mandarins are generalists. As Léon Blum says, "Political competence or even, in more general terms, managerial competence has nothing in common with technical competence since it supposes not the previous exercise of a given profession but the possession of general qualities of intelligence and character. . . . The notion of competence diametrically opposes the notion of speciality."[52]

R. Putnam has conceptualized another valuable dichotomy based on mentalities. Having distinguished between two ideal types, classical and political bureaucrats, he then attempts to see to what extent actual bureaucrats correspond to them. The classical bureaucrat is the Weberian civil servant who is above politics; the political bureaucrat accepts the inseparability of adminis-tration and politics as well as the basic premises and values of pluralistic democracy. Yet another classification could be founded on role perceptions, as the data of S. Eldersveld, S. Hubée-Boonzaijer and J. Kooiman suggest. B. Headey has taken the oppostie tack and defined a typology of ministers in order to explain the consequences for the civil service. In effect, the ministers' preoccupations determine the amount of power delegated to the mandarins: "Different role conceptions and time constraints mean that giving high priority to one role is likely to mean that other roles are down-graded and, implicitly, delegated to civil servants."[53]

I see two major types of mandarins: a traditional one on the decline and a modern one on the rise. Ambassadors, prefects, and military chiefs belong to the first; treasury inspectors, planners, heads of national agencies, managers of public enterprises, ministers' aides, and members of the *grands corps* are included in the second. A few major differences mark off these two types.

Ambassadors and military chiefs tend to come from particular social strata. Lists of French, Italian, German, Belgian, or Dutch diplomats contain a relatively high proportion of old family names, some of them from the aristocracy. Today's *Who's Who,* as compared with that of the twenties, would show that the ratio of traditional mandarins has been declining.

The modern mandarins have varied trainings: in economics, finance, or business administration. On the other hand, the traditional mandarins have a literary or legal education, and military officers have come up through Sandhurst or St. Cyr. Incidentally, European ambassadors have hardly ever been business-men as have so many American diplomats.

They are differently located. Traditional mandarins are geographically dispersed. The modern group is concentrated in capitals, sometimes in small cities like Bonn or Eur near Rome (not to mention Canberra, Brazilia, or Ottowa), but most of them work in particular districts of the old capital: the seventh arrondissement in Paris, a few avenues in old Vienna, or Whitehall.

Paradoxically, the mass media tend to pay less attention to modern than traditional mandarins. The former have less visibility because of the bureaucratic nature of their work. In effect, they function as an administrative apparatus, serving on committees and boards. They spend much of their time discussing matters around tables. In Switzerland, R. Ruffieux has counted 200 specialized committees at the disposal of the Federal Council.[54] According to T. Anton, Sweden has seventy official boards.[55] More than 4,000 persons, meeting in small groups, took part in the preparation of the French national economic plan; most of them were civil servants. On 954 boards in Norway, "78% of the civil service elite occupied 272 positions . . . ; an average of 3.2 positions each."[56] The strategic position of modern mandarins in political decision making processes contrasts with their relative anonymity in the mass media and with their self-effacing postures.

Technological developments, particularly in transportation and communi-cations, have speeded up the decline of the traditional mandarins. Napoleon created the prefectoral corps at a time when the central government did not have direct contact with the provinces; it could only appoint men of confidence. In fact, prefects had charge of territorial units measured by the time needed to go on horseback from the prefect's headquarters to the border of his administrative domain. Today, prefects are more closely supervised. Day and night, they have open telephone lines to the Ministry of Interior. They now execute orders received from Madrid, Rome, or Paris.

Communications technology has had the same effects on the job roles of ambassadors. Yesterday, ambassadors' names filled history books; recent books rarely mention them. Since the thirties, the airplane has permitted foreign ministers or heads of state to get together quickly. The ambassador, who previously had very real negotiating powers, has become merely his country's representative abroad. There is nothing surprising about the fact that graduates from the French National School of Administration no longer put priority on choosing diplomatic careers. The late President Pompidou ironically stated that ambassadors have given up "the permanent exercise of the cup of tea and biscuits."[57] In a contracting world, diplomatic representatives become figureheads. Special delegates, foreign ministers, and national leaders from various countries now negotiate with each other.

During World War I, civilian heads in the capital and military officers in the field could not maintain permanent contact; generals were entirely in charge of conducting operations. Since World War II, government leaders themselves choose military options and lead battles. Moreover, high-level technicians and engineers have a major say in military decisions, although remaining civilian officials. All this indicates how the role of military chiefs has declined.

This book deals principally with modern mandarins, so we shall look at some examples.

Treasury officials are the perfect example of powerful mandarins since they constitute an "elite within an elite." In England, S. Brittan counts about 150 of them.[58] In France, the Treasury Inspectorate does not have many more.[59] These men exercise control over the economy and finances, but the most influential among them hold positions as directors of the budget, foreign commerce, general accountancy, income taxes, tariffs, the public debt, and so on. In every country, such men play a major role in preparing the national budget and controlling expenditures in the ministries. Central bank governors, directors of nationalized banks, presidents of national credit institutions, and heads of nationalized insurance companies are, most of them, career civil servants.

In many European countries, and in the United States as well, certain economic, financial, social, and cultural activities have come to be controlled by agencies placed outside regular hierarchical channels. In general, these agencies are directly under the prime minister or president. Among institutions of this kind, we can mention the French Planning Commission, the British National Economic Development Council, the Belgian Bureau of Economic Planning, the Dutch Central Plan Bureau, the Southern Italian Developmental Agency, the French General Commission for Territorial Development, and the Italian Institute for Industrial Reconstruction. Two chapters in the present volume, those of D. Derivry and S. Passigli, deal with modern mandarins in charge of the public and semipublic sectors of the French and Italian economies.

Another chapter, by J. Siwek-Pouydesseau, focuses on members of ministerial cabinets. This latter subtype of modern mandarin works in a political rather than administrative context, thus linking the two. Having belonged to a minister's staff—the so-called ministerial cabinets—favors an individual's promotion into the highest reaches of public administration. In France, more than half the directors in the ministries thus served shortly before their appointments.

As for the *grands corps,* here is how M. Crozier describes them and their "caste privileges": "One of the nuclei of the French administrative system . . . is the existence of a certain number of closed-off *grands corps* with extremely restricted entry, whose members traditionally hoard not only top positions in the state but also most of the top positions in the nationalized sector and some within major corporations."[60]

Another even more categorical diagnosis of this privileged caste appears in a periodical under the direction of former Prime Minister Pierre Mendès-France: "A certain number of members of the *grands corps* quit the administration for important jobs in the private sector. . . . A growing number of private companies include, among their managers, men who have come from the *grands corps;* this is especially the case in banks. Thus do we see a kind of kinship develop between those who make a decision (the minister and his cabinet), those who execute it (the directors in the ministries) and those whom it concerns and who have, besides, often inspired it (businessmen). They make up a privileged, permanent, powerful, coherent group, a ruling caste." [61]

These transfers from the summit of the administrative hierarchy into the private and nationalized sectors are somewhat surprising because of the consequent loss of power, even if these men do become heads of important companies. If they were power-hungry, would they so easily leave the governmental stronghold? What really motivates them? The reply would have major implications for the theory of elites in advanced societies.

6. FINAL REMARKS

Between the two world wars, the executive power in different countries was considerably weakened by various causes; the major ones were the multiplicity of political parties and the difficulty of gathering together a stable parliamentary majority. The titles of some academic publications pointed this out: *The Crisis of Democracy and the Reinforcement of Executive Power* (E. Giraud, 1938), *The Role of the Executive Power in Modern Republics* (J. Barthelemy, 1934).

Today the opposite has happened, namely, too great an increase in the executive to the detriment of parliament. Critics do not attack the power of the ministers as much as that of the technocratic high administration.[62] Thus, a double transfer of power has taken place: from parliament to the executive, and from the executive to the top civil service. Though undeniable, this displacement has four limitations.

First, these transfers have come about in economic and financial fields, secondly in social affairs, and much less often in structural and constitutional matters.

Second, the passing of power from politicians to bureaucrats delegates authority from an elected officeholder to persons appointed—and dismissed—by him; furthermore, the politician gives up his power bit by bit, problem by problem.

Third, power is delegated not so much to an individual as to a committee, commission, or board. Within these groups, an exchange of information and opinions precedes decision. J. Lautmann remarks that consultation "has been rendered necessary by the relative decline of elective bodies . . ." and "is a substitute, in some ways, for democratic practices." [63]

Finally, only normal periods have witnessed this transfer of power to the bureaucracy. During crises, exceptional situations, or dramatic circumstances, the power of top civil servants almost disappears, and politicians—parliamentarians, ministers, or charismatic leaders—assume full power. (Military officers have also taken power in some cases.) B. Gournay emphasizes: "The high administration seems to have had no major or direct influence on the outcome of political crises in France during the last decades." [64] Most major reforms, some of a revolutionary nature, introduced throughout liberated Europe just after the war, were neither inspired nor formulated by the high administration, even though there were a few important exceptions such as the Beveridge plan for British social security. The directing staffs of political parties were, at that time, the principal actors and enactors.

In the democratic societies of Western Europe, power is not monolithic. The present volume aims at locating civil servants within pluralistic power structures.

If a sample of experts and political observers from each European nation were to ordinally name the five hundred (or fewer for the smaller democracies) most influential persons in their country's political life, what proportion of the names would be of top civil servants? Obviously, most names would belong to politicians, union officials, businessmen, pressure group spokesmen, church leaders, and many others. Of course, the choice of these experts would not necessarily depict actual power structures nor would it infallibly point out those persons at the center of power.

In fact, I did a tentative and informal survey in France some years ago. Eighteen political observers, most of them journalists or politicians, were asked to designate the 500 most powerful men in the nation's political life. In order to facilitate their choice, they received a list of 1,200 possible names. One finding of this pilot study showed that the experts could easily provide 100 or more names. Beyond that point, however, they had increasing difficulty, so much so that some admitted they could not give more than two or three hundred names with much certainty. Furthermore, the same names usually appeared among the first hundred, and there was dispersion among the second and third hundreds. Nevertheless, the proportion of high civil servants quickly rose after the first twenty or thirty names, which were mostly those of politicians. Also, the proportion stayed high in the case of those experts who listed more than two hundred. Quite significantly, the civil service position rather than the actual name of the person was frequently cited.

If a real survey of this sort were conducted in European countries, might not civil servants eventually outnumber politicians? The answer would vary with the ordinal rank of the decile chosen. Most of the first fifty names would be of politicians; but their dominance would likely diminish in the second series of fifty names where civil servants might equal them, at least in some countries. Among the first hundred or so, the highest proportion of civil servants would occur in France. Elsewhere, it would probably be higher in Sweden than Norway, Austria than Belgium, or the Netherlands than Switzerland. The Michigan group's study on the political role perceptions of top civil servants and politicians will undoubtedly furnish data capable of shedding light on this question. [65]

We may now start an interesting tour of Europe, looking through palace windows–or cabinet shutters–at the mandarins. We have expert guides. Our trip begins with James Christoph and Bruce Headey at Whitehall which, together with Tokyo's Kasumigaseki district, has the highest density of these hybrids per cubic meter. Instead of robes, they wear derby hats and carry umbrellas or, more simply, briefcases. Robert Putnam will lead us to Bonn and Rome. From there, Samuel Eldersveld, Sonje Hubée-Boonzaijer, and Jan Kooiman invite us to The Hague, and Léo Moulin and Hugo Van Hassel accompany us through politically charged Brussels. Our next stop will be at an exhibition of true mandarins in Paris where Jeanne Siwek-Pouydesseau and Daniel Derivry point out certain types. We then return briefly to Italy for a tour with Stefano Passigli before our itinerary takes us to Switzerland with Roland Ruffieux and on to Scandinavia. John Higley, Karl Brofoss, and Knut Groholt wait for us in Oslo, and Erik Damgaard will be our guide in Copenhagen. We then continue our reading travels with Radomir Lukic in Belgrade and Jerzy Wiatr in Warsaw, before returning to Paris.

NOTES

1. Figures provided by Bernard Gournay, "Les grands fonctionnaires," a paper presented at a roundtable on "La Classe Dirigeante," organized by the French Political Science Association in 1963, p. 33.

2. Among others, see: Alain Darbel and Dominique Schnapper, *Morphologie de la haute administration française* (Mouton, Paris, 1969); Jean-François Kesler, "Les anciens élèves de l'Ecole Nationale d'Administration," in Revue Française de Science Politique (April 1964): 243-267.

3. Ezra N. Suleiman, "The French Bureaucracy and Its Students: Toward the Desantification of the State" in World Politics 23 (October 1970): 149.

4. Joseph LaPalombara, "An Overview of Bureaucracy and Political Development," in *Bureaucracy and Political Development,* edited by the same (Princeton University Press, Princeton, 1963), p. 14.

5. Robert D. Putnam in this volume.

6. Brian Chapman, *The Profession of Government* (Allen and Unwin, London, 1959), p. 278.

7. Thomas J. Anton, "Bureaucrats in Politics: A Profile of the Swedish Administrative Elite," paper delivered at a meeting of the Society for the Advancement of Scandinavian Study (New York, 1972), pp. 4 and 20.

8. James B. Christoph in this volume.

9. United Nations, *Incomes in Postwar Europe: A Study of Policies, Growth and Distribution* (1967), chapter six, p. 3.

10. *Entreprise* (August 21-28, 1965) lists more than five hundred public and semipublic enterprises.

11. See William A. Robson, *Problems of Nationalized Industry* (Oxford University Press, New York, 1952).

12. On government intervention in the Italian economy, see Romolo Sartori, *Le partecipazioni economiche dello stato* (Studium, Rome, 1957).

13. Alfred Grosser, "The Evolution of European Parliaments," in S. R. Graubard (ed.) *A*

New Europe? (Houghton Mifflin, Boston, 1964), p. 228. See also: Gerhard Loewenberg, *Modern Parliaments: Change or Decline?* (Aldine Atherton, Chicago, 1971).

14. J. B. Christoph in this volume.

15. J. B. Christoph in this volume.

16. Roland Ruffieux in this volume.

17. Erik Damgaard in this volume.

18. Raoul F. Kneucker, "Austria: An Administrative State: The Role of the Austrian Bureaucracy," in Osterreichische Zeitschrift für Politikwissenschaft 2, 2 (1973): 95-127.

19. Jean-Marie Cotteret and Claude Emeri, *Le budget de l'Etat* (Presses Universitaires de France, Paris, 1972), p. 49. See also: Marie-Christine Kessler, "Pour une étude du système budgétaire français: problématique," Revue Française de Science Politique 22, 1 (February 1972).

20. John Higley, Karl Brofoss and Knut Groholt in this volume.

21. Michel Debré, "Pouvoir politique et pouvoir administratif," in La Nef (April-May 1951).

22. Alain Griotteray, "Les entreprises nationales," a report in the name of the National Assembly's Commission on Finances (Paris, 1972).

23. David Coombes, *The Members of Parliament and the Administration: The Case of the Select Committee on Nationalized Enterprises* (Allen and Unwin, London, 1966).

24. Lucien Nizard, "L'inaptitude parlementaire à influencer effectivement le processus de planification," paper presented at a roundtable of the French Political Science Association (Paris, November 1970). See also: Michel Crozier, "Pour une analyse sociologique de la planification française," in Revue Française de Sociologie 6, 2 (April-June 1965); Jean Meynaud, *Planification et politique* (Etudes de Science Politique, Lausanne, 1963).

25. Etienne Hirsch, quoted by Pierre Mendès-France in *La république moderne* (Gallimard, Paris, 1962), p. 40.

26. Mattei Dogan and Peter Campbell, "Le personnel ministériel en France et en Grande Bretagne: 1945-1957," two articles in Revue Française de Science Politique (April-June 1957, October-December 1957).

27. Jacques Lautman, "Développement économique et fonction publique en France," paper presented at the World Congress of the International Political Science Association (Munich, 1970), p. 9.

28. Mattei Dogan and Maria Scheffer Van Der Veen, "Le personnel ministériel hollandais: 1848-1958," in L'Année Sociologique (1958): 101.

29. Only one-tenth of the Fourth Republic's ministers came from the high administration, 21 individuals out of 227.

30. Ezra N. Suleiman, *Politics, Power and Bureaucracy in France* (Princeton University Press, Princeton, 1974), chapter nine.

31. On the prefects, see Brian Chapman, *The Prefects and Provincial France* (Allen and Unwin, London, 1955); and Robert Fried, *The Italian Prefects: A Study in Administrative Politics* (Yale University Press, New Haven, 1963).

32. John A. Cicco, Jr., and Kan Ori, "A New Perspective on the Japanese Higher Civil Service: An Empirical Study of its Prestige," a research paper published by the Institute of International Relations (Sophia University, Tokyo, 1974), p. 2. See also: Akira Kubota, *Higher Civil Servants in Postwar Japan* (Princeton University Press, Princeton, 1969); Mikio Higa, *The Role of Bureaucracy in Contemporary Japanese Politics* (University Microfilms, Ann Arbor, Michigan, 1970).

33. Gordon Smith, "The Bureaucratic Culture," paper presented at a panel of the European Consortium for Political Research (University of Mannheim, April 1973), p. 20.

34. R. F. Kneucker, op. cit.

35. Kurt Steiner, *Politics in Austria* (Little, Brown and Company, Boston, 1972), pp. 390-391.

36. G. Smith, op. cit., p. 23.

37. R. F. Kneucker, op. cit.

38. R. F. Kneucker, ibid.

39. K. Steiner, op. cit., p. 394.

40. Andre Molitor, "La politisation de l'administration," Res Publica 13, 2 (1971): 218-219.

41. Hugo Van Hassel in Res Publica 13, 2 (1971): 195-203.

42. Arend Lijphart, *The Politics of Accommodation* (University of California Press, Berkeley, 1968).

43. Samuel Eldersveld, Sonje Hubée-Boonzaijer and Jan Kooiman in this volume.

44. P. A. Allum, *Italy–Republic without Government?* (W. W. Norton and Company, New York, 1973), pp. 148-172; Giorgio Galli and Alfonso Prandi, *Patterns of Political Participation in Italy* (Yale University Press, New Haven, Conn., 1970), p. 161. Concerning the southern origins of most Italian director-generals, see Alessandro Taradel, "La burocrazia italiana: provenienza e collocazione dei direttori generali," in Tempi moderni (April-June 1963).

45. R. D. Putnam in this volume.

46. Under the Third and Fourth republics, transfers normally occurred between parliament and the government. Under the Fifth, a typical career begins in the high administration; afterwards the person becomes a candidate in legislative elections and, finally, minister (thus losing his seat in parliament).

47. Michel Debré, *Ces princes qui nous gouvernent* (Plon, Paris, 1957).

48. E. Damgaard in this volume.

49. Nevil Johnson, "Some Remarks on the Political Role of the Bureaucracy in Britain and Western Germany," paper presented at a panel of the European Consortium for Political Research (University of Mannheim, 1973), p. 13. By the same, *Government in the Federal Republic of Germany: The Executive at Work* (Pergamon Press, Elmsford, New York, 1973). See also: E. Blankenburg and H. Treiber, "Bürokraten als Politiker Parlamentarier als Bürokraten," Die Verwaltung 3 (1972): 273-286.

50. J. Higley, K. Brofoss and K. Groholt in this volume.

51. Frederick Ridley, *Specialists and Generalists* (Allen & Unwin, London, 1968).

52. Leon Blum, *La réforme gouvernementale* (Grasset, Paris, 1936), pp. 110, 112.

53. Bruce Headey in this volume.

54. R. Ruffieux, figures indicated in this volume.

55. T. Anton, op. cit., p. 2.

56. J. Higley, K. Brofoss and K. Groholt in this volume.

57. Georges Pompidou during a press conference reported in Le Monde (September 26, 1972): 10.

58. Samuel Brittan, *Steering the Economy* (Martin Secker and Wartburg, London, 1969).

59. On French Treasury officials, see: Pierre Lalumiere, *L'Inspection des Finances* (Presses Universitaires de France, Paris, 1959); Jean Monthen, "Un château-fort médiéval: le ministère de l'Economie et des Finances," in Esprit, special issue on the Administration (January 1970).

60. Michel Crozier, *La société bloquée* (Seuil, Paris, 1970), p. 221. See also the book published by Michel Crozier and other researchers from the National Center for Scientific Research, *Où va l'administration française?* (Editions d'Organisation, Paris, 1974).

61. "Crise de l'Etat, Crise de la Haute Administration" in Courrier de la République 85 (January 1971): 5.

62. As an example, see: Charles Debbasch, *L'administration au pouvoir: fonctionnaires et politiques sous la Ve République* Calmann-Lévy, Paris, 1969); see also: Alfred Diamant, "Antibureaucratic Utopias in Highly Industrialized Societies," in Journal of Comparative Administration (May 1972): 3-34.

63. Jacques Lautman, op. cit., p. 14.

64. B. Gournay, op. cit., p. 30.

65. For details about this study, refer to chapters in this volume by R. D. Putnam and by S. Eldersveld, S. Hubée-Boonzaijer, and J. Kooiman.

MATTEI DOGAN is director of research, Centre National de la Recherche Scientifique (Paris); director, Bureau for European Sociological Analyses (Paris); recurring visiting professor of political science, University of California (Los Angeles); former member of the French National Committee of Scientific Research; chairman, Research Committee on Political Elites, International Political Science Association; and president, Committee on Social Ecology, International Sociological Association.

1

High Civil Servants and the Politics of Consensualism in Great Britain

JAMES B. CHRISTOPH

The political roles played by British higher civil servants are complex, subtle, and frequently misunderstood. That they should be complex is not surprising, given the wide variety of tasks and powers laid on civil servants in a modern industrial state. That they should be subtle in form and nature should shock no student of the British political system, with its evolved common law assumptions and penchant for informal and imprecise operating codes. Misunderstanding is another matter, however. The sad fact is that our knowledge of how British civil servants relate to the political process has been limited by a paucity of empirical studies and a plenitude of casual observations, ranging from self-satisfied encomia to the "look, no hands" success of administrative philosopher-kings, to depictions of power-crazed bureaucratic Rasputins manipulating elected officials to their own political purposes, to hand wringing over archaic amateurism and monastic ineptitude. The habits of anonymity and secrecy for which the British civil service is known clearly carry costs, of which the risk of misunderstanding its actual functions is only one. Fortunately, though, the outside observer is now not wholly without clues. In the past decade a good deal of information has begun to come to light—from dialogues stimulated by reformist critics, official committees investigating the condition of civil service machinery, studies by social scientists, from civil servants themselves in a more open

AUTHOR'S NOTE: This article was originally prepared for delivery at the 1972 Annual Meeting of the American Political Science Association, Washington Hilton Hotel, Washington, D.C., September 5-9.

mood—sufficient to enable students to sketch a profile of bureau-cratic political life more persuasive than previous stereotypes. It is far from being a life model, but it goes some way toward elucidating the British approach to the various ways in which political and bureaucratic worlds touch and affect each other.

Fifty years ago Sidney and Beatrice Webb wrote that "The government of Great Britain is in fact carried on not by a Cabinet or even by the individual ministers, but by the Civil Service."[1] This allegation, made at a time when the scope and powers of government were comparatively small, and when the civil service was a mere fraction of its present size, has set the tone for several generations of critics of the civil service in the political system. Yet it is too sweeping and general to be entirely acceptable and useful. It conceals a host of more difficult questions that must be answered before we can appraise the extent of bureaucratic involvement in the central tasks of political decision-making and policy effectuation. Is "carry-ing on the government" synonymous with making its principal decisions, or influencing them to the elimination of all other alternatives? Are the things that modern governments do by their very nature so complex that only permanent officials can perform them successfully? Under which conditions can civil servants make as well as administer policy? Are they really equipped to do so, constitutionally and politically as well as technically? Do they desire and welcome political roles? Can they survive in a democratic system if they become identified with definite political views and contro-versial political decisions? How are their roles viewed and accepted by other political elites, and by the public at large? Above all, does it make any difference that they are British, and that the overall system in which they must operate consists of a bundle of attributes summed up as the British political climate?

The theme of this essay is that the political roles played by civil servants in Britain stem from the way demands put on the administrative sector by the increasing scope of government activity are linked with the pattern of authority and values held by governing politicians. These subsystems connect at a number of vital points; it is in this intersection where the political roles of bureaucrats are most important, if not always apparent. It is not surprising, then, to find that civil servants are called upon to perform multiple roles touching the substance of policy—some of them traditional and agreed, others less generally accepted and in the process of evolution. For despite the widespread view that the civil service is rocklike and unchanging, it has shown itself to be sensitive and responsive when confronted with sizable changes in the larger milieu of government activities. Whether or not it can respond quickly or appropriately enough is a stickier question.

1. THE POLITICAL CONTEXT OF BRITISH BUREAUCRACY

To understand the context in which civil service power is exercised requires that we look briefly first at the political environment in which it must operate. The emphasis here will be mainly on those aspects which bear directly on the evolution of the service's political roles: the doctrine of ministerial responsibility, the weakness of parliamentary supervision, the career patterns and frequent turnover of top government officials, the relationship of the bureaucracy to political parties, and the increasing dependence on consultations and bargaining with organized clientele groups.[2] Nor will we be dealing with the totality of civil servants, which on the nonindustrial side numbered 485,000 in 1971.[3] Instead, our concern is almost exclusively with the tiny group known until 1971 as the Administrative Class, the highest echelon of the service whose members are principally involved in making and implementing policy and dealing directly with political officials (ministers, junior ministers, parliamentary secretaries). It numbered about 2,800 in 1968, or less than one-half percent of all civil servants. Undoubtedly certain other officials, such as those in the higher reaches of the former Executive and Scientific classes, do more than simply carry out the directives of others and have some input to policy; but in a centralized system their political roles are quite sporadic and secondary. The Administrative Class touches the political realm much more directly. Its development, composition, and ethic remain at the center of the controversy over what a higher civil service can and should do in the modern democratic state.

By 1854, when Northcote and Trevelyan produced their famous report (which set the tone for the inner life of the service for a hundred years), the political code of the higher bureaucracy had begun to crystallize. Their recommendations, which were accepted only after the shock of the mismanagement of the Crimean War aroused Victorian politicians to the inadequacies of government personnel and machinery, established four major principles of civil service policy: (1) the service should be separated into two basic divisions, "intellectual work" being done by university graduates, and "mechanical duties" performed by a lower class of less education; (2) entry should be at an early age through competitive examinations set by a Civil Service Commission; (3) promotion should be based on merit rather than nepotism and connections, and certainly not on political considerations; and (4) separate departments should be merged into a unified service, within which transfers and promotions could be made between departments.[4] Modeled on the colonial successes of the Indian Civil Service, the report led to the institutionalization of preferred access to the Administrative Class of Oxford and Cambridge graduates, who were virtually alone in possessing the academic background to master the general and classical questions stressed in competitive examinations. By emphasizing academic ability rather than technical skills, the new system's underlying political and social philosophy confirmed the development of a top bureaucratic elite composed of intellectual generalists, interchangeable from department to department in the course of their careers, and separated from the working lives of ordinary Britons. The intrenchment of Northcote-Trevelyan attitudes gave rise to the much-quoted opening lines of the Fulton Report (1968) that it was the perpetuation of this nineteenth-century practice that "we seek to remedy."[5]

The century in which these principles have dominated the internal life of the service has brought a vast increase in the scope and complexity of government activity, and with it a proliferation of the roles required of civil servants. The regulatory functions remain, but to them has been added a range of responsibilities which with the best wills cannot be effectively kept under the thumbs of six hundred-odd Members of Parliament, or of several dozen ministers, whose tasks are also imbued with mid-Victorian assumptions. One way or another, British government disposes of about 40% of the total national budget. In addition it is involved indirectly, but not insignificantly, in the process by which a considerable portion of the remaining expenditure occurs. Britain's changing world role has diminished the demands on the two classic functions of state power—defense and foreign affairs—but their shrinkage has been overshadowed by steadily increasing involvement in a host of new activities associated with the management of the economy and the development of the welfare state, for example, the manipulation of fiscal and monetary policy, the stimulation of productivity and technological change, setting overall policy for nationalized industries, providing education, social welfare, and health services, subsidizing tourism and the arts, protecting the environment, and so on. The volume of laws, rules, and regulations needed to carry out these activities has risen astoundingly since 1945, with the result that neither parliament nor departmental ministers have had the time, information, or technical competence to cope with the details of consequential legislation. Hence the emergence of the familiar pattern: parliament lays down a framework of policy and statutorily empowers the minister to work out the details (amending existing laws to bring them up to date, creating machinery to administer the act, allowing the department to translate its broad principles into detailed rules). Inevitably, this delegated legislative power is in turn subdelegated by the minister to his top civil servants, subject only to his later confirmation and eventual responsibility to parliament for the aftereffects of delegation.

In this process civil servants play an active role. Since in almost every case framework legislation is proposed by the Government itself, civil servants will advise their ministers as to how general the general laws should be, and how much can be left in the delegated category. Their experience in administering previous policy frequently leads them to press ministers for new statutory instruments embodying accumulated administrative practices, which again will have the force of law unless subsequently overturned by parliament. It is worth noting that in both the pre- and post-legislative stages civil servants are in steady contact with those pressure groups likely to be affected by proposed changes—obtaining technical information on the anticipated effects of new rules, bargaining from the knowledge of what is apt to be their minister's final position, getting consent in advance whenever possible, satisfying the unwritten British requirement that consultation with interests precede government action, testing for their minister the temperature of the political water about to be stirred up. Aside from any technical benefits that may accrue, such consultations are meant to smooth the path of the minister in dealing with the larger political world, and to prevent embarrassing public pratfalls. The process has been institutionalized in a network of departmental and interdepartmental advisory committees, composed of spokesmen of organized pressure groups, technical and academic specialists, and lay members of the Establishment, as well as informally through fairly continuous communication between middle and high level civil servants and their "opposite numbers" in the bureaucracies of private groups.[6] The scope and character of these activities are bound to sensitize civil servants to the political world in which they are imbedded. While they adhere as strongly as ever to the view that their roles must be politically neutral and nonpartisan, in the sense of their serving ministers of whatever political stripe, higher civil servants are beginning to cast off the myth that what they do stands apart from politics, that their job is simply that of administering policies made elsewhere or of tidying up, in the name of practical realism, the loose formulations of politicians.[7] Karl Mannheim may have been correct when he wrote that "the fundamental tendency of all bureaucratic thought is to turn all problems of politics into problems of administration," but British administrative experience shows equally that problems of achieving political consensus are seldom out of the minds of higher civil servants.

This is not to say that they operate in a wholly politicized atmosphere, or that by their very situations they are free to indulge their own political tastes. Formally, civil servants are under two kinds of constraints. The lesser of them is the long-standing rule that members of the Administrative Class, though they can vote, write to the press, and be passive members of political parties, may not run for office, hold office in a political party, or engage in overtly political writing or speechmaking.[8] This is a minor constraint when seen in the strictly British context, but in comparison with the political roles open to bureaucrats in other European countries, many of whom can be and are elected to national and local political offices, it underlines the caution with which the British have approached the problem of ensuring partisan neutrality among those who stand closest to the minister's ear. The second formal constraint (which has many informal consequences) is that all official actions of civil servants must be taken in the name of their minister, who is presumed to approve of and bear responsibility for everything that goes on in his department. The consequences of the doctrine of ministerial responsibility will be discussed shortly. It deserves mention at this point, however, as it provides a benchmark from which civil servants are ill-advised to stray in the direction of making public pronouncements on partisan matters. Critics who see the civil service as closed to independent thinking, innovation, and cross-fertilization with outside professional bodies make much of the general disinclination of administrators to take identifiable positions on issues on the ground that doing so would expose their minister to the embarrassment of providing political opponents with ammunition from within his administrative family.

The critics are probably more frustrated than the higher adminis-trators themselves. There is little evidence that civil servants rankle under the strictures placed on their partisan involvement, or that they have strong partisan enthusiasms. Not much is known of the political views of members of the Administrative Class, but it is thought that they have chosen a bureaucratic career because they prefer public service without the vagaries of out-and-out political life. Consider the following excerpts from Richard Chapman's interviews with the entering class of 1956,[9] a group of Administrative civil servants now in midcareer, concerning their attitudes toward politics:

> If you are emotionally concerned about politics you don't become a civil servant.

> Party loyalties are not very noticeable—they are irrelevant when you are close to the workings of government.

> The efficiency of a Government in office tends to influence one's views . . . in many cases it is difficult to differentiate between parties—they all consist of politicians.

> Civil servants don't often discuss their party political views among themselves.

Chapman's investigation of this small but not unrepresentative group also showed that its acknowledged voting record in the 1966 General Election was "just the sort of distribution a psephologist would have expected from a sample of that age group, with that educational background, at that particular election."[10]

Although they may view party politics cynically, British civil servants are far from impatient with the overall necessity for politics or resentful of the somewhat distant popular political control of their activities. In this respect they manifest different attitudes from those of counterparts in some other European countries. A survey conducted in Britain, West Germany, and Italy by Robert Putnam revealed that antipolitical feelings were widespread in Italy but infrequent in Britain and West Germany.[11] In a significant way British civil servants have been integrated into the larger features of the country's political culture, sharing—and forming—the cluster of consensual attitudes which characterize the "style" by which decisions are made in almost all large-scale British organizations.[12]

It is not surprising that the higher civil servant is socialized into the prevailing set of political and administrative norms (though in the civil service, as elsewhere, the process "takes" in different ways with different people). The relatively closed and noncompetitive nature of the higher bureaucracy encourages the process. Most of its members enter at a tender age with the implicit assurance that theirs will be a single lifetime career. Except in wartime the service has not been hospitable to outsiders or temporary bureaucrats, and has managed in most cases to keep at arm's length the "irregulars"—academic and non-Establishment political advisers such as those imported by Harold Wilson and George Brown in the early days of the Wilson Government.[13] Until recently the idea of formal training in either the substance of policy or the techniques of administration found little more than lukewarm favor, the view being that in his formative years the newcomer could be expected to learn on the job, picking up his cues where he could find them, much as the apprentice does from the younger craftsmen, if not from the Master.[14] The crash courses in economic analysis and management techniques to which he is now exposed are not likely to replace the influence of behavior norms transmitted by peers from the stock of long-standing departmental traditions. Thus his adaption to the atmosphere of politics is likely to be more a matter of style than of substance. Accepting as he does the constitutional rightness of the politician's primacy in matters of overriding substance, he is introduced early to the folk wisdom that civil servants are repositories of the realistic way—the proper methods and procedures—needed to convert the windiness of parliamentary politics into the harder currency of applied politics (i.e., administration). It is this kind of political sense, sharpened over generations and passed on as socialization rather than training, that often incites admiration and bafflement in the outsider (that is, until the outsider reflects on his own informal education in the operating code of his corporation, or profession, or university). It is not surprising, then, that paeans abound, many from the lips of once suspicious ministers, to the frictionless way in which top civil servants have been able to refine and implement divergent policies —for example, to nationalize, denationalize, and renationalize industries as different parties come into and leave office.[15]

2. THE EFFECTS OF MINISTERIAL RESPONSIBILITY

These informal constraints on civil servants' political roles dovetail well with the omnipresent influence on their working lives of the doctrine of ministerial responsibility. It is, in the words of a political scientist-MP, "the main principle moulding the structure and outlook of the senior civil service,"[16] and a useful myth serving the joint interests of political executives and their officials. Ministerial responsibility is essentially a nineteenth-century feature of British constitutional and administrative theory. Its origin lay in the period when the House of Commons exercised considerable direct control over the details of government activity; it was devised to ensure that nothing done by officials could escape parliamentary scrutiny and, if necessary, rectification. The doctrine required that all actions of civil servants be taken in the name of the minister, who would be held accountable by the Commons for such actions and, in cases where evidence of malfeasance in the performance of duties came to light, censured or made to resign. Yet at the very time when ministerial responsibility was becoming firmly entrenched as constitutional doctrine, its meaning and function within the political system came to be changed substantially. Instead, as originally intended, of serving as a parliamentary check on ministerial and civil service power, it evolved into a force strengthening the hand of the executive and making it increasingly difficult for MPs to deal directly, or informally, with the working of the bureaucracy. The evolution of British government is full of paradoxes and ironies; few have been more important politically than the transformation of the functions of ministerial responsibility.

The original intent of the doctrine has run afoul of two major twentieth-century developments in British politics. The first is the familiar explosion in the scope and complexity of the activities of government departments, to the point where neither parliament nor the informed public expects ministers to be fully aware of, or actively approve, every action taken by their civil servants in areas not of broad policy concern, that is, matters seized upon by parliament, the media, or vocal groups. Without renouncing the doctrine, all parties have been content to accept that unintentional slippage may occur. Voluntary resignations by ministers when evidence of abuses of authority by civil servants come to light are so rare as to excite amazed admiration. When the Minister of Agriculture resigned in 1954 over revelations that some of his civil servants had exceeded their powers in the Critchel Down case, he was treated as either hopelessly naive or a quaint throwback to Victorian morality. Whatever his reasons for resigning, he was certainly not forced into it by parliamentary indignation over his failure to be properly informed on a minor land-use decision in Dorset. More serious revelations of subsequent blunders, such as the enormous errors made by the costing branch of the Ministry of Aviation in its dealings with the Ferranti Aircraft company in 1964, did not bring censure or the gate to the minister responsible. Not only has a weary recognition of the increased scope and technicality of government operations softened parliament's willingness to hold ministers carefully responsible for their officials' actions; the enforcement of the doctrine of ministerial responsibility has also been undercut by the politics of collective responsibility. This is the second important development. The tightening of party control and cabinet power over parliament has reached the point where neither the opposition nor government backbenchers can penalize a minister for departmental actions so long as the Prime Minister views such an attack as a challenge to the survival of his government, or a damaging reflection on his political management. His party's parliamentary majority, and the devices he can command to mobilize it, are normally sufficient to protect any minister faced with the ultimate test of departmental responsibility. This overlay of the doctrine of party government on the earlier precept of ministerial responsibility also affords considerable protection to civil servants, whose identity and role in possible offending actions are carefully masked through the *persona* of their political chief. Although civil servants still have the task of seeing to it that their minister suffers a minimum of political embarrassment for actions they may take, they know that the modern application of this Victorian carryover frees them in large measure from direct parliamentary scrutiny and unwonted interference by MPs in most of their actions.

The consequences of the doctrine for internal civil service relations are several. First, because all departmental actions go forth in the name of the minister and he alone is supposedly accountable for them in the world outside, civil servants cannot be summoned by parliament or any outside body to defend their views and activities. (The recent creation of a British ombudsman, to be described later, does not seriously reverse this situation.) Their anonymity not only leaves the minister's responsibility formally unchallenged. It affords them considerable freedom in their dealings with pressure groups, since they cannot be tagged with responsibility for policies considered obnoxious in the eyes of dissatisfied interests. Second, secrecy and isolation are enhanced. Because in the constitutional myth a senior civil servant cannot have a public identity apart from the minister he advises, and because it is assumed that such advice can be rendered only in the enforced privacy of internal departmental life, officials rarely are allowed to explain any but official departmental views in public. To do so might provide ammunition for those later wishing to challenge the minister's decision on either factual or judgmental grounds. Secrecy enables the minister to possess what may approach a monopoly of facts and arguments, and renders the task of those who would probe further (whether in parliament, the press, or the larger public) anything but easy. As Macintosh comments: "If the doctrine were broken and officials could explain their views freely in public, then ministers would have the much more formidable task of making their case against men who were seized of the key counterpoints and who knew their arguments were accepted by many in the ministry. It is clear why ministers, who lose only a little and gain a great deal from the doctrine, should want to keep it going,"[17]

Third, ministerial responsibility throws a cloud of secrecy over not only minister-civil servant relationships but also over negotiations with outside groups in areas where parliament supposedly has its own responsibility. It can lead to a closed relationship between pressure groups and bureaucrats which reduces parliament to a kind of post facto kibbitzer. S. E. Finer puts the dilemma succinctly: "Increasingly, what the minister presents to the Commons is a package arrangement agreed between his civil servants and the representatives of the outside groups. In the House, party discipline inhibits backbenchers from challenging their government; even if it did not, the information and evidence on which the package depends are confidential and have not been disclosed; and even if they had been, the nature of the package is so well-balanced a set of compromises that if any one part were overturned in the House the entire deal would have to be re-negotiated."[18] With neither direct access to civil servants nor their own expert staffs, MPs can serve only fitfully as informed critics of policy and administration.

Fourth, the doctrine reinforces the centralized and hierarchical nature of British administration by channeling control from above. Some semi-independent boards exist, and government as producer tends to act through nationalized industries and public corporations, for whose broad policies, but not day-to-day administration, ministers remain responsible. But in the mainstream of policy-making departments officials stand in a vertical chain, with decisions funneled up to the minister so that he can meet his formal obligation to parliament. The American or Swedish experience of administering through numerous small, fairly independent boards or agencies, or the modern management technique of appointing an official, giving him a budget and wider powers on a "show me" basis, have not been readily accepted in British public administration, ostensibly on the ground that it would vest powers of decision in officials whose public accountability, via a minister, could not be guaranteed.[19] As a result, the introduction of new policies, as well as the implementation of old ones, requires the passage through the hierarchy and onto the minister's desk of a mass of paperwork. Besides slowing the process of decision, this movement puts a premium on the talents of Administrative Class officials to sift and winnow the important from the trivial. Such skills are in part political; it takes some immersion in the political world to detect when a comparatively minor decision (in terms of the ministry's goals) carries a potentially explosive political charge. Ministerial responsibility also makes it rather difficult to graft modern business techniques onto British public administration. The Fulton Committee was told, for example, that "decisions often have to be referred to a higher level than their intrinsic difficulty or apparent importance merits because they involve the responsibility of Ministers to Parliament, and Parliamentary accountability fosters centralized control by Accounting Officers."[20]

It is difficult to believe that a major modification, or abandonment, of the doctrine of ministerial responsibility would not lead to deep changes in political relationships within the service. It is noteworthy that when, as the result of heavy criticism of the civil service by "modernizers," the Wilson Government appointed the Fulton Committee to conduct a "fundamental and wideranging inquiry" into the Home Civil Service, the Prime Minister specifically excluded from its terms of reference the examination of the working of the doctrine of ministerial responsibility, thus ensuring the limited scope of its recommendations and forcing it to question the doctrine by implication rather than directly. Given the mutual benefits of the doctrine to both ministers and civil servants, and the only mildly reformist approach to institutional change of the modern Labour Party, it was not really surprising that the committee was kept on such a short lead.

3. MINISTERS AND THEIR HIGHER OFFICIALS

The key entity in British public administration is the department, and for civil servants the key political referent in their lives is their minister. "In no European country," writes Brian Chapman, "is the civil servant's attention concentrated on the minister to quite the same degree as in Britain. European parliaments have greater powers of interfering in administration than the British parliament, and the civil servant's attention wanders accordingly."[21] This institutional fact accounts for a large share of the political roles which higher civil servants are expected to play; it also accounts for the considerable variations in civil servants' powers, since ministers are not cut from identical cloth, nor do they adopt identical conceptions of their own political missions.

Nevertheless, though as individuals ministers vary, their careers and outlooks are influenced strongly by prevailing traditions of the British political system. In contrast with continental practice, British ministers must be members of one of the Houses of Parliament, and experienced parliamentarians at that. The average apprenticeship of a new cabinet member—the period he has spent previously in one of the Houses—is fifteen years for recent governments.[22] Two effects of this convention upon ministerial attributes are worth noting. The first is the virtual exclusion from the top political executive of persons from other walks of life, such as business, law, technology, trade unionism, or academia. MPs may have begun as members of these occupations, and may retain part-time interest in them; but by the time they become ministers they are likely to have lost touch with developments in them and replaced prior skills with ones more closely associated with success on the parliamentary scene. Direct recruitment from outside parliament is extremely rare, and its results not considered so persuasive as to warrant revision of the long-standing convention.[23] The second consequence is the absence of any close fit between the minister's previous expertise and his duties as head of a government department. A certain convergence may of course occur. The minister may have been the Shadow Minister (i.e., opposition spokesman) for the subject of the department to which he is appointed, or have made a reputation as a semispecialist in its affairs as a backbencher. But the political and manpower needs of the Prime Minister just as likely may dictate his placement in a ministry whose activities are almost unknown terrain to him, especially as parliament has almost no powerful specialized committees on which he might have cut his teeth. Furthermore, only a small number of ministerial assignments are given to MPs without previous ministerial experience. This is the case particularly when his party has been in power for some years. The Prime Minister will usually construct his government by shuffling around posts among top party notables, many of whom will head two or three widely differing departments during a single parliament. (In the Wilson years, for example, George Brown was head of the Department of Economic Affairs, then Foreign Secretary; Michael Stewart was Foreign Secretary, then head of Economic Affairs; Roy Jenkins was Home Secretary, then Chancellor of the Exchequer. In his long career Sir Winston Churchill held virtually every cabinet post except Foreign Secretary.) Richard Rose has calculated that for the period 1955-70 the average tenure in the eleven departmental posts normally in the cabinet was 26 months.[24] It is misleading to characterize this as amateurism rampant, as it is to describe a higher civil servant with thirty years' experience as a sheer amateur. Nevertheless, both types of career are based on the assumption that general skills—of political and administrative management, respec- tively—are more important than subject matter expertise. With respect to ministers, one must view frequent turnover as being more related to the Prime Minister's political exigencies than to the quest for a sounder structure of public administration.

Length of expected tenure is bound to affect the relationship of a minister to his top civil servants. If he assumes, or has been chosen for, the role of maintaining existing departmental policy, his principal task is to learn and defend his legacy, which means chiefly putting his political skills at the disposal of the keepers of departmental traditions and seeing to it that departmental interests are not upset at interdepartmental and cabinet levels. For this role a two or three year stint at a ministry poses no difficult problems. If on the other hand he enters the ministry with ideas for substantial change, or a mandate from the prime minister to launch great changes, his need to press his officials quickly will be greater. Rose estimates that it takes on average three years for a minister to see a new policy to fruition, especially in view of the British penchant for elaborate interest group consultation; even this figure assumes like-minded rather than unenthusiastic civil servants. "It would take one year for the minister to understand the technical intricacies of his department sufficiently well to settle the administrative and not unimportant details of a bill, a year to push it through Parliament and/or secure Treasury authorization for expenditure, and a year to establish guidelines for administering the resulting policy."[25] Unless he can achieve this in the first several years of the life of a parliament, the minister may well find that the attention and time of his colleagues, and the House itself, are given over to issues with obvious pre-election payoff, and unless his pet measures fall into this category he finds it hard to get the requisite parliamentary time to push them through when the election countdown is on. Even if he should be fortunate enough to win the time and support for his legislation, he is apt to find that the Prime Minister's or the electorate's fancy now dictate that someone will preside over their implementation.

Even if a minister spends a number of years heading a single department, he soon finds that he can accomplish only a limited number of objectives due to the myriad claims on his time and energy. The system requires that he keep his finger in many pies, spending hours each week in parliament, in cabinet and cabinet committees, in political party meetings, in meetings with his junior ministers and top civil servants, making visits to outlying divisions of the department, consulting with pressure group spokesmen, attending official lunches and receptions, and nursing his constituency. He is also expected to deal with the paperwork that comes before him and keep abreast, by reading the heavily annotated papers which originate in the lower reaches of the bureaucracy and wend their way up to him, of the actions and proposals believed to be in need of his attention. Some of these tasks can be delegated to junior ministers, or done perfunctorily; but few can be neglected outright by ministers who wish to assert their control of departmental policy, take their accountability to parliament seriously, or have higher ambitions best served by a reputation for being a "strong" minister. Small wonder, then, that ministers (like higher civil servants) put in a 60 to 70 hour week, or that "sheer overwork, arising from the need to carry out every-increasing responsibilities, is one major obstacle to ministerial policy-making."[26] However strong his intention to bear down on his officials and impose his own stamp on his department, a British minister, like the head of any other complex organization, cannot find the time or physical stamina to cope equally with all the expectations put on him. Hence the need to set priorities and make choices. Hence also the likelihood of his strong dependence on those who have mastered the Whitehall ropes over time.

Discussions centering on "who makes policy?" in British government tend to end in fuzzy, if valid, generalizations about the pluralism of actors and forces. The question's variant for ministerial politics usually focuses on the incidence of "strong" and "weak" ministers, that is, those capable of imprinting their mark in substantial areas of policy as contrasted with those who either fail or simply carry out someone else's bidding. These concepts are necessarily vague, if only because little systematic research has been done to bring them beyond journalistic shorthand. But they do raise the important question of ministerial relationships with top civil servants, and can be useful if used cautiously. A strong minister, according to the model, knows what he wants on the large issues, comes to his department with a well-developed program, has the political weight and skill to move it through the shoals of possible opposition from cabinet colleagues, the Treasury, senior civil servants, and pressure groups, seeing to it not only that legislation and rules square with his programmatic philosophy, but also that they are administered in the same spirit. In this view the role of civil servants is largely one of informing the minister fully, analyzing his choices in terms of their technical and administrative feasibility, freeing him from trivial paperwork, and ensuring that his policies are put into effect swiftly and positively. Because they are left in no doubt over what their minister wants, civil servants act as hand-maidens rather than as brakes on the strong minister. Under the weak minister model, the minister lacks focused knowledge or concerted views of his department's mission, shows little political strength in dealing with cabinet colleagues and permanent officials, remains passive in the face of opportunities to change or rationalize major policies, becomes preoccupied with preordained routines and trivia, and so on. Opportunities for independent policy-making by civil servants are thus enhanced, if only because civil servants are forced by the absence of clear and predictable guidelines into making the running themselves.

These models are not wholly academic abstractions. One can put names under them easily from recent ministerial experience, a game at which Whitehall watchers are adept. Yet the concepts are too blunt for the intricacies of ministerial-civil servant relationships in all their forms, and too simple as explanations of the range of choices available to most ministers. Seen by civil servants, strong ministers may be those who excel in extracting funds from the Treasury for hitherto starved departmental activities, while to Treasury officials a strong Chancellor may be one who successfully resists these pressures, or rights the current balance of payments account. To the public a strong minister may be one who is able to push a fistful of popular reforms through parliament, or resists, with a maximum of publicity, pay demands from postal workers or higher rents for naval bases from the Maltese Prime Minister. To the British Prime Minister he may be one who runs a tight ship and keeps potentially embarrassing or expensive crises quietly under control. The strength or weakness of a particular minister is to some extent a matter of the vantage from which he is judged; it is also related quite directly to the sort of activities he and his department are expected to carry out. A recent study by Bruce Headey contributes to an understanding of these relationships.[27]

The paucity of hard data on policy-making at the top makes it enormously difficult to assess the extent to which ministers bow, consciously or unconsciously, to the weight of "departmental views." As civil servants speak or write infrequently of such matters, and then usually in vagueness influenced by the omnipresence of the Official Secrets Act and traditions of fraternal anonymity, most of the claims for the pressure of departmental views are based on statements from former ministers, outside critics, and "irregulars" —experts brought into Whitehall temporarily, mainly in the Wilson years, to serve as counters to the careerists.[28] Their remarks must be treated with some caution. Just as civil servants are apt to expiate their responsibility for disastrous or heavily criticized decisions by taking refuge in the doctrine of ministerial responsibility, so too ex-ministers are tempted to take the view that their best efforts were systematically scuttled by faulty information, bureaucratic intran- sigence, or deliberately slow action on the part of their officials.[29] The latter position has often been taken by observers who pinpoint the higher civil service as the secret foe of left-wing socialism, or as a short circuit in the proper implementation of party government.[30]

Lacking systematic evidence, it is not difficult to find for every example of civil servants allegedly overcoming the original views of their ministers a counter example of ministerial domination. It is commonly believed that on British policy in the Middle East, pro-Arab officials at the Foreign Office were able to bend two Labour foreign secretaries, Bevin and Morrison, to their line. But it is also believed that the Foreign Office was solidly opposed to the Suez invasion launched by Eden and Selwyn Lloyd. Chamberlain could veto the views of the Permanent Secretary and most officials at the Foreign Office at the time of Munich; but a strong departmental philosophy, such as the Foreign Office's pro-Common Market convictions in the 1960s, swept all before it (including the opposition of the Permanent Secretary at the Ministry of Agricul- ture). During the 1940s and 1950s two Home Secretaries, Ede and G.

Lloyd George, turned away from their past principles to assume the then normal departmental position of opposing the abolition of capital punishment when they came to office, only to become abolitionists again after they left the Home Office.[31] The influence of Treasury knights was held largely responsible for the fluctuations and slow growth of the British economy in the 1950s; yet in the Wilson years they were continually overruled by the Chancellor and Prime Minister in their advocacy of devaluation—a step which when finally taken in 1967 came close to resolving the perennial balance of payments conundrum.[32] It may be that these being dramatic, well-publicized decisions, ministers were just as apt to be overruled by the Cabinet as influenced by civil servants. Indeed, on more mundane, but more common, policy decisions, the impact of traditional departmental views may be greater. What does emerge from the impressionistic examples at hand is insufficient to warrant the conclusion that ministers are bound to yield to departmental views as funneled to them by their top civil servants.

What is less in doubt is that higher officials have—in fact are encouraged to have—formed views on matters of major political policy.[33] These can be called "departmental views" if they follow a single course, are not significantly challenged from within the department, and serve to narrow the minister's options. There is a tendency for them to prevail if certain conditions prevail. The first is when the minister lacks ability, experience, subject matter knowledge, time, or sufficient energy to involve himself. On many issues this kind of minister is fully aware that he is leaving the running to his civil servants. They may not be among his key issues. "What happens," writes an observant MP, "is that having to serve on many cabinet and other committees, anyone other than a top-grade and experienced minister tends to use the brief he has been given. And before every ministerial committee, an equivalent official committee meets and goes over the points, so that the whole thing can go through without a hitch to an agreed conclusion provided none of the ministers wishes to interject a personal note."[34] This situation is most likely to prevail when a political party has taken office after some years in the wilderness, when the minister lacks previous departmental experience, has been chosen for political balance rather than ability, or shows a weak political personality. Another boost to the success of departmental views occurs when the minister, in setting his priorities and husbanding his resources for a limited number of costly encounters, deliberately remains aloof from involvement in areas he judges to be politically uninteresting or self-regulating. To quote a former "key issues" minister: " . . . even after two years at the Board of Trade I had had no contact at all with the Patent Office and practically none with Weights and Measures. But I never lay awake at night thinking 'Gosh, I wonder what those chaps at the Patent Office are up to.' The only things that would keep you awake at night are sudden crises."[35]

Neither of these situations involves deliberate usurpation of power by civil servants; each is explicable by the pressures of government life or the frailties of ministerial talent. Civil servants want policies made and administered with smooth regularity, and if the minister is unable or unwilling to ride herd on them, they will carry on themselves—in the name of the minister. A more subtle problem is that of ensuring that the minister does not lose his control of events to highly confident, articulate, assertedly cautious civil servants to the point where new ventures are not risked or old agreements accepted as sacrosanct. How pervasive this problem is is difficult to ascertain, for reasons already stated. The testimony of former ministers, even when it has been discounted as containing a good deal of self-justification, shows the difficulty ministers have when faced with deeply entrenched official viewpoints. Given the uniquely elevated position of the Permanent Secretary in British departments (a phenomenon with no real counterpart in the arrangements of other European or American governments), there is some risk that what the minister is offered ostensibly as the agreed departmental view is actually only the view of the Permanent Secretary and a few of the latter's senior colleagues. Even if the minister and his political associates should wish to question every major analysis or recom- mendation coming up to them, they are too few to do the job. (Gordon has calculated that "the ratio of [top] civil servants to partisan nominees in charge of them is really about fifty to one."[36]) Furthermore, as in his relations with cabinet colleagues, a minister is unlikely to be able to engage in prolonged conflict with his higher officials on more than a handful of issues. He can do so more easily if he knows that his officials themselves are divided or uncertain—when there is not, in fact, a strongly entrenched "de- partmental view" to which all important civil servants subscribe. This occurs more often than is recognized, especially as few departments maintain a reward structure based on ideological conformity. Ministers who make a concerted effort to encourage pluralism of advice have some opportunities if they choose to use them. They may widen the circle of their advisers to include middle level as well as top level officials, make more substantial use of junior ministers, bring in outside advisers, attend personally to the views of rival pressure group deputations, and insist that the alternatives put before them represent varied views from within their department.

But there remain in British practice two formidable obstacles to the firm assertion of ministerial grip on departmental affairs: insecure familiarity with subject matter, and briefness of tenure. The latter constraint is probably the more important in the light of the well-established British convention of moving consensually whenever possible and only after thorough consultation with affected interests —meaning not only pressure groups but also kindred departments and the Treasury. Thus the temptation to build upon, or only tinker with, past policies is more easily acceded to than the call to bring forth strinkingly new blueprints, which must be years on the drawing board, or founder (as did much of Prime Minister Heath's proposed return to vigorous free enterprise) when launched without hard-won group acceptance. It is not surprising that with ministerial turnover known to occur almost every other year, civil servants should occasionally act so as to reserve some latitude for the next minister.

British government does move, however, and whatever may be the shortcomings in the policy process, it is inaccurate to portray the higher bureaucracy as obstructionist. While they cultivate a measure of independence—not unlike that of the press, another less than representative but essential estate of the political realm—civil servants seldom insert themselves in the way of a government, or a confident minister, that knows what should be done and is actively concerned with administrative affairs. Senior civil servants may resent certain strong-minded ministers, such as George Brown or Richard Crossman, who push them hard and accept few of the traditional excuses for inaction; but they are more unhappy with a minister who lacks, or fails to convey, views of what the department should be doing, who cannot stand up to the Treasury or fellow ministers, or who through inaction forces them to work overtime to fill critical vacuums. The older notion that by education, training, and situation higher civil servants were "supposed to have no pretensions to play a positive role"[37] has been outdistanced by events. It has not been replaced, however, by a policy machine equipped or willing to box in the political executive on the large issues of the shape British society is to take.

4. A GARLAND OF BUREAUCRATIC ROLES

Before we consider some of the changes made in the civil service in the past decade, it might be useful to sum up the variety of political roles that British national officials are now called upon to play, and to mention a number of roles that they do not perform, or perform in only peripheral ways. Several general observations about these roles need to be made first, however. They are made up of a mixture of requirements stemming from long-standing (or at least nine-teenth-century) government activities and ones that have developed rapidly since 1918 as the complexities of government practices have exceeded the capacity of elected political leaders to control them in any but the broadest and most sporadic way. In addition, these roles cannot be viewed as constant but are played instead in a variety of ways, depending upon the nature of a department's tasks and the orientation and skills of its presiding minister. Finally, in Britain the performance of a finite number of political roles by bureaucrats is generally accepted as legitimate by the political elite and the wider public.[38]

If politics is viewed broadly as having to do with "the forces, institutions and organizational forms . . . recognized as having the most conclusive and final authority existing in a society for the establishment and maintenance of order, the effectuation of other conjoint purposes of its members, and the reconciliation of their differences,"[39] five political roles stand out in the British higher bureaucracy:

(1) Substantive policy implementation. The traditional role of the nonelected official is to carry out the will of parliament by seeing to it that structures and personnel act to enforce the laws and policies of electorally responsible political leaders. On its face, this role might be considered as administrative rather than political, except that in contemporary Britain laws are normally stated in general terms and the burden of "middle level" interpretation put squarely on the shoulders of ministers. In addition, the volume of delegated legislative powers has increased enormously in recent years (and is bound to escalate further on Britain's accession to the Common Market), thus blending policy implementation and de facto legis-lating as political tasks for the minister and his top advisers. The minister is accountable to parliament for the execution of this mandate, but in practice much of it is carried through by his civil

servants. This is of course not unique to Britain, being characteristic of all developed industrial states.

(2) Political advising. The most exacting of higher officials' roles—the one which brings them closest to the heart of politics—is that of preparing their ministers for the making of policy decisions. In this role civil servants seldom can monopolize the field: the minister gets information and advice from members of parliament, party leaders, pressure groups, outside experts, and the press. But his single most continuous source, and the one he tends to rely upon for factual information and estimates of feasibility, is his departmental machine. To a large measure civil servants (not only at the highest level) control the content and flow of official information that wends its way up to the minister, and on them he depends for shrewd collation of arguments and alternatives. They are called upon for assessments of the probable political, as well as the administrative, consequences of actions which he may be contemplating. The skill with which this essential staff work is done has been variously evaluated, giving rise to images of the higher bureaucracy both as a highly polished engine honing down the roughness of rashly considered initiatives and of a closed monastic order producing for the minister only safe, sterilized policy choices. Whatever the truth of either interpretation, there is little doubt that to perform these tasks civil servants must be well sensitized to the political implications of all actions they recommend to the minister. Their breeding as political animals inevitably differs from that of party politicians, but their interaction requires them to be of the same species.

(3) Mutual political protection. Although top civil servants cannot be said to function as a minister's private political machine, they can respond to his need to enhance his political image. They may not be able to make him an overnight success, or to shelter him from all forms of criticism, but by ensuring that he is well fortified with neatly packaged knowledge and arguments, civil servants can underpin a confident parliamentary performance. They can see to it that he scoops up the credit for popular policies by effacing their own contribution. Habits of secrecy keep potentially damaging intelligence within the circle of insiders, most of whom can be counted on to limit its general circulation. Leaks, calculated and otherwise, do occur in Whitehall, but at nothing like the level of Washington, where they are a standard component of interdepart-

mental warfare often touching the reputations of political heads. The British relationship is symbiotic: in return for their protection and enhancement of their minister's reputation, civil servants are shielded by him from direct political interference from parliament, the press, and the public. These mutual benefits help explain the composite executive's coolness to proposals for major changes in arrangements such as scrapping the doctrine of ministerial responsibility, or less sweeping ones such as the provision of more avowedly political advisers to the minister through the introduction of French-style departmental *cabinets.* [40] In each case changes have been rejected as risking the overt politicalization of the officialdom.

(4) Advancing clientele claims. The vast majority of Whitehall departments manage policies affecting identifiable clienteles, organized or otherwise. While part of the job of civil servants is to analyze, verify, and cost the claims of such groups, and forward them to higher centers of decision, it would be unnatural if officials did not identify in some way with the interests of their clienteles, and within the overall framework of current government policy advance claims finding favor in the department. To do this is not necessarily to abandon the quest for the public interest (a task many civil servants believe they perform as well as elected politicians), but to recognize the psychological affinities created by specialization in the division of public labor. Further, the legitimacy and prestige of a civil servant's function often relates to the perceived importance of the services his department may be providing to its clientele. At one level the contribution of higher civil servants is to strengthen their minister's grasp of clientele claims to enable him to put an informed case to the cabinet, cabinet committees, the Treasury, and inter-departmental committees. At another level civil servants often employ their political skills to advance and reconcile clientele demands in the almost continual round of interdepartmental committee meetings of which Whitehall is so fond, and in subtle person-to-person encounters with Treasury officials over budgetary and expenditure matters. Increasingly the British civil servant has assumed the role of negotiator which is after all only a variant on that of the politician.

(5) Conflict management and consensus-making. The processing of clientele interests is closely related to another political role: the aggregation and reconciliation of pressure group claims on the

administrative sector. Regular links between British officials and their counterparts in the private sector have been firmly established over the past thirty years. Whitehall departments are fixed targets for a wide range of group pressures, few of them in a single direction. Both within sections of departments and in interdepartmental dealings civil servants are accustomed to bringing together competing demands and mediating among them in order to create viable "packages," which then go up to the minister for his action, or for conversion into bills and statutory instruments. To this end they are engaged in the formation and staffing of innumerable standing advisory committees, ad hoc committees, and Royal Commissions, part of whose function is to legitimate consultation with and achieve consensus among group representatives prior to the unveiling of new policies. Here, as throughout the fabric of British politics, the committee is the chief instrument of government. Such committees are not always merely vehicles for the mutual exchange of ideas and information: they often are also given responsibility for carrying out aspects of administration.[41] Civil servants lubricate this process in their own special way: they are renowned as masters of the art of committeemanship, of achieving consensus whenever possible through compromise behind closed doors. They are not the sole source of consensualism in the British political system, nor are they invariably successful: not all conflicts are neatly resolved, any more than in the more overtly partisan sectors. But to a remarkable degree civil servants are engaged as brokers bringing group representatives into contact with the political elite machinery, and pressing on them prevailing views of "administrative realism." These officials are seldom influential enough to head off persistent, large-scale conflict, such as major industrial strikes or disputes emanating from fundamental party policy. But at only a slightly lower level, they are active in ways which seldom catch the headlines. Those who welcome the muting or defusing of conflict, who are impressed with incremental change, rate this as a positive contribution of the higher bureaucracy. Those who view British politics from a more radical perspective find this subtle process insidious, especially when it results in the "de-radicalization by cooptation" of the leadership of outwardly left groups.[42]

It is also necessary to consider briefly certain other roles which British civil servants do not perform, or perform in only quite marginal ways. Five such "non-roles" are of particular interest to an understanding of the system's limits.

First, British civil servants do not substitute for a paralyzed party or electoral system. Under normal circumstances a party majority emerges easily in parliament and produces cabinets of a single party complexion, thus not posing for the higher bureaucracy the dilemma, or temptation, of having to act as preserver of the state and chief policy initiator. It may indeed act in the interestices where formal political institutions provide only general or partial guidance, and its advice may strongly mould the choices open to politicians; but this is not the same thing as assuming by default the awesome burden of overall policy initiation.

Second, civil servants rarely engage in the direct provision of goods and services. They take easily to the arts of "general administration" but seldom deal directly with the public at large. State enterprises tend to be run by nationalized industries organized as public corporations, which are only indirectly connected to the tracks of ministerial responsibility and whose managers and employees are chosen on largely technical principles and guided by standards not derived from civil service practice. Increasingly, enterprises with commercial functions are being "hived off," if not always to the private sector then to semiautonomous state corporations; witness the removal of the Post Office from departmental status in 1971. Government support of basic research, the arts, universities, and related undertakings is given through the medium of intermediary institutions such as the Medical Research Council, the Arts Council, and the Universities Grants Committee, which are not instantly amenable to civil service control. Primary and secondary education is affected by labyrinthine federal relationships between local authorities and the Whitehall ministry. In general, the power and impact of the centrl government is buffered rather than direct. These "Byzantine arrangements" (in Brian Chapman's phrase) are particularly displeasing to those who feel that civil servants lack direct knowledge of the consequences of national policies, or identification with problems of grass roots management.[43]

A third political function British civil servants do not perform to any marked extent is direct control of the populace, or of subordinate units of government. The national bureaucracy does not set mandatory production norms for industry, watch closely the behavior of average citizens, or treat the police or the courts as arms of administration. Some inspectorial functions are carried out (in factories, schools, pollution control, and so on), but they are sporadic and concerned more with uniform administration and discovery of abuses at the margin than with maintaining close tabs on the movement and behavior of citizens. Local government in Britain is not especially powerful, but it displays a variety and independence seldom found in countries where prefects act as political/administrative agents of the central government.

Fourth, because it has been traditionally a closed career, the higher civil service does not serve as an instrument for systematically recruiting talent into other elites, whether they be members of parliament, political executives, local government officials, or managers in the private sector. However attractive their skills may appear at the middle or end of their careers, few civil servants trade their places in Whitehall for ones elsewhere. Some indeed have moved into industries or universities, particularly as they approach retirement; but just as the intake of outside experts on short-term assignments has been very small, so too has been the incidence of *pantouflage*. Bureaucrats have not been coopted into ministerial posts as in Fifth Republic France, or gone into parliamentary politics as in the Bonn Republic. Higher civil servants' salaries no longer seem outrageously low when compared to those of other executives; and even when they did the security and traditions of the service have been such as to suppress the longing for other careers among those socialized into its way of life. Indeed, those who would reform the civil service have been more concerned with stimulating greater mobility in and out of its ranks than with either the threat of losing top talent or unseemly connections with other elites, public or private.

Finally, for reasons that are by now apparent, higher British civil servants do not take an active role in partisan politics. Their identification with one party over others is sublimated, both by temperament and by the requirements and etiquette of their calling. Thus they seldom bring to their tasks the passions of the true believer (at least in traditional political terms), and they cannot be appealed to easily on the basis of fraternal party ties. This disjuncture from partisanship does not, of course, mean that civil servants do not behave like political animals; but it does mean that they feel little determination to conduct a policy simply because it emanates from a particular party, or to subordinate their views to those of a minister because he is also a powerful party notable. British civil servants are apt to adopt a respectfully cynical, but not hostile, view of party politics. This attitude encourages their greater identification with the service as a more active embodiment of the public interest when compared to the comings and goings of party politicians, even though they dutifully perpetuate the canons of ministerial responsibility.

In sum, what British civil servants do falls short of being "total politics," just as it does of being "total administration." It is not strictly uniform behavior, either, without variation from department to department or from job to job. But it goes far beyond the popular myth, so assiduously cultivated by civil servants themselves, that whatever is unconnected with the manoeuvring of political parties is nonpolitical. As a global judgment, Brian Chapman's comment is only slightly exaggerated: "It is not possible for ever to evade questions about 'the right kind of society,' the purposes of the state, the basis and justification of government business. The determination of ends, the choice of means, the balance of social forces, are the stuff of politics. In these terms it is clear that some civil servants are engaged in politics. The word 'policy' is a recognition of this; it is a way of describing what civil servants do when they play a part in determining ends, choosing means and fixing priorities. It is distinguished from politics, which is limited strictly to the activities of political parties, and from administration which is the maintenance of the status quo. 'Policy' is the nothing more than the political activity of civil servants."[44]

5. REFORMERS AND REFORMS

The decade of the 1960s brought a number of changes in the British civil service, as it did in other parts of the political system. Directly or indirectly these changes affected in several ways the ability of civil servants to perform the political roles already described. How sweeping or fundamental they will turn out to be is not easy to judge; many of them have just left the drawing board. Nor are they all of a piece. In typically British fashion they have tended to emerge not so much from a thoroughgoing reappraisal of the civil servant's place in the political process as from incremental responses to a variety of stimuli. The changes that have taken place, nevertheless, are symptomatic of the British approach to modernizing political/administrative structures, and warrant mention here.

In a larger sense their adoption was related to the nagging dissatisfaction with the output of the policy machine which reached its peak in the first half of the decade. This was a period characterized by the disposition of the informed public to question and deplore traditional ways by which Britons conduct their affairs, whether in industry, commerce, education, private relations, or government. Anti-Establishmentarianism was in the air, no longer confined to just social and cultural realms. Disillusionment, centered particularly on Britain's sluggish economic performance since the end of World War II, rubbed in by comparisons with the growth and vitality shown by Western European countries in the early days of the Common Market. Both major political parties attempted to capitalize on this mood in their policies and promises—the Conservatives by attempting an incomes policy and French-style planning, Labour by making modernization a key feature of its 1964 General Election campaign. Both went in for administrative reform as one approach to modernization, but with varying emphasis and success; and neither was inclined to touch fundamentally the chief components of civil servants' political roles.

Not that civil servants did not come in for a large measure of criticism from the modernizers. They were singled out as repositories of antique amateurism, out of touch with the realities of the assembly line and the saleroom, captives of outmoded economic doctrines, ill-prepared to hold their own with European counterparts. Much of the erratic behavior of the economy was attributed to the grip of senior Treasury officials, and the Bank of England, on a dizzying succession of Chancellors of the Exchequer. The critics could not seem to agree whether the most desirable change would be to strengthen or weaken the role of the civil service (the result, perhaps, of their tendency to treat its functions apart from other elements of the political system); but some kind of reform appeared essential to cabinets of the day, for political as much as managerial reasons.

An early effort was the attempt to dilute the Treasury's dominant role in managing the economy and controlling the personnel of the national bureaucracy. In 1962 the Conservatives reorganized the Treasury into two sides (each under a separate Permanent Secretary), one to deal with economics and finance and the other with civil service management. Almost concurrently, the Macmillan government established the National Economic Development Council, a three-sided (industry, trade unions, government) committee outside the Treasury's domain, to act as a major organ of economic planning and modernization.[45] The Treasury's overall responsibility for economic policy-making was further diminished when Labour came to power in 1964 and created, side by side with the Treasury, a Department of Economic Affairs with much-publicized powers in the planning field, to which were drawn not only a number of younger civil servants but also professional economics and technical experts on temporary assignment. Wilson's cooptation of "irregular" officials, though not an overwhelming success, exposed civil servants to greater unorthodoxies, while also chastening the views of those who has previously attacked the bureaucracy from the outside. Nevertheless, Labour's middle years were dominated by the near-collapse of sterling in international trade and an unchanging low level of economic growth, and not surprisingly in this period the Treasury regained much of its former authority in the area of economic management. But in the interval it had undergone internal changes of a quieter kind, becoming more professionalized and open in its dealings with other departments and even with the public.[46]

Labour's suspicion that the composition and attitudes of the civil service were barriers to modernization of British policy-making appeared to be confirmed by the 1965 report of a parliamentary select committee, which recommended a broadly based inquiry, backed by research, into the structure, recruitment, and management of the service.[47] The Fulton Committee, which was appointed in 1966 and reported in 1968, not only took evidence from the standard sources but also commissioned studies from academics and used the services of a management consultant firm. Restricted by its terms of reference from considering basic structural features like the doctrine of ministerial responsibility (and the anonymity and secrecy stemming from it), the committee concentrated on the managerial aspects of the civil service, finding them to be grossly unfitted to the requirements of the positive state. Strongly impressed with the canons of modern business administration, it castigated "the cult of the generalist" ("obsolete at all levels and in all parts of the service"), deplored the absence of systematic professional training within the service, found little evidence of the employment of modern management techniques, alleged that scientists and engineers were relegated to second-class citizenship within its structure, condemned the infrequency and superficial nature of Whitehall's contact with the outside world, and criticized the rewarding of seniority rather than merit. The Fulton Committee's recommendations, which came under hostile attack not only from civil servants but also from academic students of administration, are too numerous to list here. Essentially they centered on the introduction of techniques of modern business management, greater recruitment of specialized rather than generally trained entrants, more delegation of budgetary responsibility to units organized around objectives, simplification of the structure of civil service classes and grades, and increased training in technical skills and subject matter.

The Wilson Government immediately accepted and moved to implement several of the committee's recommendations: the establishment of a new Civil Service Department with central authority on matters of recruitment, staffing and machinery; the creation of a Civil Service College to broaden and systematize training programs; the dedication of more resources to personnel management; and the abolition of the 47 general service and 1,400 departmental classes in favor of a unified grading structure (including the merger of the old Administrative, Executive, and Clerical classes into a new Administrative Group). The rest of the Fulton recommendations were greeted with caution, or promises that they would be treated later (if at all) in White Papers.[48] In point of fact, many of these changes were already being evolved by the time the committee sat; the committee's efforts simply gave them more impetus and legitimacy. None of them, with the possible exception of setting up the CSD, affected substantially the structure or functions of the bureaucracy. All were compatible with the doctrine of ministerial responsibility, and therefore unlikely to reorder the political roles of civil servants in any but marginal ways.

The intensification of criticism in the past decade has brought other changes. Some weakening of the propensity to governmental secrecy has occurred. Civil servants are less constrained to avoid active and vocal participation in the affairs of professional societies. A few departments have taken to issuing Green Papers—documents that raise issues and canvass a range of alternative solutions—at early rather than late stages in the drafting of recommendations to ministers, and to holding public hearings on them. The Official Secrets Act, which dates from the eve of World War I and has been a barrier to open expression by civil servants and former ministers (as well as to press reporting of government information), was sharply criticized by a lay committee under Lord Franks, which recommended a softening of its most restrictive provisions.[49] To date no governmental action has been taken on the Franks suggestion, however. Hopes for the diminution of secrecy and the enlargement of parliamentary and public input into policy-making rose with the institution, on an experimental basis, of a number of sessional select committees in the House of Commons in 1967. These committees were to be few in number and supplementary to the normal unspecialized standing committees of the House. They were established not only to enhance and improve the ability of the House to conduct its business, but also because of the rising "suspicion [among MPs] that pressure groups have an improper influence upon Whitehall."[50] Launched with considerable fanfare in the middle years of the Wilson Government in areas such as Agriculture, Science and Technology, Race Relations and Overseas Aid, these new committees did some useful work but did not really catch on, and they have petered out under the Conservatives.[51] Neither the expert staffs they employed, nor their ability to summon ministers to speak specifically about departmental actions and plans, were of sufficient strength to cut seriously into the customary relationships of officials-ministers-parliament. The specialized committee idea is not dead, but major political surgery will be required before such arms of parliament approach the scope and bite of American legislative committees. If they are to go beyond tinkering, such changes will need more wholehearted support from the political executive than has been expressed to date.

The final innovation worth mentioning here is the introduction, again in 1967, of the British Parliamentary Commissioner, or ombudsman. The origins of this office antedate the Labour government; they stem from a growing dissatisfaction in the late 1950s with the adequacy of both administrative tribunals and normal parliamentary procedures for handling complaints of maladministration. Although it bears a family resemblance to the earlier Scandinavian and New Zealand ombudsmen, the British version reflects a more limited approach to the problem of citizen grievances against the administrative process. The ombudsman's terms of reference have been circumscribed by the fears expressed in parliament that in a country the size of Britain he might be swamped with complaints and the reluctance of ministers to accept anything which would seriously impede the normal conduct of administration. Thus the ombudsman was made an officer of parliament and empowered to act only on complaints he receives through an MP, who must first be approached by an aggrieved citizen. Furthermore, the operations of certain administrative areas (the health services, housing, local government, and the nationalized industries) were excluded from his area of competence.[52] The ombudsman lacks executive power to act on his own, his duty being to investigate complaints and report to parliament on their validity, as well as the steps, if any are required, taken to rectify acts of maladministration. Maladministration is defined strictly in procedural terms. As the author of the most comprehensive analysis of the ombudsman's role puts it, " . . . if the Commissioner can find a defect in procedure, he can say there has been maladministration even if the hardship suffered by the complainant is relatively trivial. On the other hand, if he cannot find a defect in procedure, he cannot say there has been maladministration even if a complainant is suffering a hardship as a result of a decision by a government department."[53] Ministers can still veto the disclosure of any official document, thus occasionally hampering parliament's ability to debate and assess the validity of the ombudsman's decision.

Within these limits the operation of the ombudsman's office has been judged a success in its first five years, and appears to have become a fixture of the British system. It has unearthed a small, undramatic amount of faulty administrative practice and on one occasion (involving a Foreign Office decision about compensation due to men kept in a German concentration camp) forced a key ministry to back off its declared denial that nothing unusual had occurred. To the extent that no minister or civil servant wants embarrassing publicity, the potentiality of an ombudsman inquiry, like the traditional threat of parliamentary questions, serves as one more checkpoint against the uncontrolled assertion of bureaucratic power. But because it is confined to the procedural realm it does not impinge greatly on the behavior of higher civil servants and must be considered at best a minor influence on their overall political role. As with other reforms mentioned in this section, the institution of an ombudsman should be viewed as mild reformism in the British tradition rather than a major break with the past.

6. AN UNCERTAIN FUTURE

The thrust of the foregoing argument has been that the development of the British higher civil service is inseparable from the condition of the larger political system. Projections of the role of the bureaucracy into the future must therefore be based on predictions of how that system is likely to develop. In the light of Britain's recent entry into the European Economic Community such predictions may have to be carefully hedged; but certain patterns of political evolution can be assumed to continue at least into the near future, partly because they are deeply rooted in a political system which enjoys widespread popular acceptance (if not enthusiasm), and partly because the experience of the original Common Market countries does not augur an immediate transformation of long-standing civil service roles.

There is no sign that the increase of government involvement in the affairs and lives of Britons will decline in the last quarter of this century. Four years' experience under the Heath government —dominated by probably the most dogged exponent of free enterprise and private initiative come to power since the 1930s— showed how fixed is the British demand for, and acceptance of, the perpetuation of the positive state. This does mean, of course, that all government activity will continue to grow at the same rate. Expenditure on traditional foreign policy and the military is likely to taper off even more, for example. But the slack will be taken up by gradual expansion of older government functions such as education and the social services, and more dramatically by those aimed at improvement of the environment. Government's many roles as stimulus, watchdog, manager, and entrepreneur of the economy are unlikely to recede. To take but one illustration, Britain's membership in the Common Market now requires that government and industry master thousands of technical regulations and develop plans for their integration into British practice—the sort of tasks civil servants are thought to be naturally equipped to undertake with a minimum of fuss.

These are precisely the kind of tasks that parliament has shown itself to be ill-equipped, or unprepared, to carry out. The evolution of twentieth-century government has not been favorable to parliament, and there are few real signs that it will assert new powers or recapture strong initiatives in policy-making. Its function of scrutinizing the postlegislative implementation of policy is badly served by prevailing interpretations of ministerial responsibility. If parliament's role in these matters is to be upgraded, two interconnected reforms would be needed: relaxation of ministerial responsibility to the extent that parliament would be allowed to deal directly with civil servants on at least subsidiary policy questions, and development of departmental specialist committees on a more regular and comprehensive basis than now exists. The first would mean that higher civil servants would lose their anonymity and ministers their supposed power to make and answer for all decisions. Lack of enthusiasm among ministers and their top advisers is likely to stymie serious proposals for this kind of change, short of traumatic breakdown of present practices. The second reform had a trial run at an adventurous moment in the 1960s, but withered in the face of parliamentary and ministerial conservatism. The attitudes of Conservative governments toward parliamentary reform hardly presage the adoption of either reform in the foreseeable future. The Heath government, for instance, insisted that all detailed enabling legislation for Britain's entry into the Common Market be developed by ministers and civil servants rather than by parliament. Thus it is difficult to envision a reversal in the advancing trend toward reliance on delegated legislation and the crucial role played by civil servants in giving it flesh.

Public interest in the modernization of the civil service abated in the early 1970s, but the momentum continues within the service in a quieter way. Although many lines of criticism have not been accepted (e.g., many of Fulton's recommendations), some have struck sensitive chords and can be expected to motivate or accelerate internal changes. Three developments deserve watching. The first is the gradual absorption of norms and practices of administrative theory derived from the behavioral sciences and business management. Within the limits of ministerial responsibility it will still be possible to adapt elements of program budgeting, integrate scientists and technologists into the mainstream of policy-making, reduce short-term posting to departments, and add to the substantive content of in-service training. The second is a likely increase in the direct management of services by many departments now only concerned with coordinating activities of local and regional semi-autonomous boards—a change with will mean increased civil service contact with units of production and the public. There are already signs that this may occur in the management of the now highly diffused National Health Service. Should this development occur on a large scale, it could well reduce the distance between the national bureaucracy and sizable sectors of the community; it would also increase the vulnerability of civil servants to consumer criticism and put the viability of ministerial responsibility under even more strain. The third direction of change is toward greater openness, in civil service recruitment, careerism, and provision of information about official decisions. Admission to the top ranges of the former Administrative Class has widened in recent years to include a substantial influx of meritocrats of lower class origins. One can expect to see fewer higher civil servants entering directly from universities and more promoted from middle ranks or brought in as late entrants from other careers (including child-rearing). Although forms and labels may change, the use of outsiders on a temporary basis will probably continue, with efforts made to insert them into structures in a way less likely to rub the careerists the wrong way. So long as bureaucrats are involved heavily in advising ministers and negotiating with pressure groups, it is too much to expect that secrecy will disappear; but at the same time the increasing need to explain and engineer support for new policies should mitigate some of the extremes which secrecy has reached in the past. Once again, however, it must be said that changes of this sort are apt to be incremental rather than sweeping in character, more derived from the need to respond to specific conditions than from a new philosophy of governance.

How well will high civil servants, already overworked in the performance of their present tasks, be able to cope with additional political roles growing out of these changes? Can they continue to make do with the quiet consensualism of the past? Will greater openness bring more decisiveness, or paralyze an already slow-moving machine? Is administrative messiness a price one should be prepared to pay for sound and accepted decisions? At the prospect of having to propound satisfactory answers to questions such as these, the crystal ball may have to give way to the philosopher's stone. One thing seems clear, however: the higher bureaucracy in Britain will continue to be called on to carry a substantial share of political decision-making so long as no easy line between high national policy and detailed technical administration can be drawn to mutual satisfaction. It is still a share, though, not a monopoly. By temperament, socialization, situation, and resources, top civil servants are well placed to strongly influence the outcome of policy, but not to transform it into a sole proprietorship.

NOTES

1. *A Constitution for the Socialist Commonwealth of Great Britain* (London, 1920), p. 67.

2. Good recent accounts are found in R.H.S. Brown, *The Administrative Process in Britain* (London, 1970); G. A. Campbell, *The Civil Service in Britain* (3rd ed.; London, 1971); and C. K. Fry, *Statesmen in Disguise: The Changing Role of the Administrative Class of the Home Civil Service* (London, 1969). Most outlines of central administrative structure

date quickly, but for the story down to the advent of the Wilson Government see F.M.G. Willson, *The Organization of British Central Government, 1914-1964* (2nd ed.; London, 1968).

3. *Second Report of the Civil Service Department* (London, 1971), p. 59. Down about 260,000 from 1969, due to the removal of the Post Office from the civil service category.

4. *Report on the Organisation of the Permanent Civil Service, 1854* (reprinted in the Fulton Report, Cmnd. 3638, vol. 1, 1968).

5. *The Civil Service: Vol. I, Report of the Committee, 1966-68* (The Fulton Report, Cmnd. 3638, 1968), par. 1.

6. For revealing descriptions of these links, see especially S. E. Finer, *Anonymous Empire* (2nd ed.; London, 1965); Samuel H. Beer, *British Politics in the Collectivist Age* (New York, 1965); Harry Eckstein, *Pressure Group Politics* (London, 1960); Peter Self and Herbert Storing, *The State and the Farmer* (London, 1962); Edward Boyle, Anthony Crosland, and Maurice Kogan, *The Politics of Education* (London, 1971); and Political and Economic Planning, *Advisory Committees in British Government* (London, 1960).

7. The most insistent depiction of the civil servant as classical nonpolitical man is found in C. H. Sisson, *The Spirit of British Administration* (2nd ed.; London, 1966).

8. James B. Christoph, "Political Rights and Administrative Impartiality in the British Civil Service," *American Political Science Review* 51 (March 1957): 67-87. These rules do not apply to middle and lower level civil servants, whose right to engage in party politics (including candidacy for, but not membership in, the House of Commons) are acknowledged. By and large, the closer a civil servant is to the discretionary level of policy-making, the more limited the range of permitted partisan identification and activity.

9. Richard Chapman, *The Higher Civil Service in Britain* (London, 1970), pp. 116-117. Chapman's study of this cohort's career, work habits, and attitudes forms Memorandum No. 2 of Vol. 3(2), *Surveys and Investigations,* of the Fulton Report, cited in footnote 7.

10. Thirty of 35 civil servants replied; among them 17 voted Labour, 6 Conservative, 4 Liberal, 1 Scottish Nationalist, and 2 did not vote. Chapman, op. cit., p. 116.

11. "The Political Attitudes of Senior Civil Servants in Britain, Germany, and Italy," chapter 3 in this volume.

12. For an extreme argument that it is the values and methods of the civil service which more than any others set the tone for the outlook of all British elites, see J. P. Nettl, "Consensus and Elite Domination: The Case of Business," *Political Studies* 13 (February 1965): 22-42.

13. T. D. Kingdom, "The Confidential Advisers of Ministers," *Public Administration* 44 (1966): 267-274; Samuel Brittan, *Steering the Economy* (London, 1969), pp. 29-31.

14. Consider these sardonic (if now rather dated) remarks of an admirer of traditional ways in the civil service: " . . . the British administrator travelling abroad is shocked to discover that many countries are administered by men who read books about public administration. This, in the British view, is not only a surprising but a very unfortunate state of affairs, and goes some way to explain the disabilities under which foreigners, in the matter of government, notoriously suffer. The British Civil Servant does not want to suppress books of this nature. With his professional tolerance, he is not even altogether against their being read in this country—by other people. The real turpitude is for people engaged or about to be engaged in administration to read them. Such people are commiting the crime of learning from books something that one just *does*" (Sisson, op. cit., p. 28).

15. Some of the most fulsome have come from Labour Party leaders of the immediate postwar period; for example, Earl Attlee, "Civil Servants, Ministers, Parliament and the Public," pp. 16-24 in W. A. Robson (ed.) *The Civil Service in Britain and France* (London, 1956), and Lord Morrison, *Government and Parliament: A Survey from the Inside* (3rd ed.; London, 1964), pp. 320-346. See also Anthony Sampson, *Anatomy of Britain* (London, 1962), pp. 234-235, and Boyle et al., op. cit., pp. 79-80.

16. John P. Macintosh, *The Government and Politics in Britain* (London, 1970), p. 144.

See also Geoffrey K. Fry, "Some Weaknesses in the Fulton Report on the British Home Civil Service," Political Studies 17 (December 1969): 487.

17. Macintosh, op. cit., p. 143.

18. S. E. Finer, *Comparative Government* (London, 1970), p. 157.

19. The Fulton Committee's recommendations attempted to move British administration in this direction. A fuller discussion of this effort is given later in this paper.

20. Chapman, op. cit., p. 139.

21. Brian Chapman, *The Profession of Government* (London, 1959), p. 289.

22. F.M.G. Willson, "Entry to the Cabinet, 1959-1968," Political Studies 18 (1970): 236-238.

23. Some rare exceptions were Lord Mills, appointed by Macmillan as Minister of Power directly from a high post in industry; Frank Cousins, made Minister of Technology by Wilson from his position as General Secretary of the Transport and General Workers Union; and John Davies, appointed Minister of Trade and Industry by Heath from his position as Director General of the Confederation of British Industry. Each had to be found a seat in the House of Commons, or be made a peer.

24. Richard Rose, "The Making of Cabinet Ministers," British Journal of Political Science 1 (1971): 407-408. See also Anthony King, "Britain's Ministerial Turnover," New Society (Aug. 18, 1966), pp. 257-258.

25. Rose, op. cit., p. 406.

26. Bruce Headey, "What Makes for a Strong Minister?," New Society (Oct. 8, 1970), p. 624. Headey's figure of 61 hours a week was derived from interviews with fifty ministers and ex-ministers. For a graphic tale of one minister's problems, see Ernest Marples, "A Dog's Life in the Ministry," pp. 128-131 in Richard Rose (ed.) *Policy-Making in Britain* (London, 1969).

27. "A Typology of Ministers: Implications for Minister-Civil Servant Relationships in Britain," chapter 2 in this volume.

28. For example, Reginald Bevins, *The Greasy Pole* (London, 1965), chaps. 6-7; Jeremy Bray, *Decision in Government* (London, 1970), pp. 52-66; Edward Boyle et al., op. cit.; Peter Shore, *Entitled to Know* (London, 1966); Samuel Brittan, op. cit., pp. 1-35, and "The Irregulars," pp. 329-339 in Richard Rose (ed.) *Policy-Making in Britain;* and Roger Opie, "The Making of Economic Policy," pp. 53-82 in Hugh Thomas (ed.) *Crisis in the Civil Service* (London, 1968).

29. The minister "discovers that . . . great changes take time and effort to achieve. He has to prepare his case. That done, he is ever so politely informed that six of his predecessors contemplated exactly the same changes, but nothing came of them. While they would be desirable changes, the weaknesses of his arguments are gently touched upon. He smiles confidently and thinks to himself that his predecessors were not much good anyway. He argues. He is a bit irritated by the impediments that are being put up. Then his officials become evasive. They string phrases together to which he listens intently, but which he is sure have no meaning. . . . So they adjourn and his officials go off and he hears that they are having long and somewhat obscure discussions with the *élite* at the Treasury. Presently the minister asks what the position is. Then the permanent secretary is now on his well-earned leave and perhaps the minister would care to wait his return." Bevins, op. cit., pp. 57-58.

30. For an early view of the civil service as the Right's hidden weapon, see Harold J. Laski, *Parliamentary Government in England* (London, 1938), chap. 6. For a critique by an exponent of the party government model, see Michael R. Gordon, "Civil Servants, Politicians, and Parties: Shortcomings in the British Policy Process," Comparative Politics 4 (Oct. 1971): 29-58.

31. James B. Christoph, *Capital Punishment and British Politics* (London and Chicago, 1962), pp. 36-41, 110-111, 130, 136.

32. Samuel Brittan, *The Treasury Under the Tories, 1951-64* (London, 1964), and *Steering the Economy,* op. cit.; William Davis, *Three Years Hard Labour* (London, 1968).

33. Edward Boyle (Lord Boyle), Parliamentary Secretary to the Ministry of Education, 1957-59, and Minister of Education, 1962-64, has observed that "it's unreal to suppose that in any dialogue between Ministers and civil servants, the civil servants' value-judgments won't play some part as well . . . it's no enlargement of their function" (Boyle et al., op. cit., p. 75).

34. Macintosh, op. cit., p. 149.

35. Anthony Crosland, in Boyle et al., op. cit., p. 179.

36. Gordon, op. cit., p. 47. See the similar calculations of Richard Rose, "Obstacles to Party Government," New Society (Oct. 30, 1969), p. 685.

37. C. H. Sisson, op. cit., p. 38.

38. Civil servants themselves do not pretend to the "simple technician" role. For example, 92% of senior civil servants and 93% of younger civil servants in Robert Putnam's sample of the Administrative Class disagreed with the statement, "A Senior Civil Servant should limit his activity to the precise application of the law." See note 11.

39. J. Roland Pennock and David C. Smith, *Political Science: An Introduction* (New York, 1964), p. 9.

40. Always italicized, to show their foreignness. For typical civil servant hostility, see Sisson, op. cit., p. 144; and for coolness from the present prime minister, Harold Wilson's remarks in Jo Grimond, Enoch Powell, Harold Wilson, and Norman Hunt, *Whitehall and Beyond* (London, 1964), pp. 17-18. The *cabinet* idea did not appeal, either, to the Fulton Committee. See Fulton Report, par. 285.

41. A practice not followed in countries with a less pluralistic view of administration, such as France. See F. F. Ridley and Jean Blondel, *Public Administration in France* (London, 1969), pp. 320-321.

42. For a critique of the cooptation model, see Frank Parkin, *Class Inequality and Political Order* (London, 1971), pp. 133-136.

43. Brian Chapman, *British Government Observed* (London, 1963).

44. Brian Chapman, *The Profession of Government*, pp. 274-275.

45. For details of the NEDC see James B. Christoph (ed.) *Cases in Comparative Politics* (Boston, 1965), chap. 2, and the literature cited therein.

46. These events are described at length in Samuel Brittan, op. cit., and William Davis, op. cit.

47. *Sixth Report of the Estimates Committee 1964-65* (H.C. 308), p. xxxv.

48. One of the recommendations rejected by the Prime Minister was that the selection of entrants from universities be weighted in favor of those who had studied subjects thought to be closely related to civil service work.

49. Departmental Committee on Section 2 of the Official Secrets Act of 1911 (Cmnd. 5104, 1972). See also David Williams, *Not in the Public Interest* (London, 1965), and Jonathan Aitken, *Officially Secret* (London, 1971).

50. Bernard Crick, *The Reform of Parliament* (2nd ed. rev.; London, 1970), p. 269.

51. H. V. Wiseman, "The New Specialized Committees," pp. 198-223 in A. H. Hanson and Bernard Crick (eds.) *The Commons in Transition* (London, 1970); Nevil Johnson, "Select Committees as Tools of Parliamentary Reform," pp. 224-248 in ibid.; and D. R. Shell, "Specialist Select Committees," Parliamentary Affairs 23 (1969-70): 380-404.

52. Early in 1972 the Heath government announced its intention to extend the ombudsman's jurisdiction to administrative decisions in the National Health Service in 1974, and to create a team of local government ombudsmen when the Local Government Reorganisation Act takes effect that same year. The Guardian, Feb. 23, May 17, 1972.

53. Frank Stacey, *The British Ombudsman* (Oxford, 1971), p. 309.

JAMES B. CHRISTOPH is professor and former chairman of the Department of Political Science at Indiana University (Bloomington). He is the author of *Capital Punishment and British Politics* and *Britain at the Crossroads,* and he is co-editor of *Cases in Comparative Politics.*

2

A Typology of Ministers: Implications for Minister-Civil Servant Relationships in Britain

BRUCE W. HEADEY

The British constitution may be unwritten, but this has never deterred commentators wishing to cite its provisions. According to the constitution, then, cabinet ministers are responsible for all decisions emanating from government departments. Civil servants exist purely to advise on policy alternatives and implement the decisions of their political masters. Constitutional theory thus treats the minister-civil servant relationship as a constant. Political observers, on the other hand, have long recognized that the relationship is variable and have distinguished between "strong" ministers who dominate their departments and significantly influence public policy and "weak" ministers who are, in effect, run by their officials and influence policy only in detail if at all. This distinction introduces some degree of realism but is still inadequate as a basis for analyzing minister-civil servant relations. The purpose of this article is to offer a more precise fivefold typology of ministers. The data come from interviews with samples of current and former ministers and civil servants who were asked to explain their conception of their own tasks and their relationship with each other.

The relationship between a minister and his civil servants may be thought of as having both an affective or socioemotional dimension

AUTHOR'S NOTE: The data on which this article draws are more fully reported and analyzed in the author's book, *The British Cabinet Ministers: The Roles of Politicians in Executive Office* (London: Allen and Unwin, 1974). The author wishes to thank Anthony King, Maurice Kogan, Malcolm Punnett, and Richard Rose for their comments and advice.

and a policy dimension. The affective relationship is bound to have important consequences for departmental morale; in any organization morale depends greatly on relations between the boss and his immediate subordinates.[1] Morale in turn affects performance, and a priori it seems reasonable to suggest that a minister who wins the total loyalty of his officials is likely to find that the latter make efforts above and beyond the call of duty to implement his policy objectives and fight for his proposals on interdepartmental committees. By the same token, a minister who is unpopular with officials may find that the quality of the advice and assistance provided for him suffers and that crucial interdepartmental battles are lost.

The policy dimension of the minister-civil servant relationship requires some elucidation. The balance of influence between a minister and his officials is likely to change from issue to issue. It is also likely to depend, as we shall see, on the expectations, skills, and abilities of individual politicians and officials. One may further think of the former or the latter as being more or less influential at different stages of the policy-making process. The stages of the process may be conceptualized as follows: identifying a policy problem, specifying objectives and priorities, formulating alternative sets of proposals designed to achieve objectives, plotting the consequences of proposed alternatives, selecting the alternative which appears most promising, mobilizing support for that alternative within the government and among outside publics, getting one's proposals formally enacted, and last, seeking to implement them in accordance with the original objectives.[2] Conceivably, ministers or civil servants might play a dominant or passive role at any stage of this process,[3] and the object of research must be to discover what conditions affect the pattern of their relationship.

The ideal way to investigate the relationship would be to carry out case studies in "representative" Whitehall departments and in relation to a "representative sample" of issues. Apart from the conceptual difficulty of defining and selecting representative departments and issues, a research program of this kind would fail for lack of access to departmental files. It simply would not be possible to discover who influenced whom to do what when: unauthorized disclosure of the contents of files would lead to prosecution under the Official Secrets Act; and although ministers and civil servants are helpful in giving interviews, the conventions governing the anonymity and political neutrality of civil servants would mean that attempts to check on specific advice to ministers would prove abortive. This is not to imply that illuminating case studies are entirely lacking; Samuel Brittan's *The Treasury Under the Tories* and M. J. Barnett's *The Politics of Legislation: The Rent Act 1957* perhaps deserve special mention.[4] However, the case study approach is not likely to pay high dividends unless the laws and conventions of British government change.

This study deals not with actual behavior but with the *role expectations* of ministers and civil servants and their perceptions of the factors influencing their relationship. It cannot, of course, be assumed that role expectations by any means perfectly predict role behavior; but from both sides of the picture—obtained by interviewing both ministers and civil servants—it was hoped that a reasonably valid account would emerge. In 1969-70, 50 past and present ministers (27 Labour and 23 Conservatives) and 25 civil servants were interviewed by the author. The samples were not selected according to any strict randomizing procedure, but the author was conscious of the need to interview ministers with experience of different policy areas and government departments, different educational and occupational backgrounds, and varying reputations for effectiveness in office. The civil servants included 7 permanent secretaries, 5 deputy secretaries and 4 undersecretaries, and 9 officials who were then, or had recently been, private secretaries to ministers. The average interview lasted between an hour and an hour and a half, but respondents naturally differed in the amount of time they could spare. Accordingly, the best procedure was to ask a small number of standard questions, the answers to which could readily be compared and tabulated, and use the remaining time to probe further along lines of inquiry opened up by the standard questions, or to raise points on which the author believed respondents might be particularly well informed or particularly frank. Quotable responses were written down in the course of the interview but, for the most part, responses were recorded as soon as possible after interviews ended. This method of recording was not ideal in that the exact wording of replies was lost; but the interviews were, in any case, "not for attribution," and the use of a tape recorder might have precluded frankness.

1. A TYPOLOGY OF MINISTERS

Cabinet ministers have a multiplicity of tasks to perform in relation to their own departments, the cabinet, Parliament, their party, pressure groups, and publics outside Whitehall. Certain of these tasks cannot be delegated. Thus a minister is bound to attend cabinet if at all possible, and his presence at the House of Commons is obligatory for certain votes and for debates concerning subjects covered by his department. In practice it is also difficult to refuse some social invitations (cocktails at 10 Downing Street to meet a visiting Prime Minister), some requests for interviews (from a major industrialist or union leader, for example), and some speaking engagements and provincial visits. Allowing for these unavoidable commitments, sheer pressure of time means that a cabinet minister can only play an active role in the performance of a limited number of tasks and must be content to play a minor role or delegate other tasks entirely to junior ministers or civil servants. In practice it is found that individual ministers adopt different priorities. They have different *role conceptions* and seek to be effective in different ways. The role conceptions of ministers with implications for their relationship with civil servants are analyzed below. Discussion of the consequences for British government of alternative relationships is reserved for the concluding section.

The opening question put to the 50 ministers interviewed for this study was designed to elicit their role conceptions:

> What are the most important tasks a minister has to perform? In other words, what is good minister actually good at doing?

Table 1 lists the main roles cited as "important" and the number of ministers mentioning each role.

An initial point emerging from Table 1 is that more ministers (44) attached importance to departmental policy-making roles than to departmental management, cabinet, parliamentary, party, or public relations roles. The first role mentioned by 40 of the 50 ministers was concerned with departmental policy-making, and several ministers commented specifically on the preeminent importance of this aspect of their job. Thus one Conservative minister said,

> The main thing is the department. This absorbs all your energies. There is not enough time to read cabinet papers—although admittedly I'm a slow reader—and personally I always cut down on dinners and formal occasions and tell my officials that my job is here at the centre.

TABLE 1

THE ROLE CONCEPTIONS OF MINISTERS (N=50)

Classification of Roles	Number of Ministers	
I. Departmental policy-making roles:		
1. Policy initiation	23	
2. Policy selection	21	
	44[a]	(N=44)[b]
Departmental management roles:		
1. Maintain departmental morale	14	
2. Influence departmental organization and appointments	8	
	22	(N=20)[b]
II. Cabinet roles:		
1. Win cabinet battles for money, legislative time, etc.	19	
2. Contribute to cabinet decisions on a wide range of issues	5	
	24	(N=22)[b]
III. Parliamentary and party roles:		
1. Spot in advance issues likely to cause a parliamentary storm	19	
2. Mobilize parliamentary and party support for departmental measures	26	
	45	(N=36)[b]
IV. Public relations roles:		
1. Consult with the department's interest group clientele	9	
2. Sell the department, its policies, and self to relevant publics outside Whitehall	9	
	18	(N=15)[b]

a. Six ministers listed no departmental policy-making role.
b. Figures in brackets give the number of ministers who mentioned one or more roles in a particular role set.

The fact that the great majority of ministers give priority to departmental tasks lends confirmation to the view common among academics, but not always reflected in press comment, that it is within government departments rather than in cabinet, let alone Parliament, that policy objectives and programs are principally formulated.[5]

Among the ministers who cited departmental policy-making as important, 23 were concerned with policy initiation and 21 with policy selection. The distinction is crucial. Policy initiation involves setting policy objectives and initiating the search for policy programs designed to implement objectives. A minister who is concerned with policy selection is broadly content to work within the framework of existing departmental objectives and sees his role as one of selecting between policy alternatives presented to him by civil servants. In

TABLE 2

THE DEPARTMENTAL POLICY-MAKING ROLES OF MINISTERS BY PARTY (N=50)

	Party	
Role Conception	*Conservative*	*Labour*
Policy initiation	11	12
Policy selection	9	12
No mention of policy-making role	3	3
Total	23	27

other words, the distinction is between a minister who brings his "own" or his party's policy objectives to the department and a minister who lets the department bring things to him.

It is interesting that the division between policy initiators and policy selectors does not follow party lines in the way one might expect. Traditionally the Labour Party has been regarded as the party more likely to initiate change. In fact, however, this difference, if it still exists, is not reflected in ministerial role conceptions (see Table 2). Labour ministers were, if anything, slightly less likely than Conservatives to be concerned with policy initiation. Twelve out of 27 Labour ministers as against 11 out of 23 Conservatives fell in this category. In general, it was remarkable how rarely in private conversation ministers mentioned party differences or made party points. Only three ministers stated explicitly that one of their main roles was to implement party policy or take decisions in accordance with party principles. This lends support to the view that at top levels the parties have come closer together. It would be hard to imagine that thirty or forty years ago Labour leaders in particular would have omitted to mention as one of their main roles the implementation of party principles.[6]

Policy initiators and *policy selectors* form two of the categories in the typology of ministers presented below. The remaining categories are *executive ministers, ambassador ministers,* and *minimalists.* It is not pretended that every single minister fits neatly into one of these categories, but the typology is offered for its heuristic value and, one would hope, as providing a reasonable fit with Whitehall and Westminster realities.

2. POLICY INITIATORS

Not all of the 23 ministers who attached priority to policy initiation clearly regarded the role as one of overriding importance, but at least 9 did and may be classified straightforwardly as policy initiators. The approach of policy initiators may be illustrated as follows:

> One takes a few major decisions a year. I try to give as much time as possible to these decisions, particularly to getting the objectives right. All the rest is a bore: Parliament, deputations, visits, ambassadors . . . [a Labour minister]

> The minister should offer philosophical, intellectual leadership. He must think things through—the East of Suez role, the future of the Health Service, whatever it is. Only ministers can make major changes; proposals generated by civil servants are bound to put safety first. [a Conservative minister]

> There are three kinds of minister: creative ministers, administrators and those who are no good at either. A really creative minister can sometimes lead his department to reinterpret its functions. In this department we have tried to move away from the civil service norm of even-handedness in dealing with industry and to provide special incentives for firms which are efficient—particularly if they are strong on the export side. [a Labour minister of state]

These three ministers have a clearcut view of their own role in relation to their department. It is for them to state their objectives and priorities, and initiate the search for appropriate policy programs. The role of civil servants is essentially responsive. They are there to formulate proposals and administer policy in line with objectives handed down by their political master. It is interesting that the last two ministers quoted both implied some criticism of civil servants. The Conservative minister believed that, unless a politician took the initiative, "safety first" policies were bound to be pursued; and the Labour minister of state implied that civil service norms are counterproductive in the administration of industrial policy.

Despite such criticisms, however, it would be mistaken to suppose that the affective relationship between policy initiators and civil servants is necessarily a poor one. It is accepted by civil servants that policy initiation is a proper constitutional role for a minister, and various metaphors were used by officials who were interviewed to clarify the role. The minister, it was said, is the masculine principle and the department the feminine principle in policy-making. The minister must be a dynamo; he must display "fervor and enthusiasm" to drive through proposals which inevitably are greeted with caution by civil servants who have seen previous attempts at reform run aground. One civil servant spoke approvingly of the way his minister, having been defeated in cabinet on one major measure, "sulked in his tent for a week" and then returned to lay a piece of paper on the permanent secretary's desk with the words, "these are my next five initiatives."

Even if they regard ministerial policy initiation as acceptable in principle, however, there are many civil servants (13 in our sample of 25) who state that in practice it rarely occurs, or that when it does the consequences are unfortunate. Thus a former permanent secretary of a department which admittedly dealt mainly with highly technical subjects said,

> In effect it was always just a question of getting my minister to take on board policies we had in hand anyway. Of the six ministers I worked with closely, it would be hard to say that any of them made even a minor contribution to policy.

Two examples of misguided ministerial initiatives which were cited were Mr. Wilson's ban on officials discussing devaluation of the pound in 1966-67 and Mr. Maudling's "growth experiment" in 1963-64 based on the theory that an initial period of rising imports and balance of payments deficit, while industry stocked up, would give way to payments equilibrium coupled with sustained growth, provided that the Treasury did not intervene and deflate the economy in the meantime.[7] A more trivial example of ministerial impact which in his opinion was harmful was given by a former assistant undersecretary in the Home Office:

> Quite a lot of ministers have some influence, but generally in minor ways. Chuter Ede's decision not to permit graduate entrants to proceed straight to senior levels in the police force was a case in point.[8] As a Labour man his view was that they should all serve their time on the beat.

Turning from the affective to the policy dimension of the minister-civil servant relationship, we must ask what problems face the would-be policy initiator. Three questions will be raised. First, do ministers come to office with reasonably specific policy objectives which they seek to achieve? If they do, it would seem more likely that they would in practice initiate policy changes than if they only formulated "their" objectives after exposure to the influence of departmental officials. Second, do they possess the skills and abilities required to perform a policy initiation role effectively? Third, what situational constraints are liable to limit a minister's prospects of pursuing objectives to which he is committed?

On the first question, concerning policy objectives, the ministers interviewed for this study were asked:

When you were first appointed to the Ministry of ——— did you have definite policy objectives in mind, or did you have to generate your own objectives at a later stage?

The answers reported in Table 3 are classified according to whether respondents were appointed immediately after a general election or in midterm, the hypothesis being that midterm appointees would be less likely to have preconceived objectives than members of a new government who could base themselves on commitments made in their party's election manifesto. It was recognized that, in stating their policy objectives, there may have been a tendency for some ministers to lay claim to a more directive role than they in fact played. This being so, it was especially significant that 15 of the 33 ministers and 13 of 22 appointed in midterm conceded that they came to office without definite ideas about what they wanted to do. These ministers may well have simply adopted proposals which their departments already had "in the pipeline," proposals which would presumably be formulated in line with existing departmental objectives, perhaps slightly modified to fit the minister's known partisan or personal predilections.

Even if a policy initiator comes to office with specific policy objectives in mind, he may fail to translate them into administratively practical programs if he lacks the skills appropriate to the political head of a department of state. The question is: What are the skills appropriate for a minister? A hundred years ago political observers might have agreed with Bagehot that the general intelligence and knowledge of the world of the parliamentary statesman are all that is required:

TABLE 3

THE POLICY OBJECTIVES OF MINISTERS AT THE TIME OF THEIR APPOINTMENT

Policy Objectives	Time of Appointment	
	Postelection	Midterm
Claimed definite objectives	9	9
No objectives	2	13
N = 33[a]	11	22

a. This question was only put to senior Ministers who had headed their own departments and not to junior Ministers.

> There is every reason to expect that a Parliamentary statesman will be a man of quite sufficient intelligence, quite enough various knowledge, quite enough miscellaneous experience to represent effectually general sense in opposition to bureaucratic sense.[9]

Nowadays, as we shall see, sensible men differ about the attributes required for the minister's job (see Table 4). The interesting finding here is that most ministers who saw themselves as policy initiators (16 out of 23) thought that either specialized knowledge of policy areas, or executive skills, or both, are useful attributes. Specialized knowledge was said to be valuable because, as government has become more technical (economic and defense policy were mentioned particularly), lay ministers found it increasingly difficult to define their objectives with the necessary precision and to form an independent judgment about policy alternatives. Executive skills, on the other hand, were held to be an asset by 15 ministers because departments of state have developed into large complex organizations which only men with previous experience of taking decisions and securing their implementation by a large organization could expect to run effectively.

Do British ministers have specialized knowledge and executive skills? Clearly, the great majority do not. Recent exceptions notwithstanding, it remains true that nearly all ministers are recruited from those who have served a long apprenticeship on the backbenches of the House of Commons. (P. W. Buck has shown that an MP elected over the age of 40 has little chance of reaching the cabinet.)[10] Parliamentary life encourages the development of verbal, debating skills and, as one minister said, the Walter Mitty belief that a rattling good speech can solve anything. It does not

TABLE 4

RELATIONSHIP BETWEEN MINISTERIAL ROLE CONCEPTIONS AND ROLE SKILLS

Role Conceptions	Specialized Knowledge	Executive, Managerial Skills	Diffuse General Abilities[a]
Policy initiator	12[b]	10[b]	7
Policy selector	4	3	14
No policy-making role mentioned[c]	0	2	4
Total	16	15	25

a. Intelligence, character, judgment, etc.

b. Six policy initiators cited the need for both specialized knowledge and executive skills.

c. Six respondents mentioned neither a policy initiator nor a policy selection role.

encourage subject matter specialization. Nor, given the increasingly heavy demands of the parliamentary timetable, is it possible for many MPs to have a dual career and obtain experience of high level executive decision-making outside politics. Many Conservative MPs hold directorships, but these are mostly nonexecutive posts and no preparation for heading a vast department of state. It might be felt that, even if their nonpolitical careers do not develop executive skills or specialized knowledge, future cabinet ministers may acquire these attributes through "on-the-job" learning as parliamentary secretaries and ministers of state. Ideally, perhaps, this ought to be the case. In practice, however, ministerial tenure is so short that it is impossible to acquire an in-depth knowledge of the range of a department's work. Thus the median minister in Mr. Harold Wilson's Labour government remained in post only 19 months before being reshuffled. As far as the development of executive skills is concerned, ministers report that junior office is a highly variable experience. Some cabinet ministers delegate significant areas of departmental policy-making to their juniors. Others take the view that, because they and not junior ministers are answerable to Parliament, they must personally take all decisions of real importance.

Again, in so far as ministers lack skills relevant for their office, influence over policy is likely to pass to civil servants. Compared with ministers, although not compared with their counterparts in other European countries and North America, civil servants are both specialists and experienced executives.[11] It takes considerable self-confidence for the temporary political head of a great department of state to impose his policies on permanent officials.

A third rather obvious barrier to a minister's initiating policy changes may lie in the exigencies of the situation which confronts him when he takes office. Thus ministers in charge of heavy "spending" departments are likely to find their policy initiatives rejected in periods of economic stringency. Other ministers may find that reforms they intended to give priority to have to be dropped because a crisis in another area preempts their attention. Thus a former Labour Commonwealth Secretary told the author that he intended to make Indian-Pakistani relations his top priority but was prevented from doing so by the Rhodesian crisis which followed from that country's unilateral declaration of independence. Similarly, two recent Home Secretaries (Mr. James Callaghan and Mr. Reginald Maudling), whatever their intentions before taking office, had no option but to devote much of their attention to the problems of Northern Ireland.[12] Last, a minister may find that the situation which confronts him leaves him no room for manoeuvre. Thus Mr. Roy Jenkins, who clearly sees himself as a policy initiator,[13] is on record as admitting that when appointed Chancellor of the Exchequer in 1967, following devaluation of the pound, there was no room for initiatives on his part because all his officials and all competent outside observers were agreed on what his policy should be: he would need to deflate the economy and hold down wages and prices until the balance of payments improved.[14]

To summarize: policy initiation is probably the most difficult role for a minister to perform effectively. We have seen that an intending policy initiator may face difficulties in his affective relationship with those civil servants who believe that ministerial interventions are generally for the worse. Further, the balance of influence between ministers and officials is not infrequently affected by ministers' lack of specific policy objectives, their lack of relevant skills, and by situational constraints which prevent them from implementing desired policy changes.

3. POLICY SELECTORS

Policy selectors have a quite different view of the minister-civil servant relationship from that of policy initiators:

> First, you call for the facts; the civil servants provide these. Then you must make up your mind. If you can't do this you waste cabinet time. [a Conservative minister]

> You must exercise your critical faculties in analyzing papers put up by officials. You provide both an outsider's perspective and inject political judgment into the considerations of the experts. [a Labour minister]

Ministers who see themselves as policy selectors accept the objectives of the department as they find them. Their main emphasis is on the necessity of choice. The minister must take decisions and dispatch the business, not delay or vacillate. These ministers tend to see the policy-making process as falling into clearcut stages. The minister, in their view, should only be involved in "taking decisions," in selecting among policy alternatives presented by officials. Thus the very senior Conservative minister whose role conception is quoted above distinguished between the "facts" and a decision based on the facts. He dismissed as unworthy the suggestion that there was a risk of being presented only with facts which supported one particular line of analysis, or which were relevant given one definition of a problem rather than another.

The indications are that the affective relationship between a ministerial policy selector and his civil servants is likely to be good. The 25 officials interviewed for this study were asked:

> From the point of view of the department what tasks must the minister perform reasonably well?

The ministerial task mentioned first by 19 of the 25 civil servants was that of decision-making. Essentially they hoped for a minister who would expedite the flow of business as a *policy selector.* Decisiveness almost assumes the status of an ideology in the civil service,[15] and civil servants often state or imply that they constantly have to press on ministers the need to take a decision, to dispatch the business so that the department knows where its minister stands. As one very senior official put it, "the machine is geared to finding out and acting on the minister's mind." A minister who fails to dispatch the business causes serious problems both within his own department and on interdepartmental official committees.[16] Intradepartmentally, delay may mean that poorly prepared legislation reaches the statute book. Thus an undersecretary reported that his minister had kept him waiting for weeks on decisions relating to a major bill. As a consequence the bill would either fail to pass in the current Parliament or would be "a botched job containing somewhat conflicting provisions inserted by different divisions [of the department]." Interdepartmentally, officials representing a minister who has not taken a view on an issue are at an acute disadvantage. Only after the minister has clarified his position can the department swing its weight loyally behind him, prepare its briefs and press its arguments home. Officials can, of course, bluff ("I'm certain my minister would not stand for this") or reserve their minister's position, but even so battles are likely to be lost for want of a ministerially sanctioned viewpoint.

It should not be thought, however, that civil servants favor a minister who dispatches business briskly merely by dint of endorsing whatever proposals are put up to him. Almost to a man they insist they want to be put on their mettle, to have a minister who probes for weaknesses in civil service proposals, who challenges received assumptions, asks shrewd questions at "office meetings,"[17] and throws out suggestions and inquiries for his officials to follow up. In short, civil servants want their minister to perform his role of policy selector in the manner of an intelligent layman who brings with him a knowledge of the outside world, particularly the political world, and applies his outsider's judgment in assessing whatever policy proposals the department has in hand.

Turning to the question of the balance of influence between policy selectors and their officials, the chief problem a minister is liable to face is that realistic policy options may be foreclosed as a result of officials formulating a "united view" at departmental or interdepartmental level. Ten of the ministers interviewed expressed serious concern that the effect of policy options being vetoed by the departmental hierarchy of officials might mean that, on occasion, they were faced with an agreed upon set of recommendations. Alternative sets of proposals might be presented only briefly and, perhaps, tendentiously. More particularly it was argued that the preeminence of the permanent secretary could mean that the "united view" of a Whitehall department was simply the permanent secretary's view. Mr. Roy Jenkins, the former Labour minister, clearly saw this danger when he was Home Secretary:

> All advice to the Secretary of State was submitted in the form of a single co-ordinated minute under the initials of the Permanent Secretary.... I admired the speed of comprehension and decisiveness of expression on the part of the Permanent Secretary which made the system possible, but feared that the system effectively removed the point of decision from the Home Secretary. It also produced a certain reluctance on the part of officials to disagree with each other at meetings within the department. Co-ordinated views on paper tended to produce co-ordinated silence around the table.[18]

It is important to note in this context that in almost no other Western country is there a top official with as much potential influence as the British permanent secretary. Elsewhere in Western Europe and in the United States, the heads of various sections or bureaus of departments are equal in rank under the minister.[19] Several Whitehall departments have moved recently toward a more collegiate, or "management team" form of organization; but so long as the post of permanent secretary exists, the danger of ministerial policy options being foreclosed will remain.

Whether ministerial options are sometimes foreclosed on interdepartmental official committees is a more open question. It is not always realized that parallel to almost every cabinet and ministerial committee there is a committee of officials which reviews policy alternatives and generally services the cabinet committee. Official committees (as they are termed) would normally meet more often than ministerial committees and, indeed, might take six months preparing proposals which ministers would pass in a single meeting. A few ministers who were interviewed felt that the risk of this system leading to the foreclosure of options was quite high and the former Labour junior minister, Dr. Jeremy Bray, has indicated how this may be done:

> In the process of consultation between departments, officials may make accommodations which more often weaken the original proposal than strengthen it. Ministers in other departments are briefed to the weak view and told that Ministers generally find it acceptable. The sponsoring Minister can then find himself having to start by rebutting what has become an established Whitehall view of which his colleagues have been persuaded.[20]

Other ministers, including some with a reputation for being extremely able, were adamant that, in their experience, officials had never conceded points which should have been referred to ministerial level. One comment was that "any civil servant who did so would be taking a grave risk with his career." Another minister gave the matter short shift: "Foreclosed options—what are you talking about? Ask me about something else."

4. EXECUTIVE MINISTERS

Nineteen of the 50 ministers interviewed attached importance to departmental management roles. Fourteen concerned themselves with departmental morale and tried to "bring the best out of civil servants," and eight believed that they should personally supervise appointments and promotions, and occupy themselves with questions of departmental organization. The word management, is, however, slightly ambiguous. In Whitehall management is usually distinguished from policy and ministers held responsible for the latter and civil servants for the former. In textbooks on business management, on the other hand, policy-making in the sense of laying down policy objectives is generally listed as one of the main functions of managers.[21] The ministers whom we label here executive ministers (there were 5, possibly 6, in the sample of 50) have a management textbook view of their job. They believe it is a mistake to divorce questions of policy from questions concerning costing and resource control, organizational structure and personnel management.

With one exception the executive ministers in the present sample were Conservatives who had previous business experience. Their role conceptions may be gauged from the following quotations:

> In running a department one of the most important things for a minister to do is introduce proper methods of control and management. You should have a regular check that things are moving forward and that bad trends are not being established. Government statistics are not always adequate and ministers fail to observe unwelcome developments until they blow up in their face. [a Conservative minister]

> The valuable thing about business experience is that it gives you a basis of comparison for running a department. You know when to "hive off," when to set up a project team, how to evolve a cost accounting system and so forth. [a Conservative minister]

It is somewhat difficult to estimate the affective relationship between civil servants and executive ministers because there are relatively few of the latter. However, it seems reasonable to suggest that, because in the past the management of departments (narrowly defined) has been regarded as the province of the permanent secretary, a minister who takes this function on himself is likely to cause surprise if not opposition. We may also note that, in addition to any problems caused by his overlapping jurisdiction with the permanent secretary, an executive minister has to obtain the agreement of the Civil Service Department, the Treasury, or the Prime Minister before implementing many quite ordinary management decisions. He cannot, on his own authority, hire and fire staff, arrange promotions and transfers, or unilaterally decide to reorganize his department or to institute a new system for controlling the use of resources. Thus senior appointments (at permanent and deputy secretary level) are the responsibility of the Prime Minister who is advised by the Senior Appointments Selection Committee chaired by the Head of the Civil Service, and an increase in departmental staff would need the approval of the Establishment divisions of the Civil Service Department. Departmental resource management, on the other hand, is subject to control at different stages by the public expenditure side of the Treasury, the new Central Policy Review Staff located in the Cabinet Office,[22] and, of course, the cabinet itself. Last, decisions about departmental organization and the division of work between departments are ultimately taken by the

Prime Minister advised by the Civil Service Department. In short, a major difficulty for executive ministers is the number of central agencies they have to deal with and the extent to which they arouse opposition because their role conception is contrary to Whitehall expectations.

Executive ministers have an ambitious role conception, and the balance of influence between themselves and their officials is likely to depend on how much time they spare for policy questions. As emphasized above, time is an extremely scarce ministerial resource; and if a minister gets absorbed in intricate questions of departmental organization, or resource management, or attempts to introduce modern management techniques, then he may, in practice, forego the role of defining policy objectives and reviewing alternative programs. On the other hand, if an executive minister concentrates his energies by linking specific management changes to specific policy objectives, then he is more likely to make an impact. Mr. Denis Healey, for example, as Minister of Defence from 1964 to 1970, reorganized his department and borrowed Pentagon management techniques (cost-effectiveness analysis, program budgeting, etc.) as a means of achieving his principal policy aim of reducing the proportion of public expenditure devoted to defense purposes.[23]

5. AMBASSADOR MINISTERS

A fourth category of ministers, whom some observers believe are more common than the interview data suggest,[24] give high priority to their role as departmental representative or ambassador in dealing with interest groups, local government, professional associations, and other organized publics who constitute the department's clientele. These ministers may be labeled ambassador ministers. They believe that as politicians they are "specialists in persuasion,"[25] and especially competent at convincing interest group leaders to accept policies and cooperate in their implementation. Thus a Labour minister in charge of an industrial sponsoring department said,

> You have got to use a politician's ability to inspire people, not just act as a second rate Permanent Secretary. On visits to factories and so forth I have established a set pattern of always meeting people with a real job to do, including people on the shop floor.

Another Labour minister, explaining his role conception as Minister of Labour, said,

Conciliation in industrial disputes was an important part of the job. You get people off the hook—get them to relent on established positions they have taken up. . . . Industrial retraining is also important. I personally persuaded union leaders—the bricklayers were a difficult case—to agree to the schemes produced by the new Boards, which involved retraining men more quickly than the unions believed possible.

Affective relations between ambassador ministers and civil servants tend not to be particularly good. In general civil servants do not regard a minister who spends an exceptional amount of time on "public relations" in a favorable light. Inevitably, they are inclined to see such activities through departmental eyes. If a minister spends an hour reading the press in the morning, or if he spends an unusual amount of time on visits and inspections, making speeches or consulting with group leaders, civil servants regard this as time off from the real business of government, which consists of getting through the paper work and taking decisions. An exception, however, was one permanent secretary whose first comment in reply to the question about ministers' essential tasks was,

A minister must be good with people. I have known many an able minister to fall down because he rubbed people up the wrong way. Ministers in many departments have to get on well with local authorities. I remember one minister who made it obvious that he considered a deputation from the Corporation of Glasgow stupid. He was very much at fault; his department has to work with local authorities year in, year out.

More typical in his assessment of appropriate ministerial priorities was a civil servant who, remembering his period as a private secretary, said that one of his main tasks was to ensure that ministers got through the paper work and did not spend all their time "glad-handing."

The balance of influence between ambassador ministers and civil servants is bound to be weighted against the former. In so far as they do not make the formulation of policy objectives and programs their top priority, sheer pressure of time means that these tasks will tend to devolve to civil servants. An exceptional ambassador minister may be able to master policy questions, as well as to sell himself and his department to the outside world; but in the typical case, the explicit or implicit choice of a nonpolicy role means that policy is downgraded.

6. MINIMALISTS

Last, it became clear that some respondents had a rather modest conception of their job and intended to perform only the minimal roles required of a minister. What are these minimal roles? First, the acceptance of responsibility for departmental decisions; all that is involved here is signing one's initials on memoranda submitted by civil servants to indicate acceptance of their advice. Second, a cabinet minister is obliged to put up some sort of fight in cabinet to win for his department parliamentary time to pass legislation, and Treasury money to finance the department's measures. (Not to make an effort to win cabinet battles would run flatly counter to the expectations of ministerial colleagues, civil servants, and the department's interest group clientele.) Third, any minister with an instinct for self-preservation will try to avoid parliamentary trouble. He will try to spot in advance issues likely to provoke a parliamentary storm and, in general, will prepare carefully for parliamentary set pieces—debates and question time. In practice it was found that the giveaway admission of the ministers whom, for want of a more elegant label, we may call minimalists, was that the only issues they really concerned themselves with were ones Parliament might seize on. In response to the question about his most important tasks, a Conservative minister said,

> First, you must get to know the substantive side of the department's work and the kinds of issues that are politically sensitive. When I was appointed to a new department I would ask to see all kinds of papers to discover whether they were liable to cause a storm. If not—then one would not see them again.

Another Conservative minister, who was harshly dealt with by the press but showed considerable durability in office-holding terms, made this statement:

> A new minister has lunch with the outgoing minister and asks about political hot potatoes and which MPs give trouble at question time and so forth. Then you meet the permanent secretary and find out what business the department has in hand and what you have to take decisions on forthwith.

Minimalist ministers are not at all popular with civil servants. One reason is that the standing of a department in Whitehall quite largely depends on the standing of its minister. If the word gets out that a minister is run by his officials and accepts whatever advice they offer, his standing suffers and the department suffers with him. Inter-departmental battles are lost, and the minister's officials may come to be treated rather condescendingly by other officials who know that they have only to transfer a dispute to ministerial level in order to get their way.

A second reason for the disesteem in which minimalists are held is that, more overtly than other types of minister, they force officials to formulate policy objectives as well as advise on alternative programs to implement objectives. Officials prefer a minister who makes some contribution to policy if only because, as one of them put it, "that is the way the constitution is supposed to work." One final point: it goes almost without saying that ministers who come close to being self-confessed minimalists constitute only a small proportion of those who *act* as minimalists. The permanent secretary, quoted above, who claimed that, "of the six ministers I worked with closely it would be hard to say that any of them made even a minor contribution to policy," was reporting exceptional experience, but most officials refer, openly or implicitly, to previous ministers who possessed only the trappings of authority.

7. CONCLUSION

Constitutional theory regarding the minister-civil servant relationship is highly misleading. Civil servants are not always restricted to advisory and administrative roles in relation to policies laid down by ministers. On the other hand, it would be equally misleading to suggest that officials in Britain are power-mongers anxious to decide matters themselves and divest ministers of all but the dignity of office. Evidence collected for the Fulton Committee on the civil service indicates that only a small minority of officials are initially attracted to the service by a desire to influence public policy and only a few claim that the oppotunity to do so is a source of job satisfaction.[26]

A realistic picture of relations between ministers and their officials needs to recognize that ministers have markedly different role conceptions and that time constraints mean that giving high priority to one role is likely to mean that other roles are downgraded and, implicitly, delegated to civil servants. A fivefold typology of ministers has been presented, and the relationship between ministers and civil servants has been regarded as having both an affective and a policy dimension. As far as affective relations are concerned, the interview data suggest that policy selectors enjoy the best relationship with their officials, although policy initiators are looked upon as performing a perfectly proper constitutional role. The balance of influence between a minister and officials, on the other hand, does not depend merely on expectations. It is probably true that executive ministers, ambassador ministers, and minimalists generally fail to exert much influence over policy because they do not seek to do so, but other factors limiting ministerial influence are of a more objective nature. Many ministers appear to lack the skills and prior experience required to function effectively as heads of large complex departmental organizations. In any case the hierarchical structure of departments, with the permanent secretary at the top occasionally claiming to act as sole adviser, seems likely to foreclose policy options and limit effective ministerial choice. Perhaps most important, however, a majority of ministers, including some who intend as policy initiators, come to office without having specific policy objectives in mind. They intend to produce initiatives but they are not sure in what direction.

The consequences for British government of ministerial failures to define policy objectives and priorities are likely to be profound if unmeasurable. In the absence of contrary instructions from their political masters, officials normally frame policy programs which fit within the context of the existing objectives pursued by their department. Innovation and radical change are not commonly the product of proposals generated within the Civil Service.[27] New legislation, for example, is likely simply to amend existing legislation. Precedents will tend to be followed, and programs that require a department to adopt new administrative procedures will be avoided. Richard Rose has suggested that government by civil servants means government by "directionless consensus," and Charles E. Lindblom's phrase "disjointed incrementalism" would seem equally applicable to describe the pattern of change produced by such a regime.[28]

Whether one regards the prospect of "disjointed incrementalism" or government by "directionless consensus" with equanimity or dismay depends, of course, on one's political values and ideological stance. Charles E. Lindblom, for one, regards an incremental pattern of change as highly desirable and equates it with democratic change. Many left-wing critics, on the other hand, deeply regret the failure of British ministers, particularly Labour ministers, to produce more radical policy initiatives.[29] They write of a "betrayal of socialism" and loss of nerve on the part of Labour ministers in the face of the civil service and the conservatism of the so-called Establishment. An intermediate, though not ideologically neutral, position would be to recognize that different types of ministers play a worthwhile role in different departments at different times. Thus a policy initiator may be particularly valuable in a department like the Treasury which has to cope with a constantly changing environment and in which, as a consequence, new policy strategies regularly have to be worked out. Policy selectors, on the other hand, may play a useful role in a department which has an extensive backlog of legislation to get through. (The Department of the Environment and the Home Office are not infrequently in this position.) The minister in these circumstances may only need to select the measures he wishes to sponsor and take final decisions on their exact provisions. A third type of minister, the executive minister, seems most likely to make a worthwhile contribution in one of the "giant" unitary departments which have recently been founded in Whitehall as a result of the amalgamation of separate smaller departments.[30] In these departments problems of resource and personnel management are clearly going to be crucial. Next, ambassador ministers would appear to be of most use in departments like the Department of Trade and Industry, or the Department of Employment, where it is particularly important to persuade interest groups to make use of the department's services and cooperate in implementing its policy programs. Last, even ministerial minimalists may have their uses in a politically sensitive department like the Home Office if they are effective in their main aim of avoiding political controversy and defusing Parliamentary criticism.

NOTES

1. For a review of hypotheses concerning relations between leaders and subordinates, see D. Cartwright, "Influence, Leadership, Control," pp. 1-47, and S. H. Udy, "The Comparative Analysis of Organisations," pp. 678-709 in James G. March (ed.) *Handbook of Organisations* (Chicago: Rand, McNally, 1965).

2. There are, of course, many alternative conceptualisations of the "stages" of the policy-making process. Probably the best known is presented in Harold D. Lasswell, *Seven Categories of Functional Analysis* (New York: Free Press, 1956).

3. The implementation of policy programs is the stage of policy-making at which, perhaps, there is least expectation that the minister will be involved. Ministers in some departments are, however, almost bound to concern themselves with policy implementation.

Thus the Secretary of State for Employment inevitably concerns himself with the effect of particular wage claims on the government's incomes policy (if it has one) and the Home Secretary is bound to decide personally controversial immigrant deportation cases.

4. S. Brittan, *The Treasury Under the Tories* (Harmondsworth: Penguin, 1965); M. J. Barnett, *The Politics of Legislation: The Rent Act of 1957* (London: Weidenfeld & Nicolson, 1969).

5. See John P. Mackintosh, *The British Cabinet* (London: Stevens & Sons, 1962), chap. 13; L. Amery, *Thoughts on the Constitution* (2nd ed.; London: O.U.P., 1964), chap. 3; I. Gilmour, *The Body Politic* (London: Hutchinson, 1969), chap. 6. P. Gordon Walker, *The Cabinet* (London: Jonathan Cape, 1970), takes the opposite view and believes that collective deliberation in Cabinet remains crucially important.

6. See, for instance, G. H. Thomas, *When Labour Rules* (London: Collins, 1920), esp. chap. 1, "The England of Tomorrow"; C. R. Attlee, *The Labour Party in Perspective* (London: Gollancz, 1937), chaps. 7, 11.

7. On these ministerial initiatives, see S. Brittan, *Steering the Economy* (London: Secker & Warburg, 1969), chaps. 7, 8.

8. Mr. Chuter Ede was Home Secretary in Mr. Attlee's postwar Labour government from 1945 to 1951.

9. W. Bagehot, *The English Constitution* (New York: Dolphin Books, 1965) p. 232.

10. P. W. Buck, *Amateurs and Professionals in British Politics* (Chicago: Univ. of Chicago Press, 1963) p. 118.

11. See F. F. Ridley (ed.) *Specialists and Generalists* (London: Allen & Unwin, 1968), Introduction.

12. In 1972 a Secretary of State for Northern Ireland was appointed and the Home Office was thus relieved of responsibility for the province.

13. See, for example, the interview with Jenkins reported in "The Tolerant Community," Sunday Times, April 24, 1966. Jenkins argued that in order to be an effective policy initiator it was necessary for a minister, "first, not to spread one's energies too widely but to concentrate on a limited number of major issues at any one time."

14. R. Jenkins, "The Reality of Political Power," Sunday Times, Jan. 17, 1971.

15. See Barnett, *The Politics of Legislation*, op. cit., p. 29.

16. The term official committees refers to committees of civil servants.

17. "Office meetings" are meetings between ministers and departmental civil servants usually held in the minister's room.

18. R. Jenkins, Sunday Times, Jan. 17, 1971.

19. See Ridley, *Specialists and Generalists, op. cit., Introduction.*

20. Jeremy Bray, *Decision in Government* (London: Gollancz, 1969), p. 55.

21. See for example, R. Stewart, *The Reality of Management* (London: Pan Books, 1967), pp. 71-72.

22. See *The Reorganisation of Central Government* (HMSO: Cmnd. 4506, 1970).

23. For an account of Healey's period at Defence see Geoffrey Williams and Bruce Reed, *Denis Healey and the Policies of Power* (London: Sidgwick and Jackson, 1971).

24. See, for example, Brittan, *Steering the Economy,* op. cit., p. 30.

25. The phrase is Harold Lasswell's. See his "Agenda for the Study of Political Elites," pp. 264-288 in D. Marvick (ed.) *Political Decision Makers* (New York: Free Press, 1961).

26. See, R. A. Chapman, "Portrait of a Profession," *The Civil Service* (Fulton Committee) 3(2), pp. 1-29.

27. Kenneth N. Waltz's proposition that high ministerial turnover in office and low civil service turnover is a perfect formula for a low rate of policy innovation is relevant here. See Kenneth N. Waltz, *Foreign Policy and Democratic Politics* (Boston: Little, Brown, 1967).

28. Richard Rose, "The Variability of Party Government," Political Studies 17 (Dec. 1969): 413-445; Charles E. Lindblom, *The Policy of Making Process* (Englewood Cliffs, N.J.: Prentice-Hall, 1968), chaps. 4, 12.

29. Brian Lapping, *The Labour Government, 1964-70* (Harmondsworth: Penguin, 1970) reflects accurately the views of socialists disappointed with Mr. Wilson's government.

30. There are now five "giant" unitary departments: the Ministry of Defence, the Department of Trade and Industry, the Foreign and Commonwealth Office, the Department of the Environment, and the Department of Health and Social Security.

BRUCE HEADEY is lecturer in politics at the University of Strathclyde (Glasgow). He is the author of *British Cabinet Ministers: The Roles of Politicians in Executive Office* (London: Allen & Unwin, 1974).

3

The Political Attitudes of
Senior Civil Servants in
Britain, Germany, and Italy

ROBERT D. PUTNAM

1. BUREAUCRATIC RESPONSIVENESS

Can there really be much doubt who governs our complex modern societies? Public bureaucracies, staffed largely by permanent civil servants, are responsible for the vast majority of policy initiatives taken by governments. Discretion, not merely for deciding individual cases, but for crafting the content of most legislation, has passed from the legislature to the executive. Bureaucrats, monopolizing as they do much of the available information about the shortcomings of existing policies, as well as much of the technical expertise necessary to design practical alternatives, have gained a predominant influence over the evolution of the agenda for decision. Elected executives everywhere are outnumbered and outlasted by career civil servants.[1] In a literal sense, the modern political system is essentially "bureaucratic"–characterized by "the rule of officials."

The realities of power are, to be sure, too complex to be captured in any simple formulation. In varying degrees the decisions of bureaucrats are nearly always influenced by external pressures. Granted that the permanent civil service has a strategic role in the policy-making process, the central question for political scientists is: How responsive is the bureaucracy to changing social needs and political demands, and why?

AUTHOR'S NOTE: This paper is reprinted with permission from the *British Journal of Political Science* 3 (July 1973): 257-290. Pride of place in a full list of acknowledgements –too long to provide here–would go to the many generous and thoughtful officials in Rome, Bonn, and London whose cooperation alone made this study possible. My collaborators on the larger project are Samuel J. Eldersveld, Joel Aberbach, Thomas Anton, Ronald Inglehart, Archibald Singham, and John Waterbury.

In a broad sense the "responsiveness" of a government can be defined as its capacity to respond rapidly, faithfully, and effectively to the (inevitably varied and conflicting) needs and demands of the public and its representatives.[2] Responsiveness in this sense involves more than mere avoidance of wrongful acts. Discussions of administrative control and legislative oversight commonly focus on this negative aspect of the problem, revealing thus an anachronistic assumption that government's actions are more dangerous than its inactions. But as Carl J. Friedrich noted many years ago, "An official should be as responsible for inaction as for wrong action; certainly the average voter will criticize the government as severely for one as for the other."[3]

Responsiveness is in part a matter of constitutional arrangements. Bureaucracies everywhere are subject to the formal and legal authority of politically chosen executives. Ideally, Weberian bureaucrats are in the end obedient to their superiors; and if this obedience is buttressed by requirements that the career officials be nonpartisan in their loyalties, the problem of bureaucratic responsiveness would seem to resolve itself into the more familiar problem of assuring that the political executives are directly or indirectly responsible (and hence responsive) to the electorate.

Of course, there is something to this theory, as one can easily see by imagining a system of government in which the permanent officials were *not* formally bound to obey their political superiors. On the other hand, the constitutional theory of bureaucratic responsiveness is flawed by the implicit assumption that "policy" and "administration" are neatly divisible, the politicians responsible for the former, the officials for the latter. It surely does not bear demonstrating once more that this distinction is false to the realities of modern government.[4] Whatever their formal obligations to leave political matters to their political masters, civil servants are necessarily deeply involved in making policy, and formal obligations alone cannot ensure responsiveness.

An alternative theory of bureaucratic responsiveness would stress the norms and values of the higher civil servants themselves. "The essence of bureaucratic responsibility in the modern State," argued J. Donald Kingsley, "is to be sought, not in the presumed and largely fictitious impartiality of the officials, but in the strength of their commitment to the purposes that the State is undertaking to serve. . . . In the first instance, it is a matter of sentiment and understanding, rather than of institutional forms."[5] The justly renowned debate three decades ago between Carl Friedrich and Herman Finer about bureaucratic responsiveness centered precisely on how much reliance one should place on these "sentiments" and "understandings" held by officials about the social and political world around them.[6]

The responsiveness of a bureaucracy to its social and political environment no doubt also depends on an array of other factors: internal administrative efficiency; the flow of information about social and political trends and conditions; the strength and stability of representative institutions, such as cabinets and parliaments; and so on. But a major premise of this study—and one that can to some extent be tested subsequently with the data we have collected—is that bureaucrats' beliefs and values are a powerful determinant of the extent to which bureaucracy can be made compatible with democracy.[7]

2. CLASSICAL BUREAUCRATS AND POLITICAL BUREAUCRATS

Purely for expository convenience, we may imagine two polar syndromes of attitudes toward politics and political actors. On the one hand, what we may term the "classical bureaucrat" operates with a monistic conception of the public interest—the "national interest" or the "interest of the State." He believes that public issues can be resolved in terms of some objective standard of justice, or of legality, or of technical practicality. It is of such a perspective that Karl Mannheim wrote that "the fundamental tendency of all bureaucratic thought is to turn all problems of politics into problems of administration."[8] As a recent West German commission studying the higher civil service reportedly argues, such bureaucrats "frequently operate on the assumption that problems can be resolved purely objectively *[rein sachlich]*, without reference to sociopolitical considerations."[9] This presumption leads naturally to the belief that, because the bureaucrat himself is "nonpartisan," his judgment is "impartial" and "objective." Consequently, the classical bureaucrat distrusts or rejects the institutions of politics, such as parliaments, parties, and pressure groups. To the classical bureaucrat the noisy, incompetent, partisan practices of politicians seem at best senseless, at worst positively inimical to the permanent interests of the state. Thus, such a bureaucrat may well find the ideals of pluralist democracy less congenial than the quieter, more ordered, less conflict-ridden world of a benevolent autocracy.

The opposite polar type consists of what we can call the "political bureaucrat." This sort of official operates with a much more pluralistic conception of the public interest. He assumes that there can be legitimately differing interpretations of the public interest, and even genuinely conflicting interests among different groups in society. He is, therefore, both more aware of "political realities" and more willing to treat political influences on policy-making as legitimate. He recognizes the need to bargain and compromise, yet at the same time he does not necessarily shrink from advocating and even fighting for his own preferred policies. Whereas the classical bureaucrat is "procedure-oriented" or "rule-oriented," the political bureaucrat is "problem-oriented" or "program-oriented." Whereas the classical bureaucrat views the politician as a troublesome or even dangerous antagonist, interfering with the efficiency and objectivity of government, the political bureaucrat sees the politician instead as a participant in a common game, one whose skills and immediate concerns may differ from his own but whose ultimate values and objectives are similar. The political bureaucrat understands and accepts the role of such institutions as parties and pressure groups. He is likely, as well, to understand and endorse the values of political liberty and equality.

The classical ideal that officials stand apart from politics—the expressive German metaphor is *überparteilich*, "above partisanship"—has always been to some extent a myth, of course, and characteristically, though not universally, it has been associated with conservative political views. As Brian Chapman,[10] writing on the pejorative connotations of "politics" among traditional social and bureaucratic elites, has pointed out:

> This attitude towards "politics" undoubtedly has many historical overtones expressing the political resentment of a ruling class challenged by mass forces; of a social elite forced to give way to social inferiors; of conservatives, prizing above all a stable and orderly society, menaced by democrats demanding a new social pattern. Those who prefer the status quo "administer"; those who wish to change it play politics.

Despite—or more likely, because of—the rise of democratic political institutions during the nineteenth century, "classical bureaucrats" seem to have been common among senior civil servants in Europe. This is not to deny that these officials have often been deeply involved in what we might term political activity in a broad sense, but rather to affirm that they interpreted their own motives and behavior as "above politics." As Herbert Jacob concluded in his study of the Bismarckian civil service,[11] "While German administrators often played a key role in German politics, they normally viewed their activity as that of legal experts rendering judgment rather than as a politically oriented group advancing a partisan viewpoint." And in one of the few empirical studies of the topic, John Herz[12] reached broadly similar conclusions about the views of postwar German bureaucrats. They have, he argued,

> . . . a feeling of being part of a machine which, undisturbed by partisan or similar interference, is permitted to work under the control of experts. There is hardly any apprehension that absence of such interference might also mean absence of controls, particularly democratic controls. . . . By the same token, with the exception of a democratic minority of officials who recognize that institutions and parties representing the various groupings and views within the public are needed in a democracy, most bureaucrats still adhere to a deeply ingrained German skepticism toward popular participation in government. . . . Parties and parliaments are still considered "elements of disintegration." Their positive role in a democracy is not appreciated. Their existence seems to involve a threat that outside forces may intrude upon executive affairs; that "inexpert talkers" may hamper the work of the experts.

Whatever their inherent plausibility, however, the sketches I have outlined of the classical and the political bureaucrat are clearly caricatures. I have as yet offered no evidence that the beliefs and values I have ascribed to each type do indeed cohere empirically. Moreover, in the real world men and women can be found, not merely at the polar extremes, but ranged along a continuum according to the shadings of their views.

Yet this stark oversimplification may clarify the focus of our attention. Classical bureaucrats, we may reasonably assume, will not respond enthusiastically to public demands, whatever their legal vow of obedience to their superiors. Political bureaucrats, on the other hand, unhappy though they may be about specific political decisions, will be fundamentally in sympathy with the imperative of responsiveness. What evidence can we find about the incidence of these contrasting outlooks among contemporary European senior civil servants?

3. METHODOLOGY

Over the last three years a research group at the University of Michigan has been engaged in a comparative study of bureaucratic and political elites in a number of countries, representing a range of political and administrative traditions. Our research is based primarily on interviews with sizeable samples of national politicians and senior civil servants in the United States, Britain, France, West Germany, Sweden, Italy, and the Netherlands.[13] These interviews are currently being analyzed, and a report of our joint findings is expected to be completed within two to three years. The present paper is based primarily on the British, German, and Italian studies, although occasionally I will refer to data collected by my colleagues in other countries.

The methodological premise of the project is that the best way to learn how politicians and bureaucrats think is to talk with some of them. Therefore, in each country we contacted randomly chosen samples of approximately 100 senior officials, approximately 100 members of the national parliament, approximately 25 younger, especially promising civil servants, and approximately 25 younger members of parliament. As shown in Table 1, interviews in Britain, Germany, and Italy were actually carried out in 1970-71 with more than four-fifths of those contacted.[14]

Because the results to be reported here draw primarily on the interviews with civil servants, a word about the operational definition of our administrative samples is appropriate.[15] In each country we

TABLE 1
SAMPLES AND RESPONSE RATES

Country	Category	Original Sample	Actual Interviews	Response Rate (percent)
Britain	Senior civil servants	107	96	91
	Younger civil servants	29	29	100
	Members of parliament	99	80	81
	Younger members of parliament	25	17	68
Germany	Senior civil servants	110	97	88
	Younger civil servants	42	41	98
	Members of the Bundestag	98	80	82
	Younger members of the Bundestag	29	23	79
Italy	Senior civil servants	103	80	78
	Younger civil servants	29	28	97
	Members of the Chamber of Deputies	78	44	56
	Younger members of the Chamber of Deputies	23	14	61

contacted incumbents of two senior grades, so as to get some sense of the impact of differences in rank.

In Britain, the bulk of the respondents contacted were at the level of undersecretary, together with some dozen deputy secretaries. Of those at the level of undersecretary, 66 were members of the "generalist" Administrative Class, as it then was, and another 18 were members of various Specialist Classes—lawyers, engineers, scientific officers, and so on. Respondents in Britain, as in all the other countries studied, were drawn proportionately from all national ministries except those responsible for defense and foreign affairs. Virtually all the British respondents are career officials, appointed solely in terms of administratively defined merit.

In the German federal administrative structure the heads of the sections into which each ministry is divided normally have the rank of *Ministerialdirektor,* while their immediate subordinates normally have the rank of *Ministerialdirigent,* although sometimes incumbents will have a lower ranking title. While all these posts are nominally part of the career civil service, the *Ministerialdirektor* is juridically a so-called "political official." This means that he serves at the pleasure of the minister and can be asked to enter temporary retirement (with a generous pension) at any time. *Ministerialdirigenten* have, by contrast, complete job security. Of our final sample, 34 held the title of *Ministerialdirektor;* 45, that of *Ministerialdirigent;* and 18, some other title. Although posts at these levels are traditionally held entirely by career civil servants, in fact today a number of them are held by political appointees, imported more or less temporarily from outside government. Because open party allegiance and even party membership have long been common among Bonn bureaucrats, it is difficult to determine precisely the proportion of our respondents who owe their position primarily to political rather than to bureaucratic merit. This introduction of "outsiders" into the federal bureaucracy has been associated by some observers with the accession to power of the Social Democrats, but the career patterns of our respondents suggest that the tendency has developed gradually over more than a decade.

Directors general are the highest civil servants in the Italian public administration; there are approximately 110 men in all at this level. They are almost without exception career officials; but they are nominated to this peak grade by the Council of Ministers, and are thus essentially political appointees, though they are formally nonpartisan. Once appointed, however, they have tenure; and hence as a group they reflect the political sympathies of governments ranging back a decade and more. Inspectors general, the second highest ranking civil servants, are without exception career officials, nominated on the basis of seniority and administratively defined merit. This grade has often been used in recent years as a means of raising the salaries of older functionaries whose responsibilities are not as great as their formal standing suggests, particularly given the extreme centralization of authority in Italian administrative practice. Our Italian sample includes 49 directors general and 31 inspectors general.

One object of our project is to investigate generational differences among officials and politicians. We have sought, therefore, in each country to talk with a sample of the "next generation" of political and administrative leaders. In the German and Italian bureaucracies we asked a number of our senior respondents (one or two chosen randomly in each ministry) to name for us "several promising younger officials in your ministry who might well become senior officials in about ten years." Nearly all those so nominated were subsequently interviewed; and as a group, they appear to meet our theoretical criteria. Their present age distribution is consistent in each country with our requirement that they be about a decade away from senior responsibilities. On an average, they are now about two grades below the lower grade included in our sample. They seem generally very able, they are usually quite ambitious, and they are (by definition) well thought-of by their superiors. Any bias from the reputational method of selecting these samples should tend to understate differences in attitudes between the two generations, and thus should work against our hypothetical intergenerational differences.

Centralized personnel administration in Britain made a more objective method of selection practicable there. In each ministry we interviewed one or two randomly chosen assistant secretaries who had been promoted to that grade (one step below undersecretary) within the previous two years at the unusually young age of 34 or 35. We had it on excellent authority that a group so defined would fit our theoretical notion of those likely to reach the top of the administrative hierarchy within a decade—"high-fliers," as they are termed in British administrative parlance.

Response rates for all our samples were high and leave little room for significant biasing due to self-selection. In each country nearly all the interviews with senior civil servants and a number of those with senior politicians were conducted by the project director. The remaining interviews with members of the three parliaments and nearly all the interviews with the younger civil servants were carried out by local research assistants. All interviews were conducted in the native language of the respondents, and with their permission virtually all the interviews were tape-recorded, with little apparent impairment of frankness and sincerity.[16]

All the interviews followed broadly the same outline, but the questions were all open-ended, and the discussions were often wide-ranging. The topics included the respondent's background and career, his views on some contemporary public problems, his image of the policy-making process, his view of relations between the political parties, his perspectives on social conflict and consensus, on the nature of democracy, and on the proper limits on political liberty and equality, his image of his country's future, and most centrally, his interpretation of the respective roles of politician and civil servant and his analysis of the problems inherent in this relationship.

Intensive, systematic analysis of the transcripts of these interviews will provide the basis for most of our subsequent inquiry. This time-consuming process of coding and statistical analysis has only just begun, however, and at this early stage much of the rigorous support for our initial impressions must come from the responses to a written questionnaire completed by each respondent at the end of the interview. Responses to such closed questionnaires are, of course, often ambiguous; and in any event these data are much less rich than the interviews proper. Findings based solely on the questionnaire responses must be treated with due caution and skepticism, therefore; but the evidence from the questionnaire is broadly consistent with that emerging from the interviews; and the initial patterns in both sets of data in all three countries suggest some important conclusions.

4. BACKGROUNDS AND CAREERS

Before moving to an examination of our respondents' political attitudes and values, it may be informative to use evidence collected about their backgrounds and careers to sketch in broad outline the kind of men and women who lead these European bureaucracies, adding where possible comparative data from Sweden and America.[17] As the data presented in Table 2 show, the present

TABLE 2

CAREERS AND BACKGROUNDS OF EUROPEAN AND AMERICAN SENIOR CIVIL SERVANTS (in percentages)

	Britain		Germany		Italy		Sweden	U.S.
	Senior Incumbents	"High-fliers"	Senior Incumbents	"High-fliers"	Senior Incumbents	"High-fliers"	Senior Incumbents	Senior Incumbents
N[a] =	(92)	(29)	(90)	(41)	(84)	(29)	(312)	(126)
Age								
26-36	--	59	2	44	--	17	4	7
37-46	10	41	31	54	--	55	28	30
47-56	63	--	26	2	27	28	39	38
57-66	27	--	41	--	73	--	29	22
67 and over	--	--	--	--	--	--	--	3
Total	100	100	100	100	100	100	100	100
Year of First Entrance into National Administration								
1928-1939	45	--	19	--	86	3		18
1940-1949	40	--	12	--	13	28		23
1950-1959	10	88	46	27	1	52		15
1960-1969	5	12	23	73	--	17		44
Total	100	100	100	100	100	100		100
Tenure in Present Post								
0-2 years	49	84	63	64	18	36	35	59
3-5 years	31	16	21	28	28	18	27	28
6-10 years	17	--	14	8	35	46	23	9
11-30 years	3	--	2	--	19	--	15	4
Total	100	100	100	100	100	100	100	100
Service in Other Departments of National Government								
None	49	48	69	66	82	86	80	80
1-5 years	16	32	16	26	6	11	} 20	} 20
6-30 years	35	20	15	8	12	3		
Total	100	100	100	100	100	100	100	100

Education								
University								
Law	4	4	67	71	54	46	31	25
Science/tech.	20	4	9	19	23	11	33	28
Other	59	88	23	10	23	39	32	45
Secondary only	17	4	1	–	–	4	4	2
Total	100	100	100	100	100	100	100	100
Father's Education								
None or primary	31	23	34	39	13	14	37	21
Secondary	45	39	33	36	53	50	34	32
University	24	38	33	25	34	36	29	47
Total	100	100	100	100	100	100	100	100
Social Class Origin[b]								
I	35	35	42	33	42	39	42	47
II	47	54	50	51	49	47	43	35
III	18	11	8	16	9	14	15	18
Total	100	100	100	100	100	100	100	100
Parents or Relatives in the Civil Service								
Yes	36	33	40	41	52	56	22	22
Yes, but only in schools, the post office, or the nationalized industries	10	4	26	22	9	4		1
No	54	63	34	37	39	40		77
Total	100	100	100	100	100	100		100
Sex								
Male	98	93	99	98	100	93	97	98
Female	2	7	1	2	0	7	3	2
Total	100	100	100	100	100	100	100	100

a. The few cases where data are missing have been deleted in calculating percentages.
b. Social class is defined here in terms of the occupation of the respondent's father. Higher managerial and professional occupations were classified as I, all other nonmanual occupations as II, and all manual occupations as III.

administrative elites of Britain, Germany, and Italy are mostly middle-aged, mostly long-time civil servants, mostly university-educated, mostly from middle and upper middle class backgrounds, and mostly male.

Italian senior bureaucrats are distinctive, first of all, because they are older and have served, on an average, much longer in the public administration. The sclerotic stability of the Italian bureaucracy is reflected in the fact that the median senior official entered the civil service in 1936, has never served outside his present department (indeed, probably not outside his present Directorate General) and has served seven years in his present post. By contrast, the career of the average British senior official must seem kaleidoscopic, for in his twenty-five years in the civil service he has probably served five to ten years in some other department(s), and he has been in his current job barely three years. The average German senior official has served about two decades in the national bureaucracy, but the most significant fact about the German sample is the much greater range of age and tenure it reveals. This is the first of a series of hints we will encounter that our interviews caught the German bureaucracy in an extraordinary period of transition. The recency of the German officials' tenure in their present posts reflects the shake-up in the Bonn bureaucracy following the installation of the Brandt government about a year before our interviews, though evidence to be considered later suggests that this was no straightforward partisan purge.

The educational backgrounds of the respective national samples are not unexpected. The British are largely men of letters, while jurists dominate the continental bureaucracies. (The group of British respondents with a scientific or technical background reflects our decision to include some members of the "specialist" classes in our British sample.) Equally striking is the virtual absence of anyone lacking a university degree; the only (partial) exception is the small number of British senior officials who have been promoted out of the Clerical or Executive grades. There are remarkably few inter-generational differences in educational background in any country, once we take into account that specialists and people promoted out of lower grades were virtually excluded from our sample of British high-fliers.

An elite educated in the European universities of the 1930s, 1940s, and 1950s must necessarily be largely upper and middle class in origin, given the social biases in university entrance. Still, it is remarkable how similar are the social origins of bureaucrats in these four countries. What is perhaps more surprising is the relative absence of evidence that the next generation of leading administrators will be any more representative in their social origins than is the present generation.[18] Our data confirm previous findings that the civil service is frequently an inherited career, particularly on the continent. But it must be added that nearly all our respondents have climbed far above whatever rank their fathers may have had in the civil service. These are generally the sons of middle ranking, seldom of high ranking officials. And finally we must note that they are indeed almost universally "sons," rather than daughters. Sexual discrimination, at least in a statistical sense, is much greater than even social discrimination in these European bureaucracies, though there is evidence of a slight increase in female representation among the younger samples.

5. BUREAUCRATS AND POLITICS: SOME INITIAL DISCOVERIES

The central element in the distinction between classical and political bureaucrats involves their respective evaluations of their political environment. Some striking evidence of the relative proportions of classical and political bureaucrats in these three national administrations comes from the responses to the written questionnaire. One item, for example, asked the respondent to agree or disagree that "in contemporary social and economic affairs it is essential that technical considerations be given more weight than political factors." Of all Italian bureaucrats, 77% agreed, whereas only 22% of the British and 49% of the Germans agreed. Or a related example: "The interference of politicians in affairs which are properly the business of civil servants is a disturbing feature of contemporary public life." Of the Italians, 83% agreed, as contrasted with 43% of the Germans and only 9% of the British. Or a final illustration: "Although parties play an important role in a democracy, often they uselessly exacerbate political conflicts." Eighty-five percent of the Italians, 53% of the British, and only 30% of the Germans agreed.[19]

A total of six items on the written questionnaire tapped various aspects of hostility or tolerance toward the political environment, and in each country responses to these six items are intercorrelated. Bureaucrats who feel "political considerations" are less important than "technical factors" are the same bureaucrats who are disturbed by the "interference of politicians," who decry the divisiveness of political parties, and so on.[20] We can, therefore, justifiably combine responses to these six items into a single Index of Tolerance for Politics (ITP). The six components of this Index are given in Table 3, along with the distribution of responses of the British, German, and Italian civil servants, grouping together for the moment both older and younger samples for each country.

Not surprisingly, the average Italian score on the ITP (26) indicates much greater antipathy toward institutions of pluralist politics than the average score for either the Germans (59) or the British (62).[21] As these data illustrate, there are striking differences in the perspectives on politics held by British, German, and Italian bureaucrats. Most (though not all) of the senior posts in the Italian bureaucracy are held by "classical" bureaucrats; 94% of our senior Italian respondents and 90% of the Italian "high-fliers" rank below the overall three-nation mean score on the ITP. By contrast, most (though not all) of the senior posts in the British and German bureaucracies seem to be held by "political bureaucrats," at least as measured by the ITP. Of the senior British respondents, only 32% rank below the overall mean; and 7% of the British "high-fliers" are that intolerant of politics. For the German samples the comparable figures are 38% for the senior officials and 32% for the younger group.[22] I should perhaps add that the German bureaucrats show much greater diversity of opinion on these items than do either of the other two national samples.[23] We shall have occasion later to ponder this fact.

During the interview itself, as one way of tapping our respondents' attitudes toward their political environment, we asked them, "Senior officials like yourself are probably frequently involved in a grey area between the world of administration in a strict sense and the world of politics. Do you personally like the political side of your work or not?" Most of them agreed with the premise of the question, but the attitudes they expressed in response varied considerably. To some political enthusiasts, the exciting and creative world of high politics gives to the slightly humdrum job of a government official its real savour. One older British civil servant, for example, replied to my query:

> Oh, I find it really makes the job. I think it's, you know, the constant challenge it presents in how far you can go, how far ought you to go,

TABLE 3
THE INDEX OF TOLERANCE FOR POLITICS (ITP)[a]
(in percentages)

Ns: Britain = 121 Germany = 134 Italy = 102	Country	Agree	Agree With Reservation	Disagree With Reservation	Disagree
1. Basically it is not the parties and Parliament, but rather the civil service which guarantees reasonably satisfactory public policy in this country.	Britain Germany Italy	3 2 b	18 14 b	59 56 b	20 28 b
2. Often those who enter politics think more about their own welfare or that of their party than about the welfare of the citizens.	Britain Germany Italy	7 12 49	43 37 35	41 44 10	9 7 6
3. The interference of politicians in affairs which are properly the business of civil servants is a disturbing feature of contemporary public life.	Britain Germany Italy	1 16 62	8 27 21	28 32 12	63 25 5
4. In contemporary social and economic affairs it is essential that technical considerations be given more weight than political factors.	Britain Germany Italy	3 15 50	19 34 27	51 31 17	27 20 6
5. The general welfare of the country is seriously endangered by the continual clash of particularistic interest groups.	Britain Germany Italy	4 9 48	14 10 40	48 45 11	34 36 1
6. Although parties play an important role in a democracy, often they uselessly exacerbate political conflicts.	Britain Germany Italy	22 13 65	31 17 20	35 40 9	12 30 6

a. One point was given for an "agree" response to an item, three points for an "agree with reservations," seven points for a "disagree with reservations" and nine points for a "disagree." The ITP is simply the respondent's average score on the six items, multiplied by 10.
b. Italian respondents were not asked Item 1, and it was therefore excluded in calculating their ITP.

which sort of mix is the one that you really ought to recommend, even though you must consciously pull back—you know, you mustn't go over the frontier, as it were. This, I think, makes the challenge and the excitement of the job.

And a German official liked the political side of the work because it allowed for creativity:

We are not here to receive orders, mentally to click our heels, and to say, "Jawohl!"—that's not why we are here. On the contrary, if they [senior civil servants] have a different political conception [of the problem]—and they should always have a political conception—then they must, under certain circumstances, use their conception in conjunction with their expertise and simply say, "But I would propose thus and such for this reason." And if the Minister says, "No, politically we can't do that on account of these reasons," then all right, it will be done as proposed. It must be this way, because the Minister is the responsible official,who must have the last word. That can't be avoided.

To the classical bureaucrats among our respondents, on the other hand, even occasional contact with the noise, the ambiguity, and the alien ethic of their political environment was, quite literally, dreadful. An older Italian found his brushes with politics uniformly unpleasant:

Administration requires trained civil servants, who are able to apply the norms and regulations precisely. Politics introduces something else—the spirit of faction—because one who sees things politically is always looking to favor his own political movement, especially in personnel matters. These are often politically influenced, always to the detriment of the good administrator.

An Oxford educated high-flier was put off instead by the incompetence, as he saw it, of his political masters:

I don't think they are always very intelligent. . . . Since I started coming into fairly regular contact with politicians, I have not been very impressed with their quality of . . . well, the sort of political game as it's played publicly. It seems to me rather an odd way in the context of the importance of some of the issues we are supposed to be dealing with.

One Italian got onto the subject of the balance of power between ministers and civil servants.

Senior civil servants should have more power and should not be influenced either by politics or by parties . . . because, practically speaking, the minister is under the influence of the party, and hence he can give an order to a senior official which practically comes from the party. If the senior official doesn't obey the minister, he will liquidate him, in the sense of taking from him the position that he has worked so hard to gain. [We've noticed in most countries that senior officials are frequently involved in a grey area between the world of administration and the world of politics. How do you like the political side of your work?] The political side, never. An official is forced to do certain things politically, but really he should never do so. [Do you enjoy the political side?] Not at all, because things which are imposed are never pleasant.

A senior British civil servant in one of the most distinguished departments sketched very clearly the differences, as he saw them, between politicians and civil servants.

The job of a politician is talking. He is essentially an exhibitionist. . . . He has also got to be someone who is not bothered by putting expediency above principle. . . . I'd put integrity very high on the list of qualities of your civil servant. He's got to try not to be political, but to expose the facts fully and let them speak for themselves. . . . [How do you feel about the political side of your work?] It is extremely frustrating, of course. One is always fighting the feeling, "Oh, what does it matter anyway? Things are never decided properly." One becomes quite cynical about political considerations here. Perhaps civil servants are too perfectionist.

This man puts well the view of most classical bureaucrats: a perfect world would be a world without politics.

All in all, roughly three out of five British and German respondents reported that on balance they enjoyed the political side of their work, while roughly two in five reported ambivalent or negative feelings. Among our Italian respondents, the proportions were reversed, with three in five expressing aversion to politics, and only two in five feeling satisfaction with that aspect of the job.

On the basis of responses to this and several related questions, coders have tentatively rated each of our respondents on a five-point scale, according to the extent to which he "appears to be favorably disposed or hostile towards the world of politics." Table 4 shows how our senior and junior samples in each country feel about their political environment, based on their interview discussions of politics and administration.

Our confidence that these two independent measures of attitudes toward politics—one based on the open-ended interview response, the other based on the closed questionnaire—are indeed tapping a central element in our respondents' views of their environment is strengthened, first of all, by the fact that the two measures are correlated with one another in the expected direction.[24] But still more persuasive evidence of the importance of this empirical distinction

TABLE 4

ENTHUSIASM FOR POLITICS[a] (in percentages)

		Britain		Germany		Italy	
		Senior	Junior	Senior	Junior	Senior	Junior
N =		(93)	(27)	(93)	(40)	(62)	(29)
Very positive		11	26	19	22	5	- -
Moderately positive		36	37	37	32	35	48
Neutral; ambivalent		32	15	30	28	29	45
Moderately negative		21	18	13	18	21	7
Very negative		- -	4	1	- -	10	- -
Total		100	100	100	100	100	100

a. "To what extent does the respondent appear to be favorably disposed or hostile toward the world of politics?"

between "classical" and "political" bureaucrats consists in the range of other attitudes and values associated with these measures of orientation to the political environment.

First of all, political bureaucrats seem to attach much more importance to political ideals and programmatic objectives. Three of the items on our closed questionnaire tap this dimension; and although each item refers to a slightly different aspect of one's approach to policy-making, responses to the three were in fact sufficiently internally consistent to justify combining them into a single Index of Programmatic Commitment or IPC.[25] These three items, together with the responses of the three national samples to each, are given in Table 5. Those who rank high on this Index deny that the strength of a government is more important than its program, reject a merely "possibilist," short-run approach to policy-making, and discount the classical bureaucratic view that extreme positions should be avoided at all costs. A good many bureaucrats in all three countries find this sort of commitment distasteful, and endorse these antiprogrammatic questionnaire items. "If a man wants to change the world, he doesn't become a civil servant," one gruff English official explained to me. The irony is that, willy-nilly, civil servants *do* change the world. And political bureaucrats, tolerant of political institutions and at ease in the political world, are also more inclined to favor this sort of programmatic approach to policy-making than are classical bureaucrats.[26]

The contrast between political and classical bureaucrats extends to the way they interpret their own roles as civil servants. Most of our respondents rejected a questionnaire item asserting that "a senior

TABLE 5

THE INDEX OF PROGRAMMATIC COMMITMENT (IPC)[a]

(in percentages)

Ns: Britain = 120 Germany = 134 Italy = 102	Country	Agree	Agree With Reservation	Disagree With Reservation	Disagree
1. The strength and efficiency of a government are more important than its specific program.	Britain	10	41	36	13
	Germany	14	32	36	18
	Italy	39	25	23	13
2. Generally speaking, in political contro- versies extreme positions should be avoided, since the right answer usually lies in the middle.	Britain	17	55	20	8
	Germany	47	29	16	8
	Italy	71	20	4	5
3. Politics is "the art of the possible" and therefore the leaders of the country should worry more about what can be done in the short run than about ambitious ideals and long-term plans.	Britain	3	38	42	17
	Germany	8	37	33	22
	Italy	32	42	18	8

a. One point was given for an "agree" response to an item, three points for an "agree with reservations," seven points for a "disagree with reservations," and nine points for a "disagree." The IPC is simply the respondent's average score on the three items, multiplied by 10.

civil servant should limit his activity to the precise application of the law"; but those who did endorse this defensive, legalistic interpretation of the administrative process tended strongly to be "classical" in their attitudes to the political environment. Similarly, in interview discussions of "the job of a leading civil servant," classical bureaucrats stressed the need for absolute neutrality, while political bureaucrats tended to describe a more active role, seeking to solve social problems and resolve political conflicts.[27]

Moreover, in each of the three countries, these differences find resonance in current controversies about the boundary between politics and administration. In Britain, for example, political bureaucrats are more likely than classical bureaucrats to approve recent proposals for relaxing the traditional rule of official anonymity and public reticence. In Italy, classical bureaucrats are more likely than political bureaucrats to be hostile to the *gabinetto ministeriale* (the minister's personal staff), claiming that this institution illegitimately extends ministerial control into all activities of the department. On the widely debated issue of the "politicization" of the civil service in Germany, political and classical bureaucrats take opposing stands, the former favoring the trend, the latter protesting against it.[28]

These sets of attitudes seem to be linked to fundamental perspectives on human nature and social relations. Classical bureaucrats, for example, are more likely than political bureaucrats to agree with the misanthropic view that "basically no one cares much what happens to the next fellow," while political bureaucrats are more likely than classical bureaucrats to endorse the view that "it is social conflicts which bring about progress in modern society." These are only scraps of evidence, to be sure, but it is plausible that a Hobbesian view of society as fundamentally anarchic and of conflict as essentially destructive is linked to fear and distrust for the world of politics. Conversely, it is not surprising that bureaucrats who basically trust their fellows and believe in the beneficence of social conflict are more sympathetic and open-minded toward their political environment. The political implications of these contrasting syndromes are suggested by the fact that political bureaucrats are more likely than classical bureaucrats to agree with the proposition that "citizens have a perfect right to exert pressure for legislation which would benefit them personally." The classical bureaucrats' monistic interpretation of the public interest is incompatible with the fundamental ethic of pluralist politics.[29]

My introductory speculation that classical bureaucrats will be less supportive of basic democratic values than political bureaucrats also finds strong confirmation from our initial analysis of these data. In the closed questionnaire, support for political liberty was tapped by a statement that "the freedom of political propaganda is not an absolute freedom, and the State should carefully regulate its use." Not unexpectedly, the data in Table 6 show that Englishmen are warier of restrictions on political liberty than Germans and Italians. Equally significantly, however, in all three countries, classical bureaucrats are much more likely to approve "careful controls" over political propaganda.[30] Political agitation—a healthy and necessary part of the process of social communication for a political bureaucrat—is a dangerous symptom of subversion or at least of troublesome unrest for the classical bureaucrat.

Our administrators' attitudes toward politics are closely related to

TABLE 6

SUPPORT FOR POLITICAL LIBERTY (in percentages)

Ns: Britain = 119 Germany = 133 Italy = 101	Country	Agree	Agree With Reservation	Disagree With Reservation	Disagree
The freedom of political propaganda is not an absolute freedom, and the State should carefully regulate its use.	Britain	3	19	40	38
	Germany	8	25	37	30
	Italy	36	21	12	31

the warmth of their support for political equality and popular participation in government. Six items in the closed questionnaire were aimed at measuring "elitist" political values; the items, together with the responses of the three national samples, are shown in Table 7. Overall, the pattern of national differences is largely that which we have come to expect. The German and British bureaucrats are relatively egalitarian, with mean scores of 39 and 40, respectively, on the composite Elitism Index formed from these items, while the Italians, with a mean score of 50, are less enthusiastic about political equality. And once again, political bureaucrats across all three countries are the more enthusiastic proponents of democratic values. They are less likely than classical bureaucrats to believe that "certain people are better qualified to lead this country because of their traditions and family background," more likely to endorse without reservation the principle that "people should be allowed to vote even if they cannot do so intelligently," and so on.[31]

The pattern of attitudes and values we have sketched so far is coherent and intelligible, but the skeptical social scientist may wonder whether all this is related to the actual behavior of our respondents. Political bureaucrats are clearly more programmatic in their orientation to policy-making, less legalist and more activist in their interpretation of their own role, more sympathetic to an open, "political" public service, more relaxed about human relations and social conflict, more committed to the values of pluralist democracy. But in practice are they actually more responsive to social needs and political demands?

Our work so far allows only a tentative and partial, but nonetheless revealing answer to this question. Our respondents were asked to indicate the frequency of their personal encounters with a number of other participants in the policy process, including their

TABLE 7

THE ELITISM INDEX[a] (in percentages)

Ns: Britain = 121 Germany = 134 Italy = 102	Country	Agree	Agree With Reservation	Disagree With Reservation	Disagree
1. Certain people are better qualified to lead this country because of their traditions and family background.	Britain Germany Italy	1 12 27	13 13 21	31 26 13	55 49 39
2. In a world as complicated as the modern one, it doesn't make sense to speak of increased control by ordinary citizens over govern- mental affairs.	Britain Germany Italy	8 14 38	36 24 25	40 37 16	16 26 21
3. It will always be necessary to have a few strong, able individuals who know how to take charge.	Britain Germany Italy	21 23 34	55 50 34	15 19 11	9 8 21
4. People should be allowed to vote even if they cannot do so intelligently.	Britain Germany Italy	74 71 57	22 15 18	2 5 14	2 9 11
5. Few people know what is in their real interest in the long run.	Britain Germany Italy	22 23 75	35 36 17	31 30 6	12 11 2
6. All citizens should have the same chance of influencing govern- ment policy.	Britain Germany Italy	44 77 64	25 17 23	21 4 9	10 2 4

a. Nine points were given for an "agree" response to an item, seven points for an "agree with reservations," three points for a "disagree with reservations," and one point for a "disagree." Scoring was reversed for items 4 and 6, which are phrased so that to agree is to be "anti-elitist." The Elitism Index is simply a respondent's average score on the six items, multiplied by 10.

own and other ministers, the office of the prime minister, members of parliament, party leaders, interest group leaders, and ordinary citizens. In each country and in nearly every case, political bureaucrats reported significantly more frequent contacts than did classical bureaucrats.

This fact is not unambiguous, for it is not clear whether in this case attitudes precede behavior or vice versa—whether a tolerance for politics tends to increase contacts with the political world or the reverse, or indeed whether it is the politicians who shun contact with bureaucrats whose antipathy they sense. Two possible explanations can be discarded. The relationship is not a function of hierarchical proximity to the political summit, for classical bureaucrats are not concentrated in any particular grade. Nor are these sociometric patterns peculiar to a particular government, for the phenomenon occurs in Britain under the Tories, in Germany under the SPD-FDP coalition, and in Italy under the *Centrosinistra*.

This causal conundrum cannot be unraveled with the data now at our disposal, but in all likelihood each of the three possibilities previously noted is in part true. The consistency of this relationship is strong evidence that political bureaucrats make the sorts of personal contacts which allow, and presumably encourage, them to respond to the public and its representatives.

A written questionnaire is a blunt instrument for dissecting the subtleties of a personal political philosophy, and I must stress again that the results presented here are based on only a small proportion of the evidence we hope eventually to analyze. But these results are broadly consistent with the impressions my colleagues and I carried away from the fuller interviews. We have, I believe, discovered numbers of classical bureaucrats still in the upper reaches of the British, the German, and (particularly) the Italian civil services. They are distrustful of political institutions and resentful of political pressures. They disapprove of the practices of pluralism and political liberalism. They are deeply skeptical about political equality and mass political participation. They define their role as civil servants as guarantors of the permanent interests of the state, though they tend to interpret this role relatively statically and legalistically, reluctant to become actively and openly involved as program advocates, bargaining with other participants in the policy process. They are wary too of policies which seem "extreme" or "idealistic" and are more concerned about "strong government" than about the program of that government. And despite their position at the "interface" between administration and politics, their personal contacts across that interface are relatively infrequent. The responsiveness of these three bureaucracies is likely to be considerably affected by the relative balance between these classical bureaucrats and their opposites, the political bureaucrats. Let us consider each of our three countries in turn.

6. CAUSES AND CONSEQUENCES: THE ITALIAN CASE

The picture of senior Italian officials which emerges from this study would seem to confirm the sharpest censures leveled by critics of the Roman bureaucracy. The typical member of the Italian administrative elite appears here as the very essence of a classical bureaucrat—legalist, illiberal, elitist, hostile to the usages and practices of pluralist politics, fundamentally undemocratic. There are exceptions to this indictment, of course; but they are very much rarer in Italy than are political bureaucrats in the British, German, and Swedish ministries. How can we explain the attitudes of Italian bureaucrats?

One obvious explanation would simply refer to the realities of Italian politics. Perhaps, one might say, it is only sensible to be antipolitical in contemporary Italy. Italian parties *do* sometimes seem to exacerbate political conflicts; Italian politicians *do* seem often to care more for personal gain than for social progress. Yet there are two reasons for looking beyond this explanation. First, many of the views expressed by Italian bureaucrats in the interview proper make it clear that it is not merely Italian politics, but democratic politics per se which they find uncongenial. Some evidence of this appears even in the written questionnaire. A glance back at Item 4 in Table 7 will reveal, for example, that nearly half the Italian bureaucrats have reservations about the simple principle of universal suffrage.

The second reason that the classical views of most Italian bureaucrats cannot be explained away as mere reflections of reality is precisely that not all their colleagues share those views. In particular, our younger Italian respondents are systematically less hostile to pluralist political institutions, more liberal and less elitist, more committed to programmatic politics, and less legalist in their interpretation of their own role.[32] Older and younger Italian bureaucrats are responding to the same political environment, but they are not responding in the same way, because their basic values are perceptibly different.

Indeed, the values of the older Italian bureaucrats are such that they would seem more at home in the Fascist state of 1930 than in the Republic of 1970. And that is no accident, for an astonishing proportion of them in fact first entered the bureaucracy under the Fascist regime. Fully 95% of our senior sample joined the Italian civil service before 1943. Italy is administered by old men, and in 1970 older Italians had spent their formative years under a fundamentally undemocratic regime. These old men in particular had entered a bureaucracy whose operative ideals were an odd mixture of Bourbonic paternalism, Piedmontese and Napoleonic authoritarianism, and Fascist contempt for democratic responsiveness. Ideals change slowly in any human institution, and in bureaucracies perhaps more slowly than elsewhere. The Italian gerontocracy was bound to perpetuate undemocratic, classical bureaucratic ideals.

There was, of course, a political revolution in Italy in 1943; but it was never followed by an administrative revolution. The political elite of Fascist Italy was almost completely replaced with a new set of men, but the bureaucratic elite endured. As Max Weber had pointed out, "Once it is fully established, bureaucracy is among those social structures which are the hardest to destroy. . . . [The bureaucratic machine] makes 'revolution,' in the sense of the forceful creation of entirely new formations of authority, technically more and more impossible."[33] All political revolutionaries have faced this problem, Lenin and Mao no less than the young political class who constructed the Italian Republic in 1945-47. Purges are necessary, later if not sooner, but those purges seem never to have come in Italy.

Thus, ironically, the blame for the undemocratic Italian bureaucracy does return in part to the Italian political elite. Political turnover in postwar Italy has in a sense been both too great and too slight to facilitate the sort of administrative reconstruction that could have created a more responsive bureaucracy. Political turnover has been too rapid in the sense that as government has replaced feeble government, few ministers have been in office long enough to exercise their formal powers of administrative control. Today, as historically, the fragmentation of the Italian political class has allowed and encouraged the bureaucracy to "rise above politics," responsible to no higher authority and fundamentally unresponsive. And to complete the vicious circle, the inability of successive Italian governments to make the bureaucratic machine respond has condemned them to ineffectiveness. Reforms passed by Parliament, such as the recent housing program, remain unimplemented by the bureaucracy. Thus are perpetuated the social cleavages that sustain the political fragmentation that prevents the formation of strong governments that could gain control of the bureaucracy.

On the other hand, turnover in Italian politics has been too slight, in the sense that a single party has dominated all postwar governments. There are rascals in every political system and in every party, but the party system in Italy has short-circuited the normal democratic method for throwing the rascals out now and then. Italian politicians have had—and used—the power to appoint their administrative lieutenants; but they have, by and large, used this resource for maximizing short-run personal or factional gain, rather than for increasing the responsiveness of Italian government in a programmatic sense.

The strands of bureaucratic and political irresponsibility in the Italian dilemma are inextricably interwoven. Any visitor to the Roman ministries soon senses the deep and bitter alienation of the bureaucratic elite from the country's political institutions, the utter despair of finding satisfaction in public service. And our companion interviews with Italian politicians complete the picture of pathology, for the politicians reciprocate in kind the bureaucrats' distrust and contempt.

Yet the evidence of our study is in one respect encouraging about the prospects for responsiveness in Italian government. For what the founders of the Italian Republic were unable to do, and what successive governments have seemed unwilling to do, ineluctable biological processes are now about to do—to bring an end to the predominance of a bureaucratic elite reared under Fascism. If in 1970 still 95% of the elite were prewar entrants, within the next 5 to 8 years that figure must fall away to nothing, given the normal ages of entry and retirement in the Italian civil service. Of course, the successors of the present directors general will in all likelihood themselves have served three decades within the climate of opinion I have described, and thus one should not expect immediate and drastic changes in the responsiveness of the Italian bureaucracy. But our data do confirm that the young are different.

One can perhaps venture a genuine prediction, relatively rare in social science, that over the next decade Italian politicians will find the Italian bureaucracy imperceptibly but gradually becoming more responsive to social needs and public demands. Care in the appointment of successive directors general could speed up this process, if Italian politicians were to spend energy and resources in the selection of intelligent and program-oriented "political bureaucrats." The notable success of a few ministers in doing just that should encourage others. But even merely random selection from the pool of oncoming younger bureaucrats should increase the potential responsiveness of the Italian bureaucracy in the coming years.

Whether the political class can put that potential to effective use is, of course, another question.

7. CAUSES AND CONSEQUENCES: THE GERMAN CASE

The logic of the Italian case can be clarified by examining next the German results, in some ways the most surprising of all, for most observers have described the German bureaucrat as the very model of a modern classical bureaucrat. Kenneth Hanf, for example, writes of the "exclusion of social and political considerations" from the calculations of Bonn bureaucrats; and Ralf Dahrendorf, after noting that "traditional Prussian values probably no longer describe West German bureaucrats," adds immediately that "the fact remains that the administrative elite shows few traits that could permit describing it as liberal."[34] There have been few empirical studies of the values of West German bureaucrats, but several scraps of evidence from Rudolf Wildenmann's 1968 study of *"Eliten in der Bundesrepublik"* would support the hypothesis that German bureaucrats tend to be "antipolitical." More than half of his sample of leading federal civil servants agreed with such propositions as "The general welfare in the Bundesrepublik and the interests of the people as a whole are fundamentally endangered by the continual demands and altercations of interest groups," and "Basically, it is not the parties and Parliament, but rather the civil service which guarantees reasonably satisfactory public policy in the Bundesrepublik."[35] The conclusion seems clear: German civil servants should fall heavily at the "classical" end of our continuum.

The findings of our research are, of course, resoundingly to the contrary. In their responses to the closed questionnaire items, as in their much fuller discussions of these issues during the interviews proper, top level civil servants in Germany in 1970 displayed great sensitivity to and support for the imperatives of politics in a democracy. By all the measures now available, they are hardly less egalitarian, hardly less liberal, hardly less politically responsive or programmatic in outlook than their British or Swedish counterparts. Why should this be so?

The first possibility is methodological. Perhaps large numbers of "classical" bureaucrats eluded discovery in our interviews. Two decades ago the American occupiers administered *Fragebogen* to German elites, and the purposes of those earlier inquiries were less innocuous than our own. Perhaps German administrators have learned to give the "proper" responses to such questions, while privately retaining less democratic values. There is no conclusive way of discounting this possibility; but having listened carefully and skeptically to these interviews, I doubt that simple dissimulation was very common. More subtly, it is likely that a number of our respondents were indeed "playing a role" during our conversations, a role at variance with their deepest personal convictions. But in such cases, it is probably a role played well precisely because it is played often. I mean that it is the role these men normally play in their official lives; in that sense it is not false to their actual behavior, however gratingly out of tune it may be with other values they hold.

A second explanation of our findings would accept them as accurately descriptive of the federal civil service in 1970, but ascribe them to Social Democratic purges in the preceding year, purges which (by implication) could easily be followed by "counterpurges" and a return to the status quo ante. Many of the presuppositions of this theory are valid. In the first place, the SPD members and sympathizers among our respondents are markedly less "classical" in their orientations, more programmatic, more egalitarian, more libertarian.[36] Second, among our respondents, most of the recent entrants to the civil service are Social Democrats, and conversely, most Social Democrats are recent entrants.

But this is not the whole story, for eight in every nine among our senior German sample had entered the civil service before the SPD had entered the government. Moreover, we can set some outer limits on the potential effect partisan purging could have had on the composition of the administrative elite. Only 21% of our respondents claimed to be members of the SPD, and only another 6% claimed to be sympathizers. By contrast, 16% claimed to be members of the CDU, and another 27% claimed to be CDU sympathizers. Given the widespread belief that known sympathies for the ruling party can only improve career prospects, it is unlikely that many of the remaining respondents who claimed to have no firm partisan preference were secret SPD sympathizers. Hence, even at this high level in the bureaucracy and despite the rumors of purges, barely one official in four was a Social Democratic partisan.

An even more decisive bit of evidence that the traits I have ascribed to the German higher civil service are not merely epiphenomena associated with a passing Socialist government consists in the fact that while party sympathy is closely related to pro-political and pro-democratic attitudes, it is not as good a predictor as age. The younger the official, regardless of his party sympathies, the less likely he is to display the characteristics of a "classical" bureaucrat. Take, for example, responses to the item, "Basically it is not the parties and Parliament, but rather the civil service which guarantees reasonably satisfactory public policy." Overall, 16% of our total German sample agree with this statement of a "classical" bureaucratic viewpoint. But of those under 40 only 11% agree, while of those over 60, 35% agree.[37]

Correlations between attitude and age are, of course, ambiguous, for normally we cannot distinguish the permanent effects of being in a given historical generation from the temporary effects of being a particular age. But we can look more closely at this problem, and at the same time deal with the puzzling disparity between our description of the German bureaucracy and the traditional description, if we return to the evidence from the Wildenmann study of 1967-68. Fortunately, two of our questionnaire items are virtually identical. On the item just quoted, rating the civil service as guarantor of the public interest, Wildenmann found 53% agreement in contrast to the figure of 17% for our senior bureaucrats. On the item critical of interest groups as "dangerous to the country's welfare," Wildenmann found 63% agreement in contrast to 24% agreement in our senior sample.

These remarkable differences are much too great to be due to minor differences in phrasing, and they are unlikely to be due to differences in sampling frame or to sampling error. On the other hand, it is hard to imagine a trend of opinion drastic enough to explain the differences. Almost certainly the essential clue lies in the age structures of the two samples. Whereas exactly half of our senior sample is aged 50 or under, only 8% of Wildenmann's sample was that young. Even allowing for sampling errors, it seems clear that a substantial rejuvenation of the higher civil service took place in the three years between the two studies. This is consistent with the fact that 63% of our senior German respondents had been in their present posts for less than three years. Minds were not changed in this period, but official incumbents were.

There are two good reasons why such a rapid generational change could occur in the higher German civil service during these years. First of all, there is the well-known "missing generation" of the German demographic structure. This deficiency of males in the cohorts decimated by World War II meant that when men of 65 retired, they were replaced by men not of 60, but of 55 or even 50. This, in turn, meant that when the generation of prewar civil servants began to retire, changes in age structure—and therefore changes in attitude—could occur fairly rapidly.

The second explanation for such rapid change takes us back to the role played by the SPD. It seems likely—given the age structure and partisan loyalties already described—that the "purge" engineered by the new government was less a partisan purge than a generational purge. Whether new faces were brought "up" or "in," those new faces were very likely much younger than their predecessors. For demographic reasons, the generational revolution was bound to occur, but the SPD probably played a traditionally congenial role as the "midwife to history."

The transition away from "classical" attitudes is not yet complete, as is evidenced by our repeated discovery of greater diversity of opinion within the German than the British or Italian samples. Nor is there complete assurance that the transition will continue at the same pace in the future. The return of a CDU/CSU government would probably slow the process, although given the markedly less "classical" views of younger CDU sympathizers in our sample, it seems quite unlikely that the historical trend toward a more "political" bureaucracy could be reversed.

Viewed in historical perspective, it seems natural that the "classical" myth of *überparteilichkeit* should be passing. Fundamentally, this myth was based on an Hegelian distinction between State and Society and served as an ideological defense for a conservative bureaucracy against an intrusive political environment. In the first instance, as Chapman pointed out, the myth was a bulwark against the tide of the democratic revolution, and then a bulwark—breached in the end—against the almost equally uncongenial Nazi politicians. But as Germany has finally come to terms with the age of democracy during the past quarter century, her bureaucracy seems likely to continue to move toward greater responsiveness, at least insofar as this is a function of the norms and values of senior bureaucrats.

8. CAUSES AND CONSEQUENCES: THE BRITISH CASE AND SOME TRANS-EUROPEAN SPECULATIONS

British bureaucrats have long had a high reputation for responsiveness to political authority, and our data largely confirm that reputation. The historical explanation seems clear: The modern British civil service was created *after,* not before representative institutions had been firmly established. Even though higher civil servants in England have had considerable social prestige, they have rarely enjoyed the kind of public authority that has enabled large numbers of bureaucrats to play a leading role in politics in many continental countries over the past century. There was no opportunity to create a defensive myth against representative political institutions in Britain, since those institutions had greater historical legitimacy than the bureaucracy itself.[38]

But if the British findings are unproblematic at one level, at another there are some curious crosscurrents. One of the more intriguing of these involves the attitudes of the minority of specialist and technical officials included in our sample. These are the heroes of the Fulton Report—experts, not dilettantes, but historically subordinate to the generalist Administrative Class. One important, though not uncontested, theme in recent discussions of administrative reform in Britain has been a call for the enhancement of the position and power of the specialists. The preliminary results from our interviews put these proposals in a new light, for by contrast with general administrators, the specialists are distinctively more "classical"—less tolerant of political influences on policy, less wholeheartedly egalitarian and libertarian, less comfortable in the gray area between politics and administration.[39] Our sample of specialists and professionals is small and the data analyzed so far are fragmentary, but the present evidence suggests that a bureaucracy led by such men might be less responsive than one led by the "political bureaucrats" who predominate among the old Administrative Class.

The most puzzling of the findings from the British case, however, concerns not the specialists, but the high-fliers, for there is a remarkably steep age gradient in attitudes and values within the British sample, greater in fact than in either Germany or Italy. Our British high-fliers are the most politically conscious, the most programmatically committed, the most egalitarian, and the most tolerant toward politicians and pluralism of any of the groups of bureaucrats we have interviewed.[40] This finding introduces several perplexities into the discussion.

First of all, it is more difficult to account for these generational differences in terms of the recent historical discontinuities in socialization experiences which we have adduced for Italy and Germany. Of course, it is possible in Britain, as in Italy and

Germany, that the differences between older and younger officials are not generational at all, but a function of the life cycle. Perhaps when they are older and more senior, today's high-fliers will have become less enthusiastic about politics, less tolerant of politicians, parties, pressure groups, and the public. But though this possibility cannot be discounted on the basis of the data presently available, it is instructive to consider an alternative view, one that might parsimoniously account for the age-related differences we have found in all three countries.

A new type of administrative official may be emerging in Western Europe, not everywhere at the same rate, but everywhere noticeably. In each of our three countries (and in Sweden as well[41]), our younger respondents are much more open to the idea of political equality and mass participation, much less hostile and suspicious toward the political environment in which they increasingly move, much more inclined to a programmatic style of politics. Over the next decade older, classical bureaucrats will be succeeded in all these countries by younger, political bureaucrats. Perhaps the most intriguing problem to emerge so far from this study is the search for a persuasive explanation for this apparent change in the kind of men and women who administer Europe.

According to one possible interpretation, we are witnessing the playing out of the last act of the democratic revolution of the nineteenth century. Changes in political values and norms over the past two hundred years have fundamentally altered the governance of European societies. The story of this cultural revolution is so familiar that we may overestimate the rate of change in the operative ideals of those actually involved in public affairs. Perhaps by a kind of "trickle up" phenomenon the values of democratic pluralism are only now being finally diffused through the upper reaches of the European bureaucracies. The higher civil services in Europe have been among the last bastions of an older social order, at least to judge by the social origins of the incumbents; and similarly, they may be the last bastions of an older political philosophy, as embodied in the myth of the classical bureaucrat. But the bastions seem to be falling at last, dramatically as in the case of Germany at the end of the 1960s, gradually as in postwar Britain and Sweden, agonizingly slowly as in contemporary Italy.

We do not yet know enough about what values are being learned by young Europeans, either before or after they have been recruited for positions of leadership. But it may well be that those values are distinctively different from the values inculcated in today's senior officials when they were acquiring their fundamental views about society, politics, and government forty years ago. Moreover, we do not yet know much about the recruitment paths and motivations of those who have entered the public service in recent years. But it would be consistent with the little we have learned to suppose that these younger recruits have been moved more by the wish to solve social problems and to attain programmatic goals than by the desire for security, prestige, and the opportunity to "serve the nation" (in an apolitical sense) which motivated their elders.

In addition, certain structural changes may lie behind the changes in values which we have noted. Certainly, the increasing complexity of modern society and particularly the increasingly active role of government in coordinating and guiding social change require much greater interaction between bureaucracy and private groups, both institutionally and individually. As officials have to deal regularly with businessmen, shop stewards, representatives of consumer groups, local politicians, and so on, the values and habits of the officials themselves may come to change, may indeed come to resemble more closely those traditionally ascribed to politicians. It is surely significant, for example, that in each of our countries those younger bureaucrats most tolerant of politics are also the most likely to criticize the traditional barriers (such as the rule of anonymity in Britain) which have kept the official out of the world of politics, and are the most likely to prescribe an activist, programmatic, bargaining role for the bureaucrat himself. Perhaps in Britain and on the continent, too, we are seeing a gradual blurring of the strict differentiation between the role of politician and the role of bureaucrat, a differentiation altogether more appropriate to a simpler age.

This speculation raises one final dilemma in the British case. As Sir Kenneth Wheare has pointed out, "British administrative practice . . . works on the assumption . . . that people of ability, of power, and influence, in the higher civil service, can feel no sense of impropriety, futility, dishonesty, or disloyalty either to the state or to their party (if they have one) or to their consciences by working as hard as they can to execute the policy of one party and defend it against the Opposition, and then reverse the roles completely when the Opposition becomes the government."[42] Wheare was not here considering the personal commitment of officials in a political or programmatic sense, but the logic of the argument applies equally to that case. If our high-fliers maintain their present level of political involvement ("political," to be sure, in a broad and not a partisan sense), painful and perhaps irreconcilable conflicts of principle and loyalty can hardly be avoided without some bending of the service's rules of personnel management. Commitment to programs and responsiveness to public demands are not logically inconsistent with ultimate conformity to the norm of neutrality in relations with ministers; but there may well be a psychological inconsistency here. As a young civil servant is reported recently to have admitted, "Speaking personally, I find it yearly more difficult to reconcile personal integrity with a role which requires the deliberate suppression of part of what I am. It is this tension, and not overwork, which brings me, regularly, to the point where I am ready to contemplate leaving a service which I care about very deeply."[43] This dilemma poses, I think, important practical and philosophical problems that will need to be faced by the British civil service in the decades ahead.

9. UNANSWERED QUESTIONS

It has been rhetorically convenient here to summarize our initial impressions in terms of two ideal types: the classical bureaucrat and the political bureaucrat. This radical simplification will, however, probably prove inadequate for later analyses. In principle—and perhaps in our interviews as well—one can distinguish between more and less extreme classical bureaucrats (depending on the depth of their alienation from pluralistic democracy), between more and less extreme political bureaucrats (depending on the extent of their rejection of administrative neutrality). Moreover, I have here treated the domain of attitudes to politics as if it were unidimensional; and that, too, is only approximately true. For some purposes one may need to distinguish attitudes toward conflict from attitudes toward politicians and both from attitudes toward various political institutions. Our American interviews, for example, highlight the need to differentiate bureaucrats' orientations toward political leaders in the executive branch (the "Administration") from their orientations toward legislators.

Bureaucrats differ from one another in other ways that have not been adequately discussed here. Some seek discretion while others prefer directives. Some define policy problems in legal terms, others in technical terms, still others in political terms. Some give primary loyalty to their department or to "their" program, while others have a broader perspective. Some are innovative, others less so. Some are idealistic, others cynical. Some are planners while others prefer to muddle. Our interview data will speak to some of these other dimensions, too; and while they may be related to the attitudes toward politics discussed in this paper, the correlation is far from perfect. Let me take one prominent example. The evidence reported here suggests that bureaucratic activism and a tolerance for politics are positively related. But we shall nevertheless want to look closely at those respondents who are high on one of these traits and low on the other. Activists who are intolerant of politics—"technocrats" we might term them—are probably rather unlike both classical and political bureaucrats, as described here.

This report has stressed primarily cross-national differences, but of equal importance will be intranational variation and its correlates. For example, a civil servant's attitudes toward politics may depend in part on the kind of job he has and the kind of ministry he is in. (As Arthur Clun has pointed out, where you stand depends on where you sit.) Certainly, part of the folklore of each national bureaucracy is that there are substantial differences in the climate of opinion across different departments. Perhaps, too, within departments there are differences according to how routine or "unpolitical" an official's tasks are. We will also want to investigate the impact of such factors as social background, political ideology, education, and career patterns. And, finally, we will want to examine more closely the detailed links between the attitudes of bureaucrats (and politicians) and the policy process itself.

10. BUREAUCRATS AND RESPONSIVE GOVERNMENT

The main argument of this paper has been that bureaucrats vary markedly in their orientation to the world of politics and hence in their responsiveness to social needs and public demands. The assumptions underlying this argument can perhaps be clarified by restating it in terms introduced by Herbert Simon for the study of administrative decision-making. He suggests that we regard "the process of human choice as a process of 'drawing conclusions from premises.' It is therefore the *premise* (and a large number of these are combined in every decision) rather than the whole *decision* that serves as the smallest unit of analysis."[44] Some of the premises for public decisions are primarily factual, but inevitably some are evaluative. "Democratic institutions find their principal justification as a procedure for the validation of value judgments. There is no 'scientific' or 'expert' way of making such judgments, hence expertise of whatever kind is no qualification for the performance of this function. . . . Since the administrative agency must of necessity make many value judgments, it must be responsive to community values, far beyond those that are explicitly enacted into law."[45]

It is precisely in this sense that political bureaucrats, as described here, are likely to be more responsive than classical bureaucrats. Among the implicit evaluative premises that underlie policy decisions, some have the form, "Do X, because the public wants it done." For political bureaucrats this is always a persuasive (though not necessarily compelling) argument. For classical bureaucrats the premise is simply illegitimate. When the evaluation at issue is unambiguously embodied in law or in direct orders from superiors, the classical bureaucrat will normally comply, for the law is the law and orders are orders. But at the top of the administrative hierarchy matters are rarely that simple, and decisions can seldom be made by merely following orders or the law. Hence the need to be "responsive to community values," as Simon puts it, and hence, too, the greater responsiveness of political bureaucrats.

For the purposes of this paper "responsiveness" has been taken as a summum bonum. Yet how much responsiveness is desirable is a matter of judgment in individual cases for, as Friedrich pointed out, policies must meet technical criteria as well as political ones, if they are to be successful at all; and technical and political criteria will not always be perfectly reconcilable. Moreover, responsiveness to some groups in the short run may be irresponsible from a larger and longer perspective.

The relevance of these points is that any trend toward a more "political" bureaucracy is not without dangers: the danger that party patronage might gradually reduce the level of competence of the administrative elite and thereby its technical ability to be responsive on larger matters; the danger that growing political commitment on the part of administrative officials might encourage the intrusion of partisanship into those activities of the state which can and should be governed by essentially objective criteria; the danger that politicization of the higher civil service might lead over time to fragmentation and demoralization and thus in turn to a reduction in overall effectiveness; the danger that beyond some point a more political bureaucracy might be less innovative and hence less able to respond creatively to changing social needs; the danger that, as a politically aware bureaucracy comes to play a more active role in the policy-making process, the ability of the representative institutions of government to control that bureaucracy may be weakened.

These dangers call attention to the fact that bureaucratic attitudes are not the only determinant of government responsiveness, that conditions for responsiveness interact with one another, that progress along one dimension may bring difficulties along others. Subsequent exploration of the attitudes, values, backgrounds, and behavior of our samples of bureaucratic and political elites may allow us to assess more precisely these and other factors likely to affect the responsiveness of bureaucracies to people and their needs.

NOTES

1. For an interesting calculation of the balance of numbers and potential influence between elected and permanent executives in British government, see Richard Rose, "The Variability of Party Government: A Theoretical and Empirical Critique," Political Studies 17 (1969): 413-445. For a useful discussion of the power of the British civil service, see Michael R. Gordon, "Civil Servants, Politicians, and Parties: Shortcomings in the British Policy Process," Comparative Politics 4 (Oct. 1971): 29-58.

2. It would be inappropriate in this brief research report to offer an extensive theoretical analysis of "responsiveness" and of the closely related concept of "responsibility." A fully elaborated theory of bureaucratic responsiveness would have to consider explicitly the distinction between social needs and political demands, as well as the issue of differential responsiveness, for responsiveness to one group or constituency may involve systematic neglect of others. I will here leave aside these matters, along with the still knottier problem of developing operational measures of responsiveness. My working assumption is that in some generic sense we can distinguish between more and less responsive bureaucracies. I should perhaps add that responsiveness is not the only standard by which we judge bureaucracies—or governments.

3. Carl J. Friedrich, "Public Policy and the Nature of Administrative Responsibility," p. 2 in Carl J. Friedrich and E. S. Mason (eds.) Public Policy, I (Cambridge: Harvard University Press, 1940). In the present context, Friedrich's "responsibility" is equivalent to my "responsiveness." For a useful discussion of responsibility and responsiveness, see A. H. Birch, Representative and Responsible Government (Toronto: Univ. of Toronto Press, 1964), esp. pp. 17-21 and p. 170.

4. See Friedrich, ibid., for a lucid statement of the problem.

5. J. Donald Kingsley, Representative Bureaucracy (Yellow Springs, Ohio: Antioch Press, 1944), p. 274.

6. See Friedrich, op. cit., and the reply by Finer, "Administrative Responsibility in Democratic Government," Public Administration Review 1 (1941): 335-350, both conveniently excerpted in Francis E. Rourke (ed.) Bureaucratic Power in National Politics (Boston: Little, Brown, 1965), pp. 165-187.

7. Cf. C. H. Sisson's view: "The main work of government is done by an executive, and

where the work is of any complexity that executive must include a large and permanent body of officials. The triumph of democracy in Britain, if it has had a triumph here, is not to have got the work of government done by any popularly elected body but to have informed a large permanent executive with responsiveness to the moods of the elected and of the electorate." *The Spirit of British Administration* (London: Faber and Faber, 1959), p. 151.

8. Karl Mannheim, *Ideology and Utopia* (New York: Harcourt, Brace, 1946), p. 105.

9. See the report in Stern, Sept. 9, 1970.

10. Brian Chapman, *The Profession of Government* (London: Allen & Unwin, 1959), p. 274.

11. Herbert Jacob, *German Administration Since Bismarck* (New Haven: Yale Univ. Press, 1963), p. 205. A similar view seems to have prevailed traditionally in Sweden. See Joseph Board, *The Government and Politics of Sweden* (Boston: Houghton Mifflin, 1970), p. 164.

12. John Herz, "Political Views of the West German Civil Service," pp. 111-113 in Hans Speier and W. Phillips Davison (eds.) *West German Leadership and Foreign Policy* (Evanston, Ill.: Row, Peterson, 1957). I would like to avoid here the complex issue of Max Weber's view of the role of the bureaucrat; for while in some ways it is similar to that which I term "classical," in other respects it is closer to the "political" interpretation.

13. Related studies have been undertaken as well in Morocco, India, and the British West Indies, though for a variety of reasons, data from these studies are less relevant here. The project has been supported by grants to the University of Michigan from the Ford Foundation and the National Science Foundation.

14. For a variety of technical reasons, complete data are not available for each respondent. Hence, the Ns reported in this paper do not always coincide precisely.

15. The samples of politicians were simply drawn randomly from the lower houses of the national parliaments, stratified by party. The younger politicians constitute a special sample of parliamentarians aged 40 and under. The lower response rate for Italian politicians reflects the fact that Parliament was recessed for government crisis talks during much of the period of field research in Italy in the spring of 1970.

16. The one exception to the generally high levels of frankness consisted in a substantial minority—perhaps 25%—of senior Italian officials with whom the interviews were fairly formalized, with the respondents offering a "sanitized" view of politics and administration in Italy. The reticence of this minority can be attributed to the novelty of "sociological" interviewing among these Italian officials and to the climate of mutual suspicion and fear which characterizes Italian public life. The practical impact of this problem is that the Italian results probably understate substantially the alienation of the Italian administrative elite from the world of politics.

17. For a preliminary report of the Swedish data, see Thomas J. Anton, Claes Linde, and Anders Mellbourn, "Bureaucrats in Politics: A Profile of the Swedish Administrative Elite," *Canadian Public Administration/Administration publique du Canada* 16 (Winter 1973): 627-651.

18. Data from Sweden suggest that as many as a third of the younger bureaucrats there are from working-class homes—thus, the impact of more than three decades of Social Democratic rule. See Anton et al., op. cit., p. 633.

19. Some caution is appropriate in interpreting responses to these questionnaire items, for they are potentially subject to "acquiescence response set," that is, the tendency for some people to agree with such items regardless of content. This problem is much less important when analyzing responses to interview questions.

20. Across our set of three national samples the mean intercorrelation among the six items is r = .35. The Spearman-Brown internal reliability coefficient is, thus, .77. See Claire Selltiz et al. (eds.) *Research Methods in Social Relations* (New York: Holt, Rinehart, and Winston, 1959), pp. 183-184.

21. Data from the Swedish sample suggests relatively high tolerance for politics there, too; the mean Swedish score on the ITP is 58.

22. Note that the standard of comparison here is essentially a relative one: respondents are compared with the mean score (50) for the three-nation sample. However, given the scoring system for the ITP, this mean score happens to be the dividing line between those who, on balance, tended to agree with the six items, and those who, on balance, tended to disagree. Thus, it is possible to interpret this mean in an absolute sense as well.

23. The standard deviation for the ITP and for nearly every one of its component items is markedly higher for the German sample than for the other two nations.

24. Across our total sample of bureaucrats from the three countries the correlation between the questionnaire-based ITP and the measure of enthusiasm for politics is r = .25. Statistical purists may be offended by the use of interval level statistics on ordinal level data. My purpose here, however, is merely to indicate roughly the order of magnitude of the statistical relations, and in this context Pearson's r is not a misleading measure. For a recent discussion of this issue, see S. Labovitz, "Some Observations on Measurements and Statistics," Social Forces 56 (December 1967): 151-160.

25. Across our total sample of bureaucrats from the three countries, the mean intercorrelation among the three items is r = .35. The mean national scores are as follows: Britain, 49; Germany, 46; Italy, 32; Sweden, 61. By this measure Swedish bureaucrats are considerably more committed to programmatic policy-making than their counterparts in the other three countries.

26. The correlation between the ITP and the IPC across our total sample of bureaucrats is r = .50.

27. The correlation between the ITP and the "legalism" questionnaire item is r = .56; that between the measure of enthusiasm for politics and this item is r = .19. The correlation between the two measures of tolerance and enthusiasm for politics and a measure of the "activism" of the bureaucratic role described by the respondent ranges from r = .17 to r = .34.

28. The correlation between the measure of enthusiasm for politics and approval of some relaxation of the anonymity rule in Britain is r = .20. The correlation between the measure of enthusiasm for politics and approval of "politicization" of the civil service in Germany is r = .60. The comparable correlation for approval of the *gabinetto ministeriale* in Italy is not yet available, but is certain to lie within this range.

29. The correlation between the ITP and the "misanthropy" item is r = .45; that between the ITP and the "pro-lobbying" item is r = .41; that between the measure of enthusiasm for politics and the item on social conflict is r = .20.

30. The correlation between the ITP and the item on political propaganda is r = −.47.

31. The correlation between the Elitism Index and the ITP is r = −.47.

32. The correlation between age and the measure of enthusiasm for politics in Italy is r = −.22; age is correlated positively with the Elitism Index, r = .20, and negatively with the Index of Programmatic Commitment, r = −.25. The correlation between age and the item expounding a "legalist" interpretation of the role of a civil servant is r = .26. Note that even the "young" Italian bureaucrats are not so young; the median age of the Italian high-fliers is 44, as contrasted with 36 and 39 for Britain and Germany, respectively. Differences across age cohorts in data gathered at a single point in time are notoriously ambiguous. Broadly speaking, they may reflect life cycle changes, generational differences, or "natural selection." (For a detailed discussion, see my "Studying Elite Political Culture: The Case of 'Ideology'," American Political Science Review 65 [Sept. 1971]: 673.) Strictly speaking, we cannot yet exclude the life cycle explanation for these Italian data; but the generational explanation is inherently plausible, given the upheavals in Italian history in the last half century. More rigorous evidence is available for the German case, discussed below.

33. Weber, "Bureaucracy," pp. 8-10 in Rourke (ed.) op. cit. That the Italian higher bureaucracy in the past has shown a similar ability to resist the impact of political

revolutions is suggested by the fact that as late as 1937 every single one of the top 30 civil servants in the all-important Ministry of Corporations had entered the civil service before 1916. See Taylor Cole, "Italy's Fascist Bureaucracy," American Political Science Review 32 (1938): 1143-1157.

34. Kenneth Hanf, "Administrative Trends in West and East Germany," paper prepared for the Conference Group on German Politics, Western Regional Meeting, Sacramento, California, April 1, 1970, pp. 11-12. Ralf Dahrendorf, Society and Democracy in Germany (Garden City, N.Y.: Doubleday, 1967), pp. 240-241.

35. These data are borrowed from a preliminary and unpublished research report. I am grateful to Dr. Uwe Schleth for allowing me to see these results.

36. The correlation between membership in or sympathy for the SPD and the ITP is r = .25; for the IPC, r = .23; for the Elitism Index, r = −.24; for the interview-based measure of enthusiasm for politics, r = .26; for the questionnaire item on political propaganda, r = −.22.

37. The correlation in Germany between age and the ITP is r = −.30; that for the IPC is r = −.30; that for the Elitism Index, r = .21; that for the interview-based measure of enthusiasm for politics, r = −.30. These findings are broadly consistent with those reported in Thomas Ellwein and Ralf Zoll, Berufsbeamtentum−Anspruch und Wirklichkeit (Düsseldorf: Bertelsmann Universitätsverlag, 1973).

38. An alternative and perhaps complementary explanation is offered by C. H. Sisson: "The British administration enjoys an extraordinary degree of freedom from political intrusion, and there is no doubt that this freedom greatly facilitates the responsiveness of the administration to the purposes of cabinet government" (The Spirit of British Administration, op. cit., p. 112). In the subsequent analysis of our data we will want to look closely at the interaction between the values and behavior of bureaucrats and the values and behavior of politicians.

39. The correlation between "specialist" status and the ITP is r = −.26; the correlation for the Elitism Index is r = .24; for the item tapping propensity to control political propaganda, r = .25; and for answers to my question about the "grey area" between politics and administration, r = .24.

40. The correlation in Britain between age and the ITP is r = −.30; that for the IPC is r = −.37; for the Elitism Index, r = .27; for the interview-based measure of enthusiasm for politics, r = −.19. The point, of course, is not that the older British civil servants are so opposed to programs, politics, pluralism, and equality, but that the younger ones are so firmly in favor of these things. In assessing the extent of the generational differences in Britain as contrasted to the continental countries, one must recall that the Italian and German samples of high-fliers were nominated by our senior incumbents, whereas the British sample was selected by more objective criteria. Hence, the continental samples may systematically understate the real generational differences, whereas this is unlikely to be true of the British sample.

41. See Anton et al., op. cit. A similar set of findings for Sweden is reported in Ulf Christoffersson, Björn Molin, Lennart Månsson and Lars Strömberg, Byråkrati och politik (Stockholm: Bonniers, 1972).

42. Kenneth Wheare, "Seven Characters in Committee Work," as reprinted in Richard Rose (ed.) Policy-Making in Britain (New York: Free Press, 1969), pp. 107-108.

43. This statement is ascribed to the late Mr. Derek Morrell by Anthony Sampson in "The Men Who Run Britain," Observer Review (Feb. 21, 1971), p. 19.

44. Herbert Simon, Administrative Behavior (New York: Free Press, 1957), p. xii.

45. Ibid., pp. 57-58. Cf. David Marquandt's view that "there is nothing odd or distressing in politicians basing their decisions on a value judgment. One of the reasons why it is better to be governed by politicians than by civil servants is that civil servants are apt to disguise their value judgments as judgments of fact. Politicians are slightly more honest about bringing theirs into the open." "A War of Ideologies," New Society 17 (Feb. 18, 1971), p. 279.

ROBERT D. PUTNAM is professor of political science and research scientist at the Institute of Public Policy Studies, University of Michigan. He is the author of *The Beliefs of Politicians: Ideology, Conflict, and Democracy in Britain and Italy* and *The Comparative Study of Political Elites.*

4

Elite Perceptions of the Political Process in the Netherlands, Looked at in Comparative Perspective

SAMUEL ELDERSVELD
SONJA HUBÉE-BOONZAAIJER
JAN KOOIMAN

The empirical study of bureaucrats in national governments, particularly in their relationships with politicians, is just beginning to be undertaken. This effort at systematic research has occurred belatedly, despite an insistence for a long time that higher civil servants, as well as party leaders, are functionally central to effective government. A large number of scholars from Max Weber on have referred to bureaucracies in terms similar to those of Carl Friedrich, as "the core of modern government."[1] Gabriel Almond, among others, has argued the thesis that "bureaucracies tend to monopolize outputs."[2] On the other hand, many students of politics, from Graham Wallas to Maurice Duverger to V. O. Key, have insisted that party organizations and their leadership are "critical" and "strategically central" for the functioning of the political system. Wallas argued in 1908 that "the party is, in fact, the most effective political entity in the modern national state."[3]

With this emphasis on the importance of both the bureaucracy and the political party, it follows that the relationships between these two leadership structures in any political system become theoretically of great interest. Indeed, one could advance the proposition that for much of the life of the discipline of political science we have felt that one of the key problems of any government, not just "modern" governments, is how these two elite structures get along together. Fred Riggs is particularly concerned with this problem for developing societies and discusses the difficulty in maintaining a proper balance between bureaucratic power and the power and demands of partisan elites. The attempt to produce such a balance, "one of the most difficult transformations to achieve," he believes produces "inner tensions and contradictions" in the development process in these societies.[4] But one could argue that in all societies, "modern" as well as "developing," a major concern is maintaining an efficient and able bureaucracy with enough independence to do an effective job of administration, while operating in the context of a system of party politics in which (depending on the society) party leaders are competition oriented, power expansionist, patronage conscious, and reacting to the constant demands and expectations of special and general interest groups. The maintenance of a proper balance between efficiency and responsiveness in such an environment has to be achieved if the polity is to be a stable one.

The conditions or requisites for a balanced bureaucrat-politician relationship have been discussed by numerous scholars and can be summarized here. Insofar as this "balance" has been successfully achieved, it is hypothesized there will be a reduction in tensions, institutional and personal, in the relationships between bureaucrats and politicians, a mutual recognition of and respect for differential elite roles, and considerable overlap in perspectives as to how the system does function and how it should function. Essentially, patterns of elite adaptation (by bureaucrats and legislative politicians) to each other and to the system within which they have to function will have occurred in a society in which politician-bureaucrat relationships have been stabilized. In a society in which these relationships are in "imbalance," one will find the obverse of the conditions specified: tension between these elite groups, nonconvergence in perspectives about the system, disagreement on system goals and the roles of the elite actors in the system; in short, lack of adaptiveness, much conflict in political perceptions (and probably also in values), and mutual hostility rather than respect. Shils speaks of the development of the "oppositional mentality" in new states, a much broader syndrome than specified here, but a shorthand term relevant to the disjunction operationalized here.[5]

There have been many theoretical formulations of these basic prerequisites. One finds them discussed in different language in the writings of scholars already referred to, as well as others. Riggs is one among many who emphasizes the requisite of the responsiveness of the bureaucracy to political controls, without being subservient to politicians. Bureaucrats and politicians must be aware of, accept, and "legitimize" each other's roles in the system. Landau, as well as others, makes a major point of the need for the bureaucracy to accept public policy goals and act as a "change agent" applying its expertise to achieving such goals. Above all, many writers emphasize that the bureaucracy should not displace public goals with the goals of the bureaucratic organization. And Janowitz is one among many who pays attention to the "clientele group" relationships of bureaucracies, suggesting that, while the bureaucracy is attentive to interest group demands and maintains "good relations" with such groups, it is not subservient to such groups. It expects political pressure, is not antagonized by it, but maintains a neutral posture. These are some of the key conditions, factors, or expectations emphasized in the literature. But careful empirical exploration has been negligible.[6]

In the investigation of this basic theoretical concern, a comparative study of bureaucratic and legislative political elites was undertaken in nine countries from 1970 on. The professors involved in this comparative study were all on the staff of the Political Science Department at the University of Michigan. A small pilot grant from the Ford Foundation to the University, and a large National Science Foundation grant, plus additional support in some of the countries studied, provided the funding for the project. In each country a sample of members of national legislative bodies and of higher civil servants was scientifically selected, ranging in number from 100 to 300. The civil servants were selected from the two senior grades at the second and third levels below the "cabinet" (U.S.) or "ministerial" (Europe) level. Thus, in Britain the undersecretary and deputy secretary were selected; in Germany, ministerial direktor and ministerial dirigent; in the Netherlands, directeur generaal and directeur. The Ministries of Foreign Affairs and Defense were excluded from the universe of the study. The same basic sample and questionnaire design were used in each country, and the interviews taped in seven of the nine countries.[7] Two preliminary reports of the findings of the project have appeared.[8] The report presented here is part of this comparative bureaucracy series.

Our interest in this paper is with the Netherlands. We conducted from February to June of 1973 the field work for this study in The Hague. Although much of the coding remains to be completed, we will report here some preliminary findings from the closed questions of that survey. Our study included roughly one-third of the lower house of the Dutch Parliament and approximately 75 civil servants selected from two levels of the bureaucracy, as specified above. We will present the Dutch findings along with those for some of the other European countries.

The Netherlands is a particularly interesting system in which to test theoretical propositions about the attitudes and roles of the bureaucrat and his/her relationship to the legislative politician. The pluralistic features of Dutch society, especially the fragmented party system and the importance of special interest groups, combined with the alleged "pillarization" and vertical compartmentalization of social sectors provide a special system environment. Fragmentation of the parties was in 1973 perhaps at a high point, with fourteen separate parties represented in the Parliament. It required from November 1972 to May 1973 to form a coalition government and reach agreement on a new cabinet. In this diffuse and somewhat centrifugal system, the behavior of elites takes on considerable importance for the stability and functional effectiveness of the system. Lijphart has argued impressively that the accommodationist orientations and behavior of political elites in the face of great pluralist tension has been greatly responsible for effective government in the Netherlands.[9]

The basic question confronting us in the analysis presented here is how do Dutch bureaucrats and politicians behave in the context of this highly pluralized polity? Do they exhibit patterns of orientations, attitudes, and beliefs which, on the one hand, reflect the political environment, and which, on the other hand, can be construed as functional to system stability and performance? And are the orientations and values of Dutch bureaucrats and politicians, therefore, different or similar to those of elites in other European countries? Another way of posing the question is: Have Dutch elites of the type studied here evidenced a capacity for accommodating each other and for adaptive behavior in relationship to each other as well as to the system within which they are leaders? In terms of political development, we would say that we are interested in the extent to which Dutch elites reveal a capacity for growing and changing as the system changes. As Eisenstadt has said, this capacity for sustained political "growth" is "the central problem of modernization."[10] It may be also a central problem for developed, modern societies.

The Dutch civil service has been described and evaluated by many Dutch scholars, but empirical work in this area has only begun recently. And only a partial picture is available from the few studies thus far completed. In a recent paper summarizing the results of this research to date, Kooiman has specified some of the major characteristics of the Dutch bureaucracy which seem to be emerging.[11] Historically the civil service has been formally a "strict hierarchical structure," politically neutral, operating in an administrative system in which each ministry has traditionally had a great deal of "independence." The decisional role of the top civil servants can be considerable, but this is dependent on the individual minister. The "administratively oriented" ministers will maximize their decisional influence, while "professional" and "politician" types will emphasize this less.

> The core of the internal political actions or attitudes seems to be loyalty in all respects to the minister and the avoidance of even the slightest appearance of political bias. ... As far as the external political activities are concerned, the reins seem to be kept on rather tightly; not all party political activities are forbidden, but they certainly are not promoted.[12]

The work of van Braam suggests that civil servants are a fairly tightly knit social group, leading a "rather isolated social life." One gets the impression that the Dutch civil servant does indeed live in a special "world" of ideas, training, political norms, friendships, and socialization influences. Whether this is so, and whether it therefore is manifest in a homogeneous bureaucratic political culture is one of the questions we wish to put to our data.

One particular aspect of the Dutch civil service, (again varying somewhat from ministry to ministry) is the emphasis on clientele groups. Many ministries have "advisory boards" which may include representatives of interest groups. This may be an important system characteristic to keep in mind in interpreting the orientations of bureaucrats and politicians to the Dutch political process.

Kooiman's general interpretative impression is that in the Netherlands a generally "negative stereotype of the Civil Servants" exists, and that their role is not as dominant nor controversial as one might expect. "In a society with strong pluralistic characteristics, as Dutch society is, the influence of one of the pillars of the political and constitutional structure will never prevail in such a way that one can speak of a monopoly. Thus we can talk about the relative influence of the administrative apparatus with regards to other major groups of players in sharing power and influence, such as Parliament, Cabinet, pressure groups, and political parties."[13]

These observations are admittedly impressionistic, with limited data available to support them.[14] Nevertheless, they provide us with a backdrop for the investigation we conducted in 1973 into the mutual perceptions and orientations of Dutch bureaucrats and politicians. Has the relationship between bureaucrats and politicians stabilized? Have these elites developed accommodationist patterns of interaction, sharing the same perspectives towards the political system? Or are there serious and significant disjunctions, noncongruences, or even hostilities between Dutch bureaucrats and politicians? These are the basic questions we are concerned with in this preliminary analysis.

1. SOCIAL BACKGROUND AND PERSONAL CHARACTERISTICS: HOW REPRESENTATIVE OF DUTCH SOCIETY?

The Dutch higher civil servant has certain social background characteristics in common with members of other European bureaucracies and some which are distinctive. In age distribution the Dutch administrator is generally older than his/her German, British, or Swedish counterpart, but by no means as old as in Italy. The Dutch proportion below age 47 is only 13%, compared to 33% for the German bureaucracy and 26% for the Swedish (see Table 1). In striking contrast are the Dutch MPs who are relatively young—54% of our sample being at the lower age levels.

On the other hand the Dutch civil servants are, as in other European countries, the product of university education—85% in the Netherlands, which is virtually the same as in England. All civil servants in Europe seem to be highly educated which bespeaks their social and class status. Dutch parliamentarians, however, are much less likely to have a university education: only 57% reported to us such an educational background. The type of education varies greatly, however. Law training is relatively important in all countries except Britain, where bureaucrats are primarily "people of letters." In Germany, particularly, legal education is important: 67% of all German civil servants had such a background compared to 38% among Dutch civil servants. Anton reports research in Sweden suggesting a drastic decline in the proportion of lawyers in the civil service since 1917 and an increase in social and natural scientists.[15] While we do not have similar trend data for the Netherlands, it is interesting to look at the specific educational backgrounds of our Dutch elites in this connection (Table 2). Economists dominate the social science trained group among the

TABLE 1

SOCIAL BACKGROUNDS:

DUTCH ELITES COMPARED TO OTHER EUROPEAN LEADERS (in percentages)

	Higher Civil Servants					Members of the Dutch Lower House of Parliament
	Nether-lands	Britain	Germany	Italy	Sweden[a]	
Age						
36 and under	0	0	2	0	2	18
37 to 46	13	10	31	0	24	36
47 to 56	41	63	26	27	41	36
57 to 66	44	27	41	73 ⎱	32	9
67 and older	1	0	0	0 ⎰		0
Education						
University	85	83	99	100	96	57
Law	38	4	67	54	32	23
Science, technology	21	20	9	23	28	9

a. The Swedish age categories are not strictly comparable, overlapping by one year (e.g., 46 to 55, etc.).

SOURCES: Thomas J. Anton, Claes Linde, Anders Melbourn, "Bureaucrats in Politics: A Profile of the Swedish Administrative Elite," paper delivered at the Sixty-second Annual Meeting of the Society for the Advancement of Scandinavian Study, New York, N.Y., May 5-6, 1972; Robert D. Putnam, "The Political Attitudes of Senior Civil Servants in Western Europe: A Preliminary Report," paper delivered at the 1972 Annual Meeting of the American Political Science Association, Washington, D.C., Sept. 5-9, 1972.

Dutch bureaucrats. The proportion (24%) is very similar to that in Sweden (25%). Natural scientists are the other large group, somewhat less than the 28% (natural science and engineering) in the Swedish civil service. There is evidence here of comparability between the characteristics of Dutch and Swedish bureaucracies, but additional Dutch trend data are necessary to confirm this interpretation.

The Dutch parliamentarian, if he/she has gone to the university, is probably the product of one or the other of two disciplines: law or economics. Yet there are enough "specialists" with natural science, medicine, and other social science backgrounds to provide a heterogeneity of intellectual experience in the MPs' relationship with the bureaucrat. Parliament is obviously much more representative of those with lower educational backgrounds. But in addition, MPs and civil servants may reflect a type of "balance" or "congruence" in educational perspectives. Thus, one does not find MPs to be primarily lawyers while civil servants are primarily persons of technical-scientific training, or "persons of letters" (as in England),

TABLE 2

UNIVERSITY FIELDS OF STUDY OF DUTCH ELITES (in percentages)

	Civil Servants	Members of Parliament
Law	38	23
Economics	23	14
Other social sciences	1	5
Natural science	16	7
Agriculture	4	0
Medicine	1	2
Theology	0	5
Other	2	2
No university education	15	43

or vice versa. There are indeed some parallels in education which may be functional to effective elite relationships.

The middle and upper class character of the Dutch bureaucracy clearly emerges from our data. Using a six-point scale devised by Van Heek and Vercruysse,[16] we can see (Table 3) that almost 60% of Dutch bureaucrats come from the two top prestige occupational backgrounds. This means their fathers were high government officials, elective or appointive, professors or teachers in the upper levels of the educational system (but not necessarily at the university), professionals (lawyers, doctors, etc.), or holding relatively high positions in business and industry, or holding important, if not key, positions in social or economic organizations, or in the military, in the media, or in the church. The prestige level of the MPs was somewhat lower. The proportions of the "working class," however, were low in both elite structures: 11% to 20% had fathers who were "laborers." This is very similar to findings elsewhere in Europe. The Swedish bureaucrats included only 15% from working-class backgrounds.

TABLE 3

OCCUPATIONAL STRATIFICATION OF DUTCH ELITES
(Based on Father's Occupation, in percentages)

Prestige Status	MPs	Civil Servants
1–Highest	27	35
2	18	24
3	14	26
4	32	11
5	9	4
6–Lowest	0	0
% who were "laborers"	20	11

TABLE 4

RELIGIOUS BACKGROUNDS OF DUTCH ELITES (in percentages)

	Based on Total Sample		Based on Those with a Religious Preference	
	MPs	Civil Servants	MPs	Civil Servants
Catholic	30	20	52	28
Hervormd	18	31	32	43
Gereformeerd	7	8	12	11
Other	2	12	4	17
None, or N.A.	43	29	- -	- -
			N=25	N=53

The religious and partisan profiles of Dutch elites are extremely interesting, given the pluralistic character of the system (see Table 4). The Protestants have a much higher representation than the Catholics among the civil servants, while the MPs who have a religious affiliation are more inclined to be Catholic. Large proportions of both elite groups are not affiliated with a church.

The Liberal Party (VVD) has secured a disproportionate number of supporters among the higher civil servants, while the Labor Party (PvdA), the Anti-Revolutionary Party (ARP) and the Catholic Peoples Party (KVP) are "underrepresented" in the bureaucracy (see Table 5). In the absence of trend data it is impossible to confirm the direction of any tendencies; but it is fairly clear that the fragmentation of the Dutch party system over the years, but particularly recently, has found its counterpart in the civil service. Adherents of

TABLE 5

POLITICAL PARTY PROFILES OF THE HIGHER CIVIL SERVICE
COMPARED TO PARLIAMENT IN THE NETHERLANDS (in percentages)

Party	Higher Civil Service (Sample Proportion)	Parliament (Actual Proportion of Lower House)
PSP	1.4	1.3
PPR	1.4	4.7
PvdA	17.1	28.7
D'66	2.9	4.0
DS'70	5.7	4.0
ARP	1.4	9.3
KVP	12.9	18.0
VVD	25.7	14.7
CHU	5.7	4.7
Other parties	0	10.6
No preference	25.7	- -
Total	99.9	100

the new, small parties, particularly on the Left, such as PSP, PPR, D'66, DS'70, have their supporters within the bureaucracy. The general loss of strength among the large parties (except for VVD) in the country and in Parliament to the small parties has been reflected to a certain extent in the partisan composition of the bureaucracy. One could argue that the higher civil service incorporates to an amazing extent the partisan diversity of Dutch society. It does not mirror this diversity perfectly by any means. Certain small parties on "the Right" are noticeably unrepresented. But the civil service has certainly not been "colonized" by any particular party or coalition.

In sum, while the Dutch higher civil service is an "elite" in social representative terms, in no sense representative of the Dutch population, it is not a homogeneous intellectual or political elite. On the one hand it is rather well along in age, exclusively male (there were no women in our bureaucracy sample, but 14% in our parliamentary sample), university educated, and comes from non-working-class backgrounds. It has been in governmental career service a long time (84% for over ten years). But this upper bureaucracy comes from a great variety of university disciplines (law, economics, natural science, agriculture, etc.), from a great variety of religious denominations, and declares its preference for nine different political parties. Though a socially unrepresentative elite, much more so than the Parliament, it comprehends many intellectual traditions, religious beliefs, and political party orientations. In this sense it is a multivalued and "open" elite.

One final note on this: It is also a satisfied elite. We asked both groups to respond to this statement by indicating agreement or disagreement: "The disadvantages of a civil service (or political) career are more than outweighed by the personal satisfactions." The distributions of agreement, for the five countries used here, were:

Higher Civil Servants (% agreeing)

Netherlands	95
Britain	95
Germany	91
Sweden	96
Italy	57

Only three-fourths of Dutch parliamentarians felt satisfied, but members of the upper level of the Dutch bureaucracy were overwhelmingly content, indicating a degree of job satisfaction remarkably similar to that found among political elites in other European countries, except in Italy.

2. CONTACT PATTERNS: TO WHAT EXTENT DO ELITES COMMUNICATE WITH EACH OTHER?

What is the extent of bureaucracy interaction with, or isolation from, other elites and actors within the political system? If the "politicization" of the bureaucrat is occurring, theoretically one could expect evidence of considerable interaction, although this by itself is certainly not conclusive evidence. Traditionally the bureaucrat in the classical theory of bureaucracy was an "organization man," independent, aloof, belonging to a professionally autonomous elite group. To some extent scholars of the Dutch system have conceptualized the bureaucrat in the past as rather professionally and socially exclusive. If this were so in the past, there is some evidence that this is changing today, yet it is true only in a limited sense, and in relation to only certain political system actors. When asked about their frequency of contact with representatives of national organizations actively interested in departmental affairs, or what might be called "clientele groups," over 60% of Dutch civil servants indicate regular and very frequent contact (Table 6). With ordinary citizens up to 30% have regular contact, and only 7% never have contact. This suggests that the higher civil servant is not cut off from the political demand and support structure of the system completely. But in another sense, in relation to the party system, higher civil servants still appear relatively isolated. They do not admit to regular contact with party organization leaders (only 4% do), and they say their contacts with individual MPs are irregular. Up to 40% claim they are virtually isolated from parliamentary members and 80% from national party organization leaders.

There is a peculiar, and possibly significant, disjunction in the data on this point: MPs report more frequent interactions with higher civil servants than civil servants report having with MPs. Sixty-five percent of MPs say they see higher civil servants regularly (and almost 80% say they see departmental ministers regularly); but only 16% of the civil servants say they see MPs regularly. One possible interpretation of these data is that this in fact is reality. MPs may see other civil servants than those at the level of our study. That is, MPs may be in contact with ministers and/or civil servants at a lower level than those in our study. Senior civil servants just below the ministerial level appear from these responses to have infrequent contact with MPs, a finding that seems well substantiated by our data.

It is quite clear from our data that the contacts of members of

TABLE 6

PATTERNS OF CONTACT OF BUREAUCRATS AND
MEMBERS OF PARLIAMENT (in percentages)

	More Than Once a Week	Weekly	Regularly, But Less Than Weekly	Now and Then	Seldom	Never
Contacts by MPs with:						
ministers	15	34	29	15	7	- -
high civil servants	13	18	35	25	10	- -
representatives of national groups	10	21	50	19	- -	- -
national party organization leaders	33	31	26	10	- -	- -
individual citizens	64	7	17	12	- -	- -
Contacts by High Civil Servants with:						
ministers (own department)	26	19	28	15	10	1
other high civil servants	37	18	36	8	1	- -
representatives of organizations active in the department's work or area	14	10	40	21	7	7
national party organization leaders	0	1	3	16	25	55
individual citizens	12	1	16	33	30	7
individual MPs	0	1	15	44	33	6

Parliament are wide and frequent. They report that they are in regular contact with local and regional party leaders (over 90% say "regularly" or "weekly"), and with representatives of regional organizations (two-thirds report "regularly" or "weekly"). The higher civil servant, however, is in frequent interaction with his minister, with the staatssecretaris (over 50% see him regularly or weekly), and with other high civil servants. They do have "political" contacts outside the bureaucracy, but they are obviously more isolated than the MPs. Yet, one must recognize that *few of these report no contacts* with citizens, interest groups, and members of parliament. For a large majority of top level bureaucrats, then, there is some exposure to political leaders and organizations, though, with the exception of "clientele" interest groups, not on a regular basis.

It is interesting to note how civil servants report the substantive content of their contacts with civil servants. We asked them to locate on a scale the extent to which their consultations dealt with "technical-organizational aspects" or "political aspects." The results can be summarized as follows:

	Percent saying contact was inclined to deal with:		
Civil Servant Contacts with:	Technical Matters	Political Matters	Both
1. Other higher civil servants	55	35	10
2. Staatssecretaris	45	42	13

Obviously civil servants are concerned a great deal with the political aspects of administration.

3. MUTUAL PERCEPTIONS OF ELITE ROLES AND INTERACTIONS

Although Dutch bureaucrats are obviously exposed to their political environment, the key question is how do they view their relationships with other elites. Are these relationships perceived as functional and reciprocally supportive, or are they fraught with hostility reactions? We asked our civil servants to use a nine-point scale to indicate whether, at one extreme, these relationships were to be characterized as of mutual trust and effective collaboration or, at the other extreme, as being conflictual relationships in which there was a breakdown in mutual trust. Only 3% of our civil servants perceived a breakdown in trust, 17% took the midpoint on the scale, and the other 80% were inclined to see the relationships as effectively collaborative. We apparently have a higher civil service in the Netherlands maintaining considerable relationships with other political elites and groups, perfectly aware that "politics" and "administration" are not separable, and inclined in general to view their relationships with Parliament as healthy.

Perceptions by both sets of elites on the task performance of the members of Parliament demonstrate a remarkable degree of congruence (Table 7). We selected for presentation here the evaluations by civil servants and MPs of six tasks presumably carried out by the Parliament. On most tasks the evaluations are very favorable and very

TABLE 7

MUTUAL PERCEPTIONS OF PARLIAMENTARY TASK PERFORMANCE (in percentages)

Specific Task of Parliament	Evaluation Scale[a]				
	Very Poor	Poor	Pro-Con	Good	Very Good
Making laws					
MP[b] view	0	4	2	84	9
CS[c] view	0	10	10	77	3
Supervising, controlling the government					
MP view	0	28	18	48	7
CS view	0	12	14	73	0
Dealing with citizen complaints					
MP view	0	24	12	58	7
CS view	0	25	17	56	2
Handling conflicting group demands					
MP view	0	19	23	53	5
CS view	2	40	16	42	0
Influencing governmental policy					
MP view	0	27	16	55	2
CS view	0	7	10	83	0
Maintaining contacts with voters					
MP view	0	22	21	55	2
CS view	2	32	16	51	0

a. We used again a nine point scale, but collapsed the scale points to five in this table.
b. MP=member of Parliament
c. CS=civil servant

similar. Only a minority of the civil servants feel that the Parliament is doing a poor job in the performance of these six tasks. There is most concern in the parliamentary handling of group conflicts and differences, where two-fifths feel Parliament does a poor job. But given the expectation in terms of classical theory of much more skepticism by bureaucrats of the functioning of legislative politicians, the extent of affirmative evaluations by higher civil servants revealed by these data is striking. In law making, policy determination, and control of the governmental apparatus, the civil servants think the politicians do a very satisfactory job. MPs are much more self-critical, actually. They are not as sure as civil servants that they are supervising or checking the administration, nor are they as confident that they are doing a good job in making policy. But both sets of elites have very similar views as to the functioning of the Parliament. There appears to be no major disagreement.

Perhaps a better test of the degree of accord between bureaucrats and politicians are the answers to this question: To what extent do the two elites agree on the actual, and desired, influence that top civil servants and parliamentary experts *do have* and *should have* on parliamentary decisions? Table 8 reveals again a strikingly high convergence of opinion. Over 80% of the MPs feel that the civil servants do have influence on policy, and almost 80% that they should have such influence. Further, most civil servants (92% to 96%) readily admit that members of Parliament who are policy experts do have influence and should have influence on decisions. Again there is no basic disagreement. Certainly the images of mutual role perceptions in relation to the national policy process are remarkably similar. When evaluating each other pragmatically, civil servants and legislators know who has and should have power in the Dutch system.

Both MPs and civil servants are also realistic about the roles of other groups and sectors. We actually asked both to indicate their opinions of the influence they thought other categories of people should have. There were 14 such groups, ranging from cabinet ministers to newspapers, radio, television and even public opinion research. The results show a strong congruence in perceptions. The proportions of respondents supporting the influence of a particular

TABLE 8

PERCEIVED ACTUAL AND DESIRED ROLE FOR CIVIL SERVANTS, AND
PARLIAMENTARY EXPERTS, IN PARLIAMENTARY DECISION-MAKING
(in percentages)

	Very Little Influence	Little Influence	Pro-Con	Some Influence	Great Influence
Actual Role of:					
1. Civil servants					
MP view	0	9	7	82	2
CS view	2	22	13	62	2
2. Parliamentary experts					
MP view	0	4	7	81	7
CS view	0	2	6	88	5
Desired Influence Role of:					
1. Civil servants					
MP view	5	5	11	72	7
CS view	3	8	6	75	8
2. Parliamentary experts					
MP view	0	0	0	95	5
CS view	0	0	4	84	12

group varies, but there are only a few instances of sharp differences of opinion, and even these are not "all or none" differences. The interesting differences occur for cabinet ministers, voters, party organization leaders, and public opinion research (Table 9). The MPs have a peculiar reluctance to say that cabinet ministers should have a great deal of influence over parliamentary decision-making. They, however, do not say ministers should have no influence (only 2 to 4% do), but they are much more likely to place them at scale positions 4, 5, and 6. The "dualistic" character of the Dutch parliamentary system is no doubt largely responsible for this expectation by MPs, but it is a political norm not accepted by the civil servant apparently. The reliance on voters, on the other hand, seems more important to the MP than to the civil servant, which is also true for the role of national party organization leader. Again, these are not "all or none" differences. It is significant that 55% of Dutch civil servants feel voters demands should be relatively influential, and virtually none of the civil servants discount voters

TABLE 9

INFLUENCE RANK ORDER OF SOCIAL AND POLITICAL GROUPS AS PERCEIVED BY BUREAUCRATS AND POLITICIANS IN THE NETHERLANDS (Percent of Civil Servants and MPs who feel each actor or group should have "considerable influence," i.e., located them at scale positions seven, eight, or nine on our nine-point scale.)

	Civil Servants Rank Order	MPs Rank Order	
1. MP policy specialists	87	91	1. MP policy specialists
2. Cabinet ministers	83	71	2. What MPs hear from voters
3. Other higher civil servants	65	52	3. Other higher civil servants
4. What MPs hear from voters	55	52	4. Trade unions
5. Public opinion research	41	48	5. Political party organization leaders
6. Trade unions	34	41	6. Cabinet ministers
7. "Middle class" organizations	33	28	7. Action groups
8. Employer organizations	31	28	8. Middle class organizations
9. Newspapers	29	26	9. Employer organizations
10. Churches	28	26	10. Newspapers
11. Political party organization leaders	27	23	11. Farm organizations
12. "Action groups"	22	16	12. Churches
13. Farm organizations	21	11	13. Public opinion research
14. Press, radio, TV	19	11	14. Press, radio, TV

completely. Similarly, the influence of party leaders is played down by civil servants: 17% say they should have little influence, 56% place them at or near the midpoint of the scale, and 27% believe they should have considerable influence. Interestingly, civil servants believe more in the importance of public opinion research, no doubt reflecting a greater concern for building a scientific component into parliamentary decision-making.

There are no serious disjunctions here in influence perceptions of civil servants and politicians. There are certain indications in the data that civil servants are not, aside from their support for MPs, as interested in recognizing the role of certain "political" actors. And there is some antiministerial feeling among MPs. But generally there seems here to be high agreement on what the political terrain looks like and who should be influential in the political arena. What is agreed upon may be more important than the differences in opinion. It is clear that only a small minority of either elite group wishes to give church denominations, newspapers, radio, or TV a dominant role in parliamentary decision-making. Supporters for a great deal of influence for interest groups—unions, farmers, employers, middle class, action groups—are relatively small in number in both groups. Only a third of our respondents feel that the representatives of these groups should play a major role. Yet, very few feel these groups should have no influence or very little influence (scale positions 1 to 3). This finding can be summarized as follows:

| | *Percent feeling group should have minimal influence* *(scale position 1-3)* | |
	MPs	*CS*
Trade unions	4	8
Employer organizations	14	6
Middle class organizations	14	6
Farm organizations	10	11
Action groups	4	21
Churches	25	23

Thus, while most Dutch political and administrative elites feel "interest groups" should have some influence, few of them feel they should have great influence. Basic governmental policy is viewed as the prerogative of MPs (and their response to the electorate is considered particularly important), and higher civil servants. Other actors and interest groups should have an input, should have a role in the process, but this role should not be definitive.

4. PERCEPTIONS OF POLITICAL CONFLICTS

Thus far the image that has emerged is one of two elite structures in the Netherlands, MPs and higher civil servants, which are socially and politically heterogeneous in composition; which, though revealing different contact patterns, do interact with each other occasionally (and for some more frequently); and who, to a considerable extent, share each other's views as to role and influence in the system. This suggests, perhaps prematurely, a "healthy," "friendly," mutually supportive relationship between the two. To test this further, we now need to ask how these elites view the system itself and the nature of "politics" as it is found in the Dutch society, and the *manner* in which bureaucrats take part in the political system.

First as to ideological orientation toward the intervention of the state in social and economic affairs, our Dutch leaders are strongly supportive (Table 10). They generally do not fear state involvement. Indeed, of all the countries in our study, the Dutch are most "collectivistic" and "welfare oriented," (based on these short answer items[17]). The Swedish elites are much more inclined to be concerned about state intervention, and the Germans and British are virtually split 50-50 in their responses to this item.

Because our Dutch elites are high in socioeconomic status, as are the elites of the other countries in our study, it is surprising to see such high support for governmental intervention in the society and economy in the Netherlands. An explanation for this finding is elusive and will have to be pursued in subsequent analysis.

The Dutch leadership's feeling as to the existence of conflict between the government and private enterprise, however, differs for bureaucrats and politicians. Most MPs see a conflict; most civil servants do not. Swedish and Dutch civil servants are very similar in this respect. We will return to these conflict perceptions in a subsequent section.

There is one other item on which Dutch elites differ: the importance of "efficiency" versus the importance of "program." The Dutch civil servant favors "efficiency" (65%); the MP, "program" (72%). Commitment to "program" is interestingly greater among all parliamentarians in our study than among all civil servants, in all our countries, including Italy.

There is some evidence here, then, of "tension" or difference in orientation between the Dutch civil servant and the Dutch MP. The

TABLE 10

ELITE VIEWS OF GOVERNMENTAL GOALS AND MEANS: THE NETHERLANDS
COMPARED TO OTHER EUROPEAN NATIONS[a] (in percentages)

Item	Netherlands MPs	Netherlands CS	Sweden CS	Britain MPs	Britain CS	Germany MPs	Germany CS
1. Favors state intervention into economic and social affairs.	81	68	33	44	53	45	43
2. No conflict of interest seen between government and private enterprise.	39	67	71	b		b	
3. Abstract principles of right and wrong seldom help in solving social problems.	50	62	63	b		b	
4. Politics is the "art of the possible"— leaders should work on short-run, not long-term plans.	19	25	10	39	48	52	47
5. The strength and efficiency of a government are more important than its program.	28	65	24	42	58	43	50
6. When one group or individual gains something, it usually means that another loses.	31	36	31	26	44	23	27

a. A four-point agree-disagree scale was used, but dichotomized for presentation here. The
percentages used here represent those who agreed or agreed with reservations (or disagreed,
and disagreed with reservations) to the statement submitted to them.
b. Statement not used in this study.

MP seems less "pragmatically" interested in a strong and efficient
government and more interested in its program. Another item we
used ("Politics is the art of the possible and therefore leaders should
work for short-term plans, not long-term plans") did not produce
such striking differences, although again the MP was less interested in
only short-term plans. It is a difference in orientation which is only
apparent in terms of the valuing of governmental efficiency over
program, not whether it is a "short-term" or a "long-term" program.
In other respects Dutch elites see system "goals" and "means" very
similarly (in Table 10).

Because the Netherlands is theoretically such a "conflicted" and
pluralized system, it is instructive to return to the question of

conflict perceptions. The Dutch civil servant is obviously opposed to political conflict. He has a consensual view of how the system should function optimally. He sees social conflicts as not necessary to progress (69%), he feels extremism should be avoided (82%), and he is inclined to feel that the "clash of particularistic interest groups" is dysfunctional (57%). The Dutch MP is much more consistently supportive of conflict and sees it as functional to progress and to the general welfare. Here is apparently a major "tension" and disjunction in the perspective of these two elite groups.

Dutch civil servants, if looked at in comparison to those in other Western European countries, are less supportive of conflict and more preoccupied with the clash of interest groups than in other countries, except in Italy. The bitterness of Italian political life has apparently resulted in elite opinions, held by both MPs and bureaucrats, that extreme positions should be avoided and that group conflict is harmful to the society. The same seems to be true, though somewhat less overwhelmingly so, for Dutch bureaucrats, but not for Dutch politicians. The Swedish, British, and German civil servants are much less concerned about the harmful effects of interest group conflicts than are Dutch civil servants. Only the Swedish civil servants, however, question the functional utility of social conflicts, as do the Dutch, while British and German civil servants (and MPs) feel such conflict may have utility. We see then not only a difference of perspective between Dutch civil servants and politicians on conflict perceptions, but some dissimilarities with other European bureaucracies. Dutch civil servants prefer consensus, not conflict, and apparently do not see political conflict as healthy. One cannot conclude this for British and German bureaucrats; they are much less concerned about conflict. Swedish bureaucrats have a mixed set of perceptions, but on balance, as Anton has reported, seem consensual in their preferences.[18]

5. PERSPECTIVES ON THE ROLES OF PARTIES AND INTEREST GROUPS

We noted earlier that neither higher civil servants nor MPs in the Netherlands felt that specialized groups (labor unions, employer groups, farmer organizations, etc.) should have great influence in authoritative, parliamentary decision-making. This question is particularly important in the Netherlands where the pressure from these groups, as well as newly recognized "action groups," has increased and where, in fact, their role in a sense has been legitimized by the creation of the Dutch Social Economic Council. The major question remains: In the face of the continued pressure from such groups, as well as the emergence of new parties in recent elections, what do Dutch elites feel is the role and function of these groups? We can only begin to get some feeling about their views from our closed questions (Table 11). First, it is obvious that there is a sizable current of opinion among Dutch elites that parties "uselessly exacerbate" political conflicts. Even 50% of the MPs agree to this proposition. Three-fourths of the civil servants agree. Similarly, as seen in Table 12, a third of the MPs and over 50% of the administrators are concerned about the "continual clash of particularistic interest groups." Nevertheless MPs and civil servants by no means feel that the civil service should displace parties and Parliament as the arena of decision-making. And both elites are overwhelmingly supportive of a

TABLE 11

THE ROLES OF PARTIES AND INTEREST GROUPS (in percentages)

	Netherlands		Sweden	Britain		Germany		Italy	
Item	MPs	CS	CS	MPs	CS	MPs	CS	MPs	CS
1. Basically, it is not the parties and Parliament but rather the civil service which guarantees reasonably satisfactory public policy.	7	46	27	19	24	4	17	a	a
2. Although parties play an important role in a democracy, often they uselessly exacerbate political conflicts.	50	74	53	44	62	32	31	54	88
3. Relations of close collaboration between a ministry and the groups or sectors most affected by its activity are improper and unnecessary.	7	14	5	13	4	17	2	45	24

a. No data on this item for Italy.

TABLE 12

ELITE PERCEPTIONS AND EVALUATIONS OF THE NATURE AND ROLE OF CONFLICT IN THE POLITICAL SYSTEM (in percentages)

Item	Netherlands		Sweden	Britain		Germany		Italy	
	MPs	CS	CS	MPs	CS	MPs	CS	MPs	CS
1. Only by social conflicts can progress be a achieved in modern society.	52[a]	31	14	70	54	70	73	b	b
2. In political controversies extreme positions should be avoided since the right answer usually lies in the middle.	52	82	74	57	76	82	77	77	95
3. The general welfare of the country is seriously endangered by the continual clash of particularistic interest groups.	38	57	25	25	21	21	24	56	89
4. To compromise with political adversaries is dangerous because it normally leads to the betrayal of one's own side.	24	7	14	38	11	22	15	34	62

a. These are percentages of each elite group who agreed with the statement.
b. Statement not used in Italy.

"clientelistic" relationship between ministries and interest groups. Less than 15% of either elite group disapprove of close collaboration between administrators and interest groups. This seems, thus, to be a fairly sophisticated and carefully drawn set of views. Dutch elites are concerned about meaningless and dysfunctional group conflict (and civil servants are especially worried), but neither group wishes to reduce such groups to governmental impotence nor to cut off the influential contacts of such groups with the Dutch governmental system.

Comparatively speaking, Dutch elites look similar to those in other countries, in some respects, but distinctive in other respects. Italian elites also reflect a high level of concern about party conflict, which might be expected in a society with such a polarized and unstable party system. British and Swedish civil servants are also greatly concerned (62% and 53% respectively, feel parties "uselessly exacerbate political conflicts"). But German elites are much less worried. Dutch civil servants are more inclined to feel that their own role in public policy is important, compared to that of the parties and Parliament, than are civil servants in other European countries. Swedish, British, and German civil servants are much more self-effacing than are the Dutch.

Some cumulative evidence of differences in perceptions and preferences for Dutch MPs and civil servants continues to develop, therefore. Added to the much lower estimate by civil servants of the role that national party organization leaders should have in policymaking (Table 9), and the consensual and "anti-group conflict orientations" of civil servants (Table 12), are their views that party conflict is inclined to be dysfunctional and for a sizable minority (46%) that the civil service has a more basic role to play in the system than parties and Parliament.[19] These are merely intimations of noncongruent perceptions derived from our closed questions for the Dutch samples. They certainly need to be more carefully analyzed and verified in our more elaborate analysis which will follow.

6. VIEWS OF CITIZEN INVOLVEMENT:
HOW "ELITIST" ARE DUTCH ELITES?

Previously we reported that over half (55% of civil servants and 71% of MPs) of Dutch elites felt that the content of voters communications to Parliament should have considerable influence in policy-making. It is necessary to probe further their views on mass participation to discover whether they feel citizens can be intelligently informed about public affairs, whether they have the basic right to political involvement, and whether in the final analysis they can have an impact on governmental action. Is there a consistent pattern of responses to these queries?

What is remarkable is the high level of congruence for Dutch elites on the items concerning mass involvement. The bureaucrats are inclined to be slightly less citizen-oriented than the MPs on most of the statements. But the differences are not great, except possibly for item 6 (Table 13). Civil servants are more in favor of strong leadership than are MPs. Both are very "paternalistic," but civil servants more so (item 4: "Few people know what is in their real interest in the long run"). But despite such paternalism, Dutch elites reject social aristocratic notions, feel that citizens have the right to exert pressure, to influence policy, and to vote even if they are not well informed on public issues. There is close to 100% agreement on some of these statements. We do not report here all of the nuances of their feelings on these questions, and certainly they do indicate agreement "with reservations"; but on balance they appear egalitarian and very supportive of citizen participation, as a matter of principle.

Comparing Dutch elites with those of other European countries produces interesting observations. Swedish bureaucrats are more citizen-oriented, or less "elitist" perhaps, on all of the comparable items than Dutch civil servants. The Dutch are also somewhat less in favor of citizen participation than British civil servants. But the Dutch are very similar to German bureaucrats, if we compare their extent of agreement on these "elitism" items. On the other hand, the Dutch MP is consistently more "democratic" or "nonelitist" in his orientations toward citizen involvement in politics. This is particularly so in comparison with the German and Italian MP, although it is also in an item-by-item comparison with the British MP. The differences are not great (except comparisons with Italy), but they are part of the same pattern. The Dutch MP is an egalitarian with anti-elitist orientations, based on these data. On 21 item-by-item comparisons, he is less elitist on 16 than his European parliamentary confrères.

The Italian elite orientations are not as strikingly contrasted on some of these items as one might expect. Italian bureaucrats are obviously much more worried about increasing citizen control, and are also more supportive of aristocracy, and more paternalistic. But they, too, overwhelmingly support the citizen's right to vote and to influence policy.

Two final observations on Table 13. There is a remarkable similarity in elite orientations cross-nationally in Europe as to citizen involvement. The British MP and civil servant diverge from the pattern on one or two items, and the Italians slightly more so. But generally proportions of agreement to these items are at very similar levels for all countries. A second observation is that in all countries

TABLE 13

COMPARATIVE PERCEPTIONS OF CITIZEN INVOLVEMENT (in percentages)

	Netherlands		Sweden[a]	Britain		Germany		Italy	
Item	MPs	CS	CS	MPs	CS	MPs	CS	MPs	CS
1. In a world as complicated as the modern one, it doesn't make sense to speak of increased control by ordinary citizens over governmental affairs.	39	34	19	29	45	18	38	48	65
2. People should be allowed to vote even if they cannot do so intelligently.	100	97	b	92	97	82	88	98	74
3. All citizens should have the same chance of influencing governmental policy.	100	96	b	85	66	96	95	95	89
4. Few people know what is in their real interest in the long run.	59	80	53	37	60	61	65	79	92
5. Certain people are better qualified to lead this country because of their traditions and family backgrounds.	16	24	12	30	16	21	27	20	54
6. It will always be necessary to have a few strong, able individuals who know how to take charge.	64	89	66	74	83	67	76	48	69
7. Citizens have a perfect right to exert pressure for legislation which would benefit them personally.	88	79	88	99	98	80	84	66	46

a. The Swedish statement differed as follows: "Every individual citizen has a perfect right to attempt to influence decisions of public agencies."

b. Not used in the study.

civil servants are consistently less citizen-supportive, or more "elitist," than MPs. In 28 item-by-item comparisons, there were only five instances where civil servants supported the citizen's role more than MP. This is as expected and documents the "democratic" social origins and linkages of parliamentary elites with their publics.[20]

7. THE BUREAUCRAT'S TOLERANCE OR INTOLERANCE OF POLITICS

We have already presented evidence that most Dutch civil servants are opposed to political and social conflict, and are concerned about the role parties and interest groups play in accentuating such conflict (Tables 11 and 12). This raises the basic question of whether or not civil servants are tolerant of political party leadership and the way it functions in the system. The "classical" profile of the bureaucrat has emphasized, for example, his obsession with the technical aspects of public problems, rather than the political aspects.[21] One key item we used to test this hypothesis was: "In contemporary social and economic affairs it is essential that technical considerations be given more weight than political factors." To this item 79% of Italian civil servants agreed, 46% of the Germans, but only 32% of the Dutch agreed. Only the British civil servant seems more tolerant of politics in this respect than the Dutch civil servant. On the other hand, the Dutch MP is the most opposed to transforming political questions into technical problems, and only 13% support the idea of giving greater weight to technical considerations.

On the other items in our study exploring the "tolerance of politics," we find a similar pattern of response. Very few (17%) of the Dutch civil servants feel that politicians are interfering in their affairs. However, a majority (54%) agree that politicians are too often solely interested in their own welfare, a finding similar for the other countries. What stands out in this analysis is the congruence, or mutual tolerance, of Dutch elites. The Dutch higher civil servant and MP seem to respect each other and not to feel much hostility or sense of improper interference. In this respect the Dutch are very similar to the British.

The most dramatic contrast in these data is with Italy. The bitterness of feeling is manifest in the responses to these items. The Italian civil servant has little respect for the MP, feels policy should be made by technicians, and resents the interference of politicians.

On the other hand, the Italian MPs resent the interference of bureaucrats. The contrasts with the Dutch (and British) are overwhelming. Thus, 79% of the Italian civil servants resent the interference of politicians (and 82% of the Italian MPs resent the interference of bureaucrats) compared to percentages of 17% and 22%, respectively, in the Netherlands, and 11% and 37%, respectively, in Britain. Clearly the pattern of bureaucrat-MP relationships is of a different order in Italy.

An "index of tolerance of politics" was developed, using the three items in Table 14, plus three other items.[22] Italian bureaucrats had the highest mean score (70), followed by the Dutch (47), the Germans (42), and Sweden and Britain (38). The placement of the

TABLE 14

THE TOLERANCE OF POLITICS–BY BUREAUCRATS AND POLITICIANS
(in percentages)

Item	Netherlands		Sweden	Britain		Germany		Italy	
	MPs	CS	CS	MPs	CS	MPs	CS	MPs	CS
1. In contemporary social and economic affairs it is essential that technical considerations be given more weight than political factors.	13	32	32	26	24	29	46	33	79
2. The interference of politicians (or civil servants) in affairs which are properly the business of civil servants (or politicians) is a disturbing feature of contemporary public life.	22	17	37	37	11	62	47	82	79
3. Often those who enter politics think more about their own welfare or that of their party than about the welfare of the citizens.	20	54	55	29	52	22	54	61	83

Dutch in this index is largely a function of the Dutch civil servants' fear of party and interest group conflict compared to other countries, with the exception of Italy. This aspect of the Dutch bureaucrat's political culture perhaps stands out as much as, and probably more than, any other. The Dutch bureaucrat accepts the role of MP and is not concerned a great deal about the interference of politicians. In fact he believes their role in the system is paramount. What he is concerned about is conflict per se, and party conflict particularly.

8. CONCLUDING OBSERVATIONS

Dutch higher civil servants seem to have adapted well (or have been socialized to) the realities and norms of Dutch political life. They are by no means a socially representative elite. Their contacts with party leaders are rather limited, although extensive with interest group representatives. But they clearly recognize the role of parliamentary party leaders in policy-making and generally feel they do a good job. Dutch civil servants are "state interventionist" in ideology, but may be inclined to prefer pragmatic and efficiency goals rather than program goals, although the evidence on this is not completely clear. An outstanding feature of bureaucratic orientations in the Netherlands is the overriding concern with political conflict. Dutch bureaucrats feel parties "uselessly exacerbate political conflicts," and they feel the clash of interest groups is dysfunctional to the general welfare. Yet, the role of interest groups is overwhelmingly defended. The right of citizens to "pressure," and the collaboration of ministries with "client" interest groups is strongly endorsed. Generally, Dutch civil servants support the citizen's role in the system, as a matter of principle, though perhaps from a somewhat paternalistic perspective. In all of this, the Dutch higher civil servant and member of Parliament display a very high congruence in orientations toward politics. The MP is more likely to "play down" the role of the minister in policy-making, and to place more importance on the role of party leaders in the process, to be less concerned about conflict, indeed to see conflict as functional to process, and to be less "elitist" in his perceptions of what the citizen's role should be. But the differences are not sharply delineated except for a few items, particularly with reference to the role of conflict and the place of parties in the policy-making process.

There are tensions manifest in the orientations of these two groups, but there is virtually no evidence of overt hostility, nor of a basic difference in images of the system, analytically or normatively. There is, on the other hand, much mutual respect, great tolerance, and political accommodation between the Dutch civil servant and MP.

Ever since Max Weber the concept of the "classical bureaucrat" has been used to characterize public administrators. Robert Putnam has argued that his data show that this type of civil servant is still common in Italy but much less so in Germany and Britain.[23] The components of the "classical bureaucrat" syndrome are many, but presumably the emphasis is on "technical" approaches and solutions to public policy problems, the distrust of politicians, aversion to popular participative forms of democracy, preoccupation with rules and procedures, and preoccupation with bureaucratic organizational goals and "efficiency" in its operations rather than governmental "programs." These and other components (some of which scholars disagree on) are meant to distinguish the "classical bureaucrat" from the "political bureaucrat" who exhibits opposite characteristics. Where does the Dutch higher civil servant seem to fall if we look at these first data from our study? The answer is that the results are mixed, that there obviously still are "classical bureaucrats" in the Dutch system, but that there are also many higher civil servants who do not have the characteristics of the "classical bureaucrat." Thus, 65% are "efficiency" conscious, but 35% see efficiency as less important than program. One-third appear to be fairly "elitist" in their views of the proper citizen role in the system; but two-thirds are not "elitist" in this sense. One-third also think technical considerations should take precedence over "political" considerations. They are as a group not very relaxed about political conflict (up to three-fourths are not) and thus do not qualify as "political bureaucrats" in this respect. They oppose controversy and taking extreme positions (82%). And 46% think the civil service is a better guarantor of public policy than the parties. On some dimensions, therefore, from two-thirds to three-fourths of the Dutch civil servants seem to be "classical bureaucrats"; on other dimensions, as few as one-third seem to be. Pending a more thorough analysis, one interpretation that may be acceptable is that the level of "classical bureaucratic" orientations in the Dutch civil service is probably at the level of one-third but that the special conditions of Dutch politics naturally lead civil servants, as well as others, to be preoccupied with political conflict and its exacerbation. This does not mean that they are not "liberal democrats" necessarily. Indeed, we have presented considerable evidence that the majority of Dutch civil servants recognize the proper role of parties, interest groups, and citizen action as legitimate aspects of the Dutch system. While they endorse mass and political group participation in the political process, they cannot be relaxed about the fragmentation of the Dutch system and the consequences of social and political conflict.

Cross-nationally Dutch civil servants emerge as much closer to Sweden and Britain, and in some cases to West Germany, than to Italy. The dimensions in Table 15 graphically demonstrate this. On the first five dimensions we selected, the Dutch are located second to Sweden or Britain. These are key dimensions in the "classical bureaucrat" syndrome. On all of these German and Italian civil servants are more "classical": more interested in "technical" approaches, more resentful of political interference, less interested in increased citizen control. They are also more willing to see social conflict, in general terms, as functional to progress (on this the Swedish and Dutch civil servants are much more "consensual" than others), and more willing to have political leaders work for long-term plans and goals. On three other dimensions, however (items 6, 7, and 8 in Table 15), the Dutch civil servants are much closer to the Italians. In both Italy and the Netherlands, civil servants are similarly opposed to interest group conflicts, the exacerbation of conflict by parties, and prefer "efficiency" objectives as opposed to "program" emphases.

Significant patterns of association have been discovered, therefore, in the orientations of civil servants in five European nations. Significant differences country by country have also appeared in our data. Having identified and described some of the key characteristics of Dutch elites in comparison with Western European elites, and particularly the patterns of interaction and congruence between top civil servants and members of Parliament, it is now necessary to look at the relevant conditions and factors which may help explain these similarities and differences. Particularly important in this respect will be the political system environment within which these elites must work together in order to achieve a functional, effective polity. The relevance of systemic variables, among others, will have to be explored in the process of explaining these preliminary comparative observations.

TABLE 15
PLACEMENT OF CIVIL SERVANTS FROM FIVE COUNTRIES ON POLITICAL DIMENSIONS

Dimension:	0%			50%				100%

1. Priority of Technical over Political Considerations (% favoring technical considerations)

Priority of Political Considerations   B   S,N   G   I   Priority of Technical Consideration
24%   32%   46%   79%

2. Resentment of Interference of Politicians (% concerned about interference of politians)

Does not Resent Politicains   B   N   S   G   I   Resents Politicians
11   17   37   47   79

3. Increased Citizen Control (% against more citizen control)

Pro Citizen Role   S   N   G   B   I   Vs. Citizen Role
19   34   38   45   65

4. Necessity of Social Conflict for Progress (% favoring conflict)

Vs. Conflict   S   N   B   G   Pro Conflict
14   31   54   73

5. Whether Political leaders should work for short term or long term plans (% favoring short term plans)

Long Term Plans   S   N   B, G   I   Short Term Plans
10   25   48,47   77

6. Clash of interest groups (% concerned about conflict)

Not Harmful   B   G   S   N   I   Harmful
21,   24,25   57   89

7. Whether Parties exacerbate Conflicts (% concerned about Parties role)

Party Conflict Role not Serious   G   S   B   N   I   Party Conflict Role is Serious
31   53   62   74   88

8. "Efficiency" in relation to "Program" (% favoring "efficiency")

Pro Program   S   ;   B   N   I   Pro Efficiency
24   50   58   65   68

Code:

B -- Britain
G -- West Germany
I -- Italy
N -- Netherlands
S -- Sweden

NOTES

1. Carl Friedrich, *Man and His Government* (New York: McGraw-Hill, 1963), p. 464.

2. Gabriel Almond and G. Bingham Powell, Jr., *Comparative Politics–A Developmental Approach* (Boston: Little, Brown, 1966), p. 153.

3. Graham Wallas, *Human Nature in Politics* (New York: Knopf, 1921), p. 103; M. Duverger, *Political Parties* (London: Methuen, 1951), pp. 352 ff; V. O. Key, *Politics, Parties and Pressure Groups* (New York: Crowell, 1958), p. 12. See also Avery Leiserson, *Parties and Politics* (New York: Knopf, 1958), p. 35.

4. Fred Riggs, *Administration in Developing Countries* (Boston: Houghton Mifflin, 1964), p. 237.

5. Edward Shils, *Political Development in the New States* (The Hague: Mouton, 1968), pp. 34-36.

6. See among other sources, for collections of materials and special studies relevant to this summary of "prerequisites," Joseph La Palombara, *Bureaucracy and Political Development*, (Princeton Univ. Press, 1963); Irving Swerdlow (ed.) *Development Administration: Concepts and Problems* (Syracuse Univ. Press, 1963); Morris Janowitz et al., *Public Administration and the Public* (Ann Arbor: Institute of Public Administration, 1958); Riggs, op. cit.; Ferrell Heady, *Public Administration: A Comparative Perspective* (Englewood Cliffs, N.J.: Prentice Hall, 1966) for a summary of much of the literature as of that date.

7. As of mid-1973 the field work had been completed in the following countries: United States, Britain, France, Germany, Italy, Sweden, Netherlands, Morocco, and Jamaica. We hope to complete the study eventually in Japan and India.

8. Thomas J. Anton, Claes Linde, Anders Melbourn, "Bureaucrats in Politics: A Profile of the Swedish Administrative Elite," paper delivered at the 62nd Annual Meeting of the Society for the Advancement of Scandinavian Study, New York, N.Y., May 5-6, 1972; Robert D. Putnam, "The Political Attitudes of Senior Civil Servants in Western Europe: A Preliminary Report," paper delivered at the 1972 Annual Meeting of the American Political Science Association, Washington, D.C., Sept. 5-9, 1972.

9. Arend Lijphart, *The Politics of Accommodation* (Berkeley: Univ. of California Press, 1968).

10. In *Bureaucracy and Political Development*, op. cit., p. 104.

11. Jan Kooiman, "The Higher Civil Servant in Holland: Role, Status and Influence," paper prepared for the European Consortium for Political Research, Mannheim, Germany, April 1973.

12. Ibid., p. 16.

13. Ibid., p. 2.

14. Kooiman does draw on empirical studies to document the low prestige status of civil servants. In a 1970 national sample of voters, only 24% saw the influence of higher civil servants as "great," compared to 72.5% for government ministers, 70% for Parliament, 67% for political parties, 57% for big business, 53% for trade unions, 45% for radio and TV, and 40% for newspapers.

15. Anton et al., op. cit., pp. 16-17.

16. F. van Heek and E.V.W. Vercruysse, "De Nederlandse Beroepsprestigestratificatie," pp. 11-48 in F. van Heek et al., *Sociale Stijging en Daling en Nederland*, Vol. 1 (Leiden: Stenfert Kroese, 1958).

17. Subsequent analysis of our interviews using the open-ended questions, not yet coded, will be needed, of course, to confirm this finding.

18. Anton et al., op. cit., p. 20.

19. The actual distribution for Dutch civil servants on this item (item 1 in Table 12) was:

> Agree, 6%
> Agree with reservations, 40%
> Disagree with reservations, 35%
> Disagree, 19%

20. An "elitism index" was constructed for all these countries using the first six items in Table 13. The Dutch MPs scored low with a mean score of 33.5; for bureaucrats, the Italians were high with a mean score of 50, Germans at 39, the British at 40, and the Dutch at 42. See Putnam, op. cit., pp. 20-22, for a discussion of the index and the scores.

21. Karl Mannheim, *Ideology and Utopia* (New York, 1936), p. 105.

22. See the first two items in Table 11, plus item 3 in Table 12.

23. Putnam, op. cit., passim, and p. 23.

SAMUEL J. ELDERSVELD is professor and former chairman of the Department of Political Science, University of Michigan. He is also a former mayor of Ann Arbor, Michigan. His book, *Political Parties: A Behavioral Analysis,* won the Woodrow Wilson Award for the best political science book in 1965.

SONJA HUBEE-BOONZAAIJER has taught at the University of Leiden in the Netherlands.

JAN KOOIMAN is professor of public administration in the Graduate School of Management, University of Delft. He is former secretary of the Parliamentary Group of the Dutch Labor Party, and has been a fellow at the Netherlands Institute of Advanced Studies in the Social Sciences.

5

The Politicization of the Administration in Belgium

LÉO MOULIN

The politicization of public administration in Belgium seems to have become so general and so acute that an equivalent situation can hardly be found elsewhere.

The purposes of this study are: (1) to see whether facts confirm this impression; (2) to explain what reasons have created such a situation; (3) to bring to light the advantages and disadvantages or, more precisely, the assets and liabilities of this system, as well as its social and human costs; and finally (4) to disengage as much as possible the somewhat homeostatic "brakes" which, by acting in the very center of the force field created by the extreme politicization of Belgian public administration, ultimately ensure the validity of this administration and, consequently, of the national community.

1. DEFINITION

To politicize is "to give a political role or nature to."[1] For example, to politicize trade union elections is basically the equivalent of clericalism on the political level—the desire to have the clergy participate actively as clergy in the political life of a country. Clericalism, like politicization, exists when the boundary commonly agreed upon by a given society at a given time as marking the limits of this kind of action is trespassed. The two words are accordingly endowed with a pejorative complexion. When applied to an administration, politicization may be seen from four complementary approaches:

(1) Politicization exists when recruitment or promotion of government employees is made mainly or solely on the basis of political criteria, in other words, when membership, usually militant, in one or another political party or in one or another union (itself highly politicized) is the decisive criterion for recruitment or promotion. This is what the Anglo-Saxons call patronage, so cherished during the nineteenth century.[2]

(2) Politicization exists when a civil servant thus appointed or promoted introduces partisan factors into the public authority's decision-making processes, that is, when, by pursuing political or trade union activity within the very center of the public services, he endeavors to orient the decisions of the ministers or the ministries in a direction conforming to the political directives of his party; or if he opposes ministerial initiatives, as much as he can, whether by alerting the press or members of parliament belonging to his party or even by sabotaging a project at the administrative level.

(3) Politicization exists when a civil servant informs his party or union of the scope of what a minister or the administration is preparing[3] and, for this purpose, does not hesitate to make use of confidential documents coming into his possession during the fulfillment of his duties.[4]

(4) Finally, politicization exists (although in the reverse sense) when a civil servant helps his party or union prepare its platform, whether by drawing its attention to the administrative obstacles it risks meeting on the way that leads to the realization of its objectives or by designating the objectives which are politically, technically, and administratively possible under the given conditions. Of course, these activities take place during work hours with the help of documents, skills, studies, information, statistics, and so on, and with the material means, typewriters, stenciling machines, paper, postage, and the like placed at his disposal by his job.[5]

Taken in this fourfold sense, the politicization of administration, whether public or semipublic, in Belgium is an undisputed and now well-known fact.

I said at the start that these four approaches are complementary. Obviously, a party or union supports only the candidacies of those members who have given proof of their loyalty by rendering services of the kind just described. Likewise, a party or union evidently intervenes to place its own people at strategic points in the administrative and political decision-making process.

A certain amount of political or union activism (but I underline the fact that the two big unions in Belgium are openly politicized: one is Socialist; the other, Christian Social) is accordingly a sine qua non condition for administrative success. A successful career, a prestigious *cursus honorum,* now no longer results without party or union support. In any case, they cannot be achieved against the consent of these powers.[6] As formerly any grenadier carried a field marshal's baton in his cartridge case, so today any civil servant has a magnificent administrative career before him, provided he is sufficiently politicized.

2. A NOVEL FACT?

Is this an entirely new fact? In the extreme, systematic, conscious and general form that it has assumed in Belgium today, without any doubt, yes. But for all that, we should not think that the nineteenth century never heard of it. In fact, the British concept[7] of an administration being entirely neutral from the political point of view and faithfully executing the wishes—whatever they be—of the executive, a conception systematized and idealized by Weber, has not been able to be imposed at any given moment in history. As found in the *Dictionnaire politique* of 1842:

> Government is the will that directs. Administration, as an instrument of this will, is limited and must limit itself to the pure and simple role of an executing power.

M. Block states precisely, "At all times and in all countries, administration has been the devoted assistant of politics." Its mission has always been "to infuse details with the principles and doctrines of the government," in effect, of the classes in power. And he candidly adds, but in those days intellectuals had a good conscience and, "having the same origin, marching towards a common goal, being animated by the same spirit, these two powers (i.e., government and public administration), each in its own spheres and with similar means, have fulfilled the role of the state."[8]

Reflecting the oligarchy installed in power and being very often recruited from within it,[9] the magistrature, teaching profession, clergy, and public service were all the more able to serve the state without difficulty and with complete objectivity, and thus the national community (for the two were confused at that time), insofar as their interests coincided with those of the governing class and their vision of the world with that of the bourgeoisie from which it emanated. The administration could be neutral because its neutrality served the interests of the class in power, as was most often the case, of the same class from which it originated. The army could be mute because the society—or, at least, the minority claiming to represent society in its entirety—spoke for it.[10] Besides, thoughtless indiscretions were severely punished; and this was usually sufficient to being to heel those who had lost their class sentiments. As for those who refused from the start to play the game, they were automatically excluded from the Establishment and from paths leading to power, or they were expelled.

3. FOR A NEW SOCIETY, A NEW ADMINISTRATION

This politically and socially homogeneous society-in-power has been succeeded by another society in which the antagonistic forces harbored in the life of the past century have become embodied within political parties and professional organizations purposely organized and structured to accent class differences and conflicts and to defend, most often fiercely, class interests.

In a divided society, such as the Belgian society, where the social common denominator is very small (we shall see why), in a state conceived as an arena for strife and antagonism, unions and parties quite logically endeavored to impose the placement of their own members at all levels and at all "hot" junctions in the decision-making process, whether to politicize the administration's action in the way they desire or, if necessary, to paralyze and sabotage the "politicizing" action of opponents. Because of this, public administration has ceased being unconsciously politicized, as it was during the preceding century, in order to become consciously politicized.

4. SOCIALISM AND PATRONAGE

The will to control the paths leading to power and power itself, inasmuch as it depends on the public services, quickly came to depend on the loyalty that the lower classes, greedy to feel protected, reassured, insured, and patronized, have given to left-leaning groups.

The Socialists and Communists have been the most eager of all the parties to politicize the civil service. For instance, from 1944 to 1959, appointments invoking Article XVIII, which permits sensation "parachutings," are distributed as follows:[11]

| Socialist | 39 | Communist | 14 |
| Liberal | 24 | Christian Social | 14 |

An official is "parachuted" from one administrative branch into a higher position within another—or the same—branch, thus avoiding (evading or transcending) the usual rules for promotion and for interdepartmental transfers. These figures point out that in fifteen years, "leftists" have appointed 77 civil servants whereas the Christian Social Party, the largest party, has appointed only 14, as many as the miniscule Communist Party.

How can this phenomenon be explained? To begin with, by the fact that the Marxist vision of the world tends to see state and public administration as the means *par excellence* of social repression in the hands of the class in power or as the means for the conquest and control of socioeconomic activity when placed in the hands of various struggling classes. Consequently and advisedly, the party should "stuff" the civil service with members capable of making state affairs favor or stress the direction desired by the party or capable, if necessary, of controlling and paralyzing the policies proposed by the opposition. In the second place, it can be explained by the fact that the leftist parties, originally at least, did not recruit their members from within the Establishment nor among the students at Belgium's "Ivy League" schools; therefore, that membership in and fidelity to the party, rather than social origins or past education, should serve as the criteria for selection and advancement seemed normal in their eyes. It can be still further explained by the fact that the clientele of the left are deprived more than any others of such "social contacts" and "relations" as facilitate successful careers. At a time when the fundamental equality of all people is being stressed, these "social orphans" have naturally placed all their hopes for success in the support which the "feudal" system of political or union life grants them. Finally, socialist avidity, to use the term of the "rightist" press, is further explained by the fact that the left lagged considerably behind the "bourgeois" parties in matters of appointment, promotion, and infiltration.[12]

5. THE PUZZLE

Officiously if not officially, each civil servant, public official, magistrate, and teacher in Belgium is labeled, catalogued, and classified not only according to his political and union affiliations, linguistic group, religious practices, and the university where he did his studies, but also according to the region where he was born, the faction within his party or union where he is active, the "patron" who protects him, and a hundred other variables, *ejusdem farinae.*

Should a civil servant happen to disappear prematurely, administrative brains, better equipped (in a different way) than the most powerful computers, begin to whir. Naturally, to calculate the chances of the successor in terms of merit or competence never enters the head of any Belgian citizen, even if he is politically illiterate. In order to take X's place, everybody knows that, taking into account the disposition of the minister most directly concerned, he cannot be So-and-so, who is Walloon, or Flemish; So-and-so, who has completed his studies at the Freemason University in Brussels (since a Catholic is needed); So-and-so, who has received his education in French and who speaks French at home with his wife of French origin; or even So-and-so, because he comes from a section of Flanders that the minister, also Flemish, cannot stand; and so on. Everyone deduces that only two or three candidates have any chance. Indeed, the most glorious, and least savory, eating contest of grab-as-grab-can occurs between these two or three. Their merits and abilities only enter as one of the arguments, certainly not as the most, let alone the only, decisive factor.

Moreover, the vanquished in this plebian tournament does not completely loose his stake of intrigues, procedures followed, visits, telephone calls, dinners, immodest reminders of services rendered to the party, the country, the Resistance, Mr. X or Y, et cetera. He stands a good chance of being consoled by some promotion or other, certainly minor compared to what he was eyeing, but full of promise—at least to believe his minister's declarations.

The most important skill in this little social game is to fit such a large number of rare variables that you automatically become "the right man in the right place." Or also, the minister may impose so many conditions of his own choosing that practically none of the possible candidates can satisfy them except one who, for example and as if by chance, belongs to his staff. This man alone can complete the puzzle. He is accordingly indispensable, and providential.

In this respect, the ideal in Belgium is to be, all at once: a Fleming, a nonbeliever, a leftist, a graduate of whatever university (provided it is not the Catholic University at Louvain), a factotum of a major union leader, and a member of a ministerial staff. From that moment on, you are a rare specimen of a seldom found fauna. You then have every chance of success, whatever your abilities or merits.

However all these "qualifications" may not suffice. Your minister may be weak or ungrateful; politically speaking, he may be less powerful than the homochrome minister supporting your rival. Or, he may insist on keeping you on his staff; that does happen. On the other hand, ministers have been known to support the nominations of people whom the party had imposed on them at the time of the formation of the ministry but whom they wanted to get rid of because they judged them to be incompetent or lazy, or both at once. That is the reason the sole fact of being one of the members of a ministerial staff does not always suffice to ensure a promotion.

6. STRUCTURES OF POLITICIZED SELECTION

All the same, this selection system is well organized. A. Molitor, one of the most competent men in Belgium in the field of administrative sciences, has stated that:[13]

> It's a secret to no one that a nonofficial ministerial committee was established within the government in order to deal with judicial reform and the appointments resulting from it. Here was organized, if I may say so, the proportioning of appointments. Studies can also be made of the manner in which an apparatus for screening and selecting candidates for various offices has been set up in each of the large, so-called traditional, parties.

Farther on, he spoke about the "nominations stock exchange" held at the ministerial staff level.

Making appointments progressively as they occur "in any old order" is not the procedure. In effect, any ministerial team formed (and, in Belgium, taking into account the forces confronting each other, this team is always the result of an alliance) or, better still, dissolved calls for a series of appointments, promotions, and parachutings for all categories of officials from the lowest echelon to the highest level. This series must ensure and respect the equilibrium implied by the rising or setting political constellation.

These equilibriums are not established within each ministry, one after the other. A good number of ministries by tacit tradition in the hands of one or another party have, in fact, a very politically homogeneous personnel. To expect that the party controlling such a ministry will accept the appointment there of a civil servant from the other side, especially among the higher ranks, is quite unrealistic. For this reason, with ministries as a whole taken into account, these equilibriums are achieved by including semipublic and international organizations in the "appointment policy." For instance, a Belgian holding a position in an international organization will not receive a post within the civil service.

Hence, we can pass judgment as to whether a given equilibrium is accurate or well founded only by keeping in mind an overall picture of the list of appointments, promotions, transfers, and parachutings without forgetting the honorary "dead-end" posts and sinecures.

7. TIME, A POLITICAL DIMENSION

Furthermore, candidates are not chosen only for the present. The future is another dimension of the problem. Accordingly, the following are sometimes predicted years in advance: vacancies in various positions, organizations yet to be created (which automatically imply new nominations and promotions), deceptions which will not fail to appear, youthful ambitions which must be rewarded, and sons who will have to be placed.[14]

Here is another method of subtle scheming. The party may present a candidate knowing full well he has no chance. It then waits for a refusal. But in exchange for its agreement, out of principle, on the appointment of a candidate presented by the party in power (in principle, the opposition parties have no chance of having a candidate appointed, however worthy he may be), it can obtain the assurance either that it will dispose of the next important appointment or that its "unlucky" candidate will receive some sort of promise or even some scraps to calm his hunger. It can always cash in on a foreseen and sometimes willed defeat.

That is what meets the eye, but there are also some things which cannot be seen. For example, a certain promotion which may appear, today, very paltry in the eyes of the uninitiated has a future full of promise, while the promotion given to another man rising as fast as a comet may well signify the sad end of a career.

All that makes for a very subtle game requiring a Saint-Simon to describe as it merits. Specialists, journalists, and staff members take special pleasure in deciphering the obscure movements which accompany nominations and promotions and in thus calculating the future chances of each person and the stability of the equilibrium thus defined.

Of course, the public knows nothing about all these "goings-on," and it is left in its ignorance. It certainly senses, at a distance, that all does not take place as democratic morality would like; but it has no idea, happily for its illusions, of what really takes place. In this matter, as in many others, democratic control is impossible.

8. INSTITUTIONALIZE POLITICIZATION?

This state of affairs is so firmly anchored in actuality (the innumerable reforms[15] elaborated as remedies having failed) that some observers have thought of institutionalizing this politicization of civil servants in the same way that linguistic differences have been recognized in Belgium by creating Dutch and French "linguistic roles."

Such a proposition evidently raises some serious objections. Will political affiliation be a sine qua non condition for being appointed or promoted? If so, what would become of the civil servant who refuses to register in a party or to publicly declare the party where he has registered? Or who registers in a party vowing opposition? Would an employee have to remain unconditionally faithful throughout his service to the party he adhered to when entering the administration? Or is he allowed to evolve, and to be converted? And what of those who change sides in the case of victory by one or another political party?

Moreover, such institutionalization of political allegiances would obviously accent even more the cleavages that characterize political and social life.

In fact, Belgium possesses political parties born from confessional struggles which, during the preceding century, transformed this country into a battlefield for *Ligueurs* of every stripe, clerical and anticlerical, each one more upright than the next. To these political parties have become agglomerated (when not secreted by them) social, family, and trade union organizations: child-care centers, sanitariums, clinics, maternity and rest homes, vacation centers, mutual fund services, cooperatives, and all kinds of powerfully organized insurance agencies, usually prosperous, active, and rich. This sense of the "gold-mine"—of visible and palpable realization—is a particular feature of the Belgian genius. All these are politically stamped.

For its part, the educational system tends to perpetuate the existence of two major spiritual families, Catholic and non-Catholic, sharing among themselves the entire school-age population. Today, these two families live in peace but only after having, for nearly a century, engaged in ferocious ideological, political, economic, and, of subsidiary importance, religious battles.

This ensemble of rigid conditions has created an extremely dense network of allegiances of every sort which encloses the life of a Belgian citizen from his birth to his death and from which, supposing he would wish to do so, he would have a hard time escaping. After all, he does not want to very much. He prides himself, especially if he is a "progressive," on voting as his father and grandfather have always voted! Nine-tenths of Belgian citizens are instantly labeled. They are hardly disposed, aside from badly looked upon exceptions, to deviate from the line traced for them since childhood.

To institutionalize such a situation by asking candidates for the civil service to make an oath of political allegiance at the very start of their careers and to, in some way, make such an oath one of the conditions for their careers would only harden and calcify even more the extreme "segmentarization" of Belgian society.[16] Is this desirable?

9. THE PLACEMENT OFFICES

The situation being what it is, political parties and unions have logically become "placement offices," in addition to their roles of being a resonance box, an amplifier, for the aspirations and wishes of a portion of public opinion, or providing a simplified guide for channeling public opinion at election time, or protecting the "social orphans" in question. But what preoccupies us most is their role as placement offices. That is the way the immense majority of Belgian citizens, especially those who use them as such (and most civil servants do), view them. The parties themselves have hardly any illusions about the nature of the bonds linking them to civil servants. All they need do is observe what becomes of these unconditional loyalties when they are not satisfied and rewarded as expected—or when, after all, they are.

10. THE PRICE OF COMMITMENT

The government employee who puts himself at the service of a party or union has some merit. To serve a party (without a lot of illusions), he is most often condemned to lose in vain, or almost so, a good part of his time, his grey matter, and his intellectual liberty—all without being assured of gaining much profit. Indeed, what will be the constellation of forces within the party the day a chance of being granted a promotion occurs? At that moment, which will be the winning "clan"? Just belonging to a party does not imply support: he must be in the right clan the day the richest spoils are divided. Will the dotard he has cajoled throughout the years pay him with ingratitude (ingratitude is a royal virtue)? Will his son-in-law not happen to be well placed in the race?

Thus snubbed and deceived, thought little of, and seldom listened to, in addition, this civil servant runs the risk of not always being compensated for having accepted to write what he did not believe or for not having written what he did believe, sometimes even the risk of betraying his duties toward the state.

All the same, there undoubtedly are some citizens who are active within the ranks of a political party without any ambition for being compensated. This is possible. But, aside from the young (but yet!) and those militants with the most rigid mentality, who are usually found in parties and small groups incapable of ever becoming placement offices, I know of hardly any. In any event, the careers of these pure among the pure scarcely suffer from their purity.

11. THE MEANS OF SUCCESS

There is no reason to be indignant about such a way of thinking. The "dirty jobs," which Molière spoke about, have always permitted people to push themselves forward in the world. Intrigues, patronage, traps laid for "friends," flattery, beauty and youth of women, corruption, family ties, and obsequiousness have always been part of the arsenal of *arrivistes*. Undoubtedly, the mistake, which takes no account of human nature, is to want an apoliticized, disincarnated civil service. The Belgian Camu Reform (1937) wished to set high normative standards. It ignored, or wanted to ignore, that politicizing mechanisms were functioning in that somewhat imaginary England used as a model where belonging to a certain social circle, having studied at certain schools, speaking with a certain accent, and dressing in a certain way constituted social criteria as precise and effective as membership in a political party.

12. FORCE COUPLES

Belgian history explains the presence and virulent action of antagonistic "force couples": the coupling of Walloon and Flemish linguistic forces, of progressive and reactionary ideological forces, of clerical and anticlerical, left and right, communal and central, and so on. Acting on one another in sometimes convergent but more often contradictory combinations, these couples have as effect, first, to produce permanent ideological divisions and, thereafter, to intensify politicization.[17]

By constantly putting in question the unity of the Belgian nation and the homogeneity of its society, this state of permanent warfare has incited citizens to fall back into those fortresses close and familiar to them. They use their communes, local clubs, and local branches of parties, unions, and churches as means of defending themselves against the state's pretensions, which are always considered exorbitant. This situation explains why political parties are organized so as to permit citizens to live in their care from cradle to grave.[18]

All of which very logically explains what can be observed in this country: partisan allegiances, unconditional vassalage to some political or union nitwit, and clannish attachments to particular powers rather than to the society, to a region rather than to Belgium, to local rather than to central power. Such allegiances, vassalage, and local partisan and fragmentary attachments are so powerful that even the consciousness of belonging to a community, which is not (needless to say) Belgium, does not always succeed in dominating them. Sooner or later new dissensions arise under the impulse of other allegiances and other force couples equally anchored in this country's past and equally as vigorous as those which helped build it. The same holds true for the Flemish even though their community feeling, sparked by the fights they had to carry out to turn to account their right to a national life and culture, is very strong. What to say then of the Walloons and Brusselites, and herein lies the tragedy, regularly overcome by forces of dissension sweeping away those of consensus?

It is no surprise that the politicization of public administration is four-dimensional, as already described at the start of this study, and that politicization even has a tendency to become more important as the game of force couples unfolds. Indeed, why would a civil servant not prefer to serve his party, a reality more visible to his eyes and more consistent with his profound aspirations, rather than to serve the state, a cold and distant monster? Athens, Rome, and Florence experienced similar states of mind at the time their decadence set in. Farther on, I will tell why I believe Belgium will be able to escape this fate.

13. LIABILITIES OF THE SYSTEM

The dangers inherent in such a system are evident:

(1) At the communal and provincial levels and in the public sector, it creates veritable fiefs which almost escape, or systematically strive to escape, from the central power's controls and directives. Within each ministry, it permits the creation of cells of administrative resistance capable of sabotaging the policies of ministers not on the same side. (Therein lies the necessity, which I will come back to later, for ministers to set up a "counteradministration" in the form of vast and powerful private staffs.)[19] The system favors political action by civil servants within their administrative functions, action which may and often frequently does go so far as to orient a minister's decisions in a partisan direction or to stress the partisan character of his decisions.

(2) For want of having established a total spoils system, this system costs a lot; but the high cost of solutions is one of the characteristics of the Belgian polity. (A look at the School Pact will convince anyone of this.) Entire networks of government employees may, in effect, be more or less stranded or detoured around because they do not have the same political inclinations as their ministers. These administrative "desert crossings" can be so total that some employees have used them to take up or continue, very easily, university studies (and finish them with success) while lying in watch for the moment a more favorable political climate would allow them to resume their careers.

(3) Furthermore, this placement office role of parties and unions does not contribute one little bit toward degrading their "quality" images perceived by a citizenry already deprived by tradition of many illusions, and not only by the citizen but also by civil servants who, however much they benefit (sometimes) from the system, do not suffer less, on other occasions, from the counterblows (always unjustified in their eyes). After all, the scorn inspired in the average citizen by these practices, when he, all of a sudden, feels a pang of civic pride, is quite naturally—and unjustly it must be added—directed against the entire civil service, which public opinion has a tendency to see as a very costly group of people having no other merit than knowledge of how to plot around the ministers. Obviously, all that is not healthy.

(4) Last but not least, among the most unfortunate effects of politicization are the serious traumas inflicted on the civil service, traumas which can lead to the actual destruction of this administrative tool. A confirmed statistic shows that only 60% of civil servants use politics to ensure their careers.[20] This means that the 40% who do not, feel severely wounded by the humiliating and deceiving effects of such interventions.

This comes about because, as I have already said, the most meritorious, intellectually and administratively speaking, are not generally the ones who resort to political means in order to advance themselves, quite the contrary. Neither are they those who have the highest opinion of the public services, nor even those who believe politics is clean, and certainly not those who are the most disinterested. Those civil servants with traditional views about the public service and good citizenship feel the shock all the more brutally. Some such employees do exist even yet, although this rare species is on its way to extinction.

This situation creates surges of bitterness, rancor, tension, and vengeance which imperil the very foundations of public administration. A man as informed about administrative realities in Belgium and, thus, as restrained in the expression of his judgments as is A. Molitor goes so far as to say, "We are in the right to fear that an atmosphere of insidious civil war may reign in the public services some day."[21]

To give a remedy for such a situation is difficult if not impossible. Some have suggested maximizing the advantages of the system while at the same time minimizing "the disadvantages of political appointments as a factor in the demoralization of state employees."[22]

This is wishful thinking which does not give the least notion of the solution to be applied to this sorry problem.[23]

14. THE MINISTERIAL STAFFS

A minister's fear of seeing his actions sabotaged by a hostile civil service gives rise to an actual counteradministration in the form of a private ministerial staff, a cabinet, composed of employees politicized enough in order that the minister may trust them, as well as of fanatical supporters coming from the outside.[24] In accordance with this system's logic, both have to be rewarded with all kinds of promotions and parachutings which strongly contribute toward further stressing the politicization of public administration.

Such wariness is certainly far from being justified all the time. Indeed, it is sustained in the minister's mind by those very ones, activists, civil servants, union leaders, who have some reason for doing so, even if their reason is only self-interest—in order to be on or to place a friend or coreligionist on the staff. Furthermore, there are a good number of "civil servants at the middle or lower levels who are perfectly loyal in their relations" with their ministers.[25]

But, whether justified or not (for may part, I believe it excessive), such wariness is founded on the fact that a minister knows by experience (if only by having himself generously contributed toward creating a like state of affairs) to what degree his ministry is so very completely politicized and how much party attachment overrides loyalty to the country—undoubtedly for one or another employee and not for all. But how is he to know the one who will divert a certain confidential plan from its lawful route to the opposition press? This has happened a hundred times. Or the one who will not sabotage ministerial undertakings? Or who will execute his decisions without any disparaging hidden motives? Or better yet, who, with all his heart, will help him carry out his responsibilities?[26]

Not being certain about his lines of communication and, also, wanting to please his political friends, a minister will urgently look for "the employees in his ministry who have the wanted label or, at worst, the same ideas, the same ties, as himself." The high official, who analyses the situation thus created in those terms, continues his exposé by emphasizing that "in defiance of any hierarchical procedure, such a civil servant will very likely have to deal with issues" that his superior who has been "shoved aside" will not even have the opportunity to examine. The normal path for administrative documents is thus short-circuited. And he concludes, "The superior waits for a more favorable political formation—a minister of the same tendency as his own."[27]

Understandably, a like state of affairs, which is not uncommon, creates the conditions for latent war between the civil service and the cabinet, a war in which the latter does not win each battle. Obviously, this kind of insidious conflict neither raises the prestige nor increases the output of public administration. All it does is accentuate the politicization of the latter and of its action on society.[28]

15. ASSETS OF THE SYSTEM

No matter how serious certain aspects of such a situation might be, it has some advantages:

(1) The diversity of these placement offices assures a representation, however rudimentary and self-interested, within the very center of the administration of all political, religious, and union tendencies. Consequently, this diversity creates an equilibrium in actual fact and represents a micropublic opinion by definition more sensitive to the movements of public opinion than would be an administration ideally isolated from the rest of the nation.[29] In some ways, this balance protects democracy from political accidents and arbitrary governmental decisions.

(2) Politicization may also ward off the temptations of technocracy, inevitable temptations in the case of an administration, and thus shelter citizens from its effects. The multiplicity, technicality, and complexity of questions dealt with by the state increase the risk of seeing a veritable "technobureaucracy" installed.[30]

(3) By guaranteeing a minimum of power and social protection to those not having them, politicization gives civil servants the chance of being (more or less!) protected from the predominance and abuses of ministerial power, since parties and unions watch over their flocks.

(4) Politicization tends to create poles of activity and motivation which administrative deontology, or civil feeling alone, does not always succeed in arousing. Politically motivated personnel may sometimes be more capable of initiative, even if unilateral and partisan, than a lot of government employees waiting around for orders. Moreover, to the very degree that employees are politicized,

they have an interest in keeping their party from remaining inactive or from blindly launching headfirst into inordinate ventures which are contrary to existing legislation or which are very likely to seriously clash with the civil service or public opinion.

On the whole, politicization of the civil service is a brake or a motor, depending on the case, on ministerial activity.

16. CHECKS ON THE SYSTEM

The application of politicization contains several powerful checks within itself.

(1) One of the very first, and not the least, derives from the fact that partisan allegiances are nearly always made with the most impudent political amoralism. They are formed without illusion, without enthusiasm. Hence, a party cannot count on the unconditional devotion of those who think only of using its power, particularly when the party is "in a sufficiently advanced state of decomposition so that the most political, or at least the boldest, civil servants can turn a deaf ear to its fiats or instructions."[31]

(2) In addition, there are "states of grace." No gamekeeper is as intractable as an expoacher. Likewise, a party activist, once appointed, can, with experience and age helping, prove to be excellent, competent, heedful of the common good, sensitive to civic imperatives, and all the more independent with regard to his party because he no longer expects anything from it and the long haggling sessions (and the deceptions) staking out his career have finally nauseated him. Aside from several "party creatures," the chief secretaries, provincial governors, magistrates, and members of the State Council and Audit Office, all of whom are, despite what they say, appointed with a party's seal of approval, illustrate this metamorphosis rather well. We often enough see a minister very considerably deviate from the objectives fixed by his party, thus entering the ranks of statesmen.

(3) Another brake on this system, a counterweight opposing the total invasion and domination of administrative life by politicization, is the very fact that the government employee who, by reason of his political identity with a minister or of his instantaneous capacity for mimicry, has direct access to the minister's cabinet and who can therefore short-circuit one or another of his superiors with political allegiances contrary to his own, knows very well that the tactical

advantage he enjoys may be put in question tomorrow by elections or by a cabinet reshuffle. Thus he does not uselessly provoke whoever has some chance of rebecoming his full-time superior at any moment. He will "manage" him, administratively speaking, by keeping him informed about the intentions and plans of the minister (of course, as long as no promotions are in sight). Such politico-bureaucratic "buddyship" contributes somewhat toward attenuating the effects of excessive politicization.

(4) Also to be taken into account is the fact that "the great majority of civil servants suffer"[32] from this extreme politicization and resist it with all their might.[33] Again, A. Molitor:

> The sense of one big administrative family, the mutual esteem beyond disagreements, the solidarity created from common interests and work done side by side, have, until present, frequently held in check the germs of internal division which infiltrate from the outside.

(5) The extreme segmentarization of Belgian society automatically creates a series of brakes which oppose (and with what vigor!) an adversary's decisions which are judged to be too partisan.

(6) Also worth noting is that, however great the dangers that politicization may cause for the smooth functioning of institutions, such dangers are somewhat limited by the fact that fundamental political options never result from the civil service alone. The civil service or, to be more exact, an administrative section within a ministry on the same political wavelength as its minister, can propose such or such a measure, inspire such or such a policy; but it does not have the power to impose them unless stealthily, almost without the minister's knowledge. Under the control of the minister's cabinet, the civil service must apply decisions made, even if they are politically rather than administratively sound. Perhaps, with all things considered, we would be more correct to speak of the politicization of civil servants rather than of the civil service. Thanks to this state of affairs, any minister coming into office can legitimately hope to find among the ranks of his ministry a chain of employees devoted to his policies; but the Council of Ministers makes the decisions. At the very most, the civil service may accentuate technocratic or "partisan" aspects of proposed measures.

(7) Lastly, the extreme politicization of Belgian society appears to me to contain several homeostatic checks. According to pure logic, the henceforth recognized right of civil servants to be partisans before being state employees implies that every member of the

national community may enjoy the right to break, on his own authority, the bonds which tie him to the community. Teachers can indoctrinate pupils entrusted to them. Scientists and economists may spy for a foreign company or power. Officers can publicize their political opinions. Priests can throw themselves into urban guerilla warfare. Magistrates can fight against the laws. How can we decide that certain groups have the right to be politicized, to go on strike, to inflect or oppose government policies, whereas others do not have these same rights? In the name of what principles can we establish such discrimination?

If the rains and squalls of permanent strife and extreme politicization are continuously eroding away the community's richest soil, what can be put in place of the civic ties which necessity imposes on all life in society regardless of the regime's philosophy? Consciousness of such a peril is a beginning of wisdom for Belgians who, after all, if they like to quarrel a lot, doubtlessly value living together much more, even if only in order to be able to quarrel as they have been doing for centuries.

17. DEMOCRACY AND MERITOCRACY

Meritocracy, a system of selection based only on merit, usually intellectual, has an aristocratic or elitist aspect and, for that very reason, is haughty and aloof. This goes against the egalitarian sensitivity of our times.[34]

Like it or not, the level of a child's intelligence, like his aptitude for pursuing studies, strictly correlates with the socioeconomic level of his parents.[35] Consequently, even if gifted children of the working class succeed in overcoming the obstacles created by these initial differences, selection according to the sole criterion of past education is still not less a selection by class to some degree. Furthermore, to recruit the best is to openly declare as incapable those not chosen. A society where full and real equality of chance would exist at the starting point, where, as a consequence, no social factor could any longer be invoked to explain failure, and where, in Plato's words, "justice would consist in treating unequal things unequally" and therefore in pushing the incapable back onto lower levels, would undoubtedly be an inhuman jungle without pity and without remorse.

Such a perspective goes against the egalitarian, democratic, and sympathetic sensitivity particularly widespread in Belgium. At the point from which we are actually looking, such a perspective discourages, irritates, and scandalizes all those for whom poor intellectual endowment, lack of personality, or scarcity of social contacts constitute obstacles to advancement. For these people, party and union take the place of social connections and make up for the merits and qualifications they lack.

As the effects of what is conveniently, although quite inaccurately, called the democratization of education are increasingly felt, this process of politicization will very foreseeably continue gaining importance in Belgian public life. Social success obtained by all possible means (notably political) will increasingly replace promotion by competitive selection or seniority. And, from fear of being unjustly outdistanced by political parasites, the best civil servants will, in turn, finally enlist (if they have not already done so) in the ranks of a political party—the most powerful, by preference, the most promising for the future, at least in its capacity for promotions—thus accelerating the rhythm of politicization in Belgium.

In order to be otherwise, Belgian society would have to cease being impregnated with this democratic-egalitarian idealism that animates it; mediocre men would have to renounce any ambitions; parties and unions would have to stop acting like pressure groups without direct responsibilities; and their leaders would have to be able to count on sources of loyalty other than services rendered, as is the case today. All that is very unlikely.

Hence, this politicization is the logical outcome of the social, no longer liberal, democracy under which we are living. There is thus little chance that we will ever retrace our steps toward a past which, as we have seen after all, was far from being as asceptic, politically speaking as "apoliticized," as is wont to be said.

NOTES

1. Le Robert's French dictionary.

2. Cf. *A Dictionary of the Social Sciences* by J. Gould and W. Kolb.

3. The passing on of information in the case of Communist civil servants can evidently go farther and raise the question of espionage.

4. R. Massigli, *Sur quelques maladies de l'Etat* (Paris: Plon, 1958), p. 20:

The notion of the state has been so emptied of substance that those who serve the state have gone so far as to be unaware of the essential requirements of this service. The observance of secrecy is only the first of such requisites. To acknowledge that any servant of the state, minister or functionary, whatever his rank, is bound by it is to recognize that no one is free to define it as he finds most convenient.

I believe I can say that in Belgium the problem has been resolved in a diametrically opposed sense: the party has a (quasi) monopoly on secrecy and information.

5. Cf. L. Moulin, "La politisation de l'administration," Revue Générale (Jan. 1970). By the same author: "Les institutions politiques à venir," Analyse et Prévision (April 1966); "La décision politique en Belgique," Res Publica, no. 2 (1966); and pages 167-189 in Res Public, no. 2 (1971). The biggest part of this latter issue is devoted to a conference dealing specifically with politicization in the public services.

6. R. Massigli, op. cit., pp. 60-63:

Today the head of an administration, who is conscious of the traditions which honor the service to which he belongs, discovers with a mixture of astonishment and inconvenience that seeking after political support is not reserved for aspiring janitors and doorboys.

7. Cf. B. Chapman, "La Politique et l'Administration," Revue Internationale des Sciences Administratives, no. 1 (1958): 1-15.

8. M. Block, Dictionnaire politique, 1863. The fact that the term patronage clearly belongs to the vocabulary used during the last century confirms our thesis.

9. If they were not, they had in their pockets at least a proof of social conformity that the Establishment had granted them: a certificate of political or religious affirmation, most often both.

10. Even though there have been "lodges" of officers and also civil servants, cf. Res Publica, no. 2 (1971): 227. But differences of opinion and Weltanschauung remained, in spite of everything, of minor importance.

11. La Relève, no. 13 (March 28, 1959).

12. The same explanation appears in R. Williams, "Modernisation de l'administration publique britannique," Revue Internationale des Sciences Sociales 21 (1969): 114-125.

13. A. Molitor, in Res Publica, no. 2 (1971): 219. Also refer to "L'administration dans la société belge" by the same author in Aspects de la société belge (Brussels: Bibliothèque de L'Institut belge de Science politique, 1958), pp. 113-133.

14. For nepotism characterizes all periods and all societies. In "Bureaucracy" in The Encyclopaedia of Social Science, H. Laski, who does not say a word about the politicization of public administration, affirms that cases of nepotism are rarer in our society than under the Ancien Régime.

15. "A general reform is claimed on all sides," wrote Senator V. Leemans in a report made in 1959 for the Commission of Finances, "but as soon as work begins, it runs up against a general inertia." This happend because a good many civil servants have an interest in not seeing the services depoliticized, this politicization giving them chances for advancement which their merits alone would not give them. See also: V. Crabbe, "Considérations sur la bureaucratie: ses causes sociologiques et ses motifs politiques," Revue de l'Institut de Sociologie, no. 2 (1955).

For a historical account of administrative reforms, see, for example, the report by Minister Lilar to the Senate on March 10, 1959, or "Le Rapport de la Commission Max-Léo Gérard" in Moniteur belge, Oct. 21, 1954, or yet again "Le Rapport fait au nom de la Commission des Finances du Sénat de Belgique" by Senator V. Leemans (February 3, 1960 sitting). The very multiplicity of these reports—The first goes back to 1859!—and their unanimity clearly underline the irreversible continuity of this phenomenon. For a defense of the "apoliticism" of the civil service, see D. Norrenberg in Res Publica, no. 2 (1971): 173-180.

16. V. Lorwin, "Segmented Pluralism: Ideological and Political Cohesion in the Small European Democracies," Comparative Politics (Jan. 1971): 142-155, has established that the degree of this "segmentary pluralism" is much higher in Belgium than in Switzerland,

Austria, or Holland. Eighty percent of activities in Belgium—education, mass media, leisure, bureaucracy, and the like—rate high, that is, reach a very high degree of "segmentarization," whereas the rate for Holland is 61%; Austria, 50%; and Switzerland, 25%. Two out of fourteen are medium in Belgium against seven in Austria, five out of thirteen in Holland and six out of twelve in Switzerland.

17. Res Publica, no. 2 (1971): 206.

18. To follow this logic strictly, not only must the Flemish and Walloons have their own formations, as is already true, but additional ones would have to be created for members of the Socialist, Christian Social, Liberal, and other parties. However, the most ardent partisans of total politicization hesitate to propose this. Indeed, the most intrepid minds in this field are asking that "rupturing forces be neutralized not only at the level of the state and senior civil service but also in the army, national police and magistrature" (Res Publica, no. 2 [1971] : 231). This is understandable.

19. Tradition has entrusted certain ministries to one party rather than another, for example, francophone education by preference to a Socialist, agriculture to a Catholic. Thus, Socialist or Catholic employees form the largest part of the personnel of these two ministries. The ministerial puzzle may require that a traditionally "leftist" ministry be entrusted to a "rightist" minister, hence the need for the minister to be able to count on a large and active cabinet of his own.

20. Estimate put forward by A. Molitor, Res Publica, no. 2 (1971): 207.

21. A. Molitor, "L'administration," p. 131.

22. Res Publica, no. 2 (1971): 232.

23. Witnesses are numerous and unanimous on this point. From among many others, see: A. Molitor in Res Publica, no. 2 (1971): 22, and in "L'administration," pp. 130-132; "Nous n'aurons plus de grands commis," La Relève (April 5, 1958).

24. The minister does not discreetly choose the members of his staff. The party intervenes to propose to him—and impose on him, if such be the case—some of those persons on its "waiting list." For its part, the union behaves the same. Of course, these waiting lists are the products of innumerable and prolonged intrigues. Cf. Res Publica, no. 2 (1971): 235.

25. Res Publica, no. 2 (1971): 235.

26. For R. Massigli (op. cit., pp. 48-50), the cabinet has become the "minister's brain and, with relation to the civil service, the master's eye. A study bureau on the one hand, an organ for control on the other." The same idea is expressed in a communiqué issued by the Association des Fonctionnaires Généraux de Belgique (Le Soir, Feb. 18, 1971) which speaks of the "curtain hung by the private staff between the minister and the public services." Likewise, see R. Grégoire, La Fonction publique (Paris: Colin, 1954).

27. Res Publica, no. 2 (1971): 235.

28. Note that to counterbalance the actions of these private ministerial staffs, "occult ministries" are created with circuits drawn parallel to those traced by the private staffs. Cf. Res Publica, no. 2 (1971): 234.

29. R. Williams (op. cit., p. 123): "The British Civil Service seemed to be too isolated from the community, a fact more serious than any other."

30. See: C. Macpherson, "Progrès technique et décision politique," Revue Internationale des Sciences Sociales 3 (1960): 389-401; C. Langrod, "Rationalisation des méthodes et des moyens d'action dans l'administration publique," ibid., pp. 402-418.

31. P. Lévy, "Les silences de la RTB," La Revue Nouvelle (Sept. 1969): 193.

32. A. Molitor, "L'administration," p. 131.

33. Res Publica, no. 2 (1971): 226.

34. Cf. M. Young, The Rise of the Meritocracy, 1870-2033 (London: Thames and Hudson, 1958).

35. L. Moulin, "La démocratisation des études: limites et possibilités," Revue Générale (April 1969): 5-27.

LÉO MOULIN is professor of sociology at the Collège d'Europe (Bruges), president of the Belgian Institute of Political Science, and chief editor of *Res Publica*. He is the author of *L'Aventure européenne, Le monde vivant des Religieux,* and *De Robespierre à Lénine.*

6

Belgian Civil Servants and Political Decision Making

HUGO VAN HASSEL

Persisting historical mythology depicts Belgian civil servants as neutral guardians of the public interest. Such a picture is drawn from a normative interpretation of the past applied to present and future behavior. It is a comfortable cover for pragmatic conduct since it does not conform to facts. This mythology follows from the Weberian ideal of bureaucracy as highly rationalized organization and the bureaucrat as the personification of perfect objectivity. Recruited because of his technical competence, the bureaucrat has been trained for a definite position where he performs in a strictly logical manner by applying general rules to specific situations. Without any subjectivity, he executes whatever hierarchy dictates; but he dare not do any more than that.[1] This conception only fits into a system for which Weber foresaw a homogeneous elite at the top. In the "disenchanted" world of down-to-earth affairs, this elite of the elite makes the best decisions for people living in this most rational democracy. The elite manages society by using bureaucracy as its chosen instrument. Members of such an organization are completely integrated in that they identify themselves with the ruling elite and cut themselves off from the rest of the community. Only in this way do they become valuable, full-fledged members of the organization. Thus, public bureaucracy drifts from its Hegelian role of mediation between political leadership and citizenry and becomes a means of domination. In fact, the prerequisite of bureaucratic neutrality closes the system to pluralism.

During the nineteenth century, this model held in Belgium if we believe certain observers.[2] Moulin points out:[3]

Reflecting the oligarchy installed in power and being very often recruited from within it, the magistrature, teaching profession, clergy and public service were all the more able to serve the State without difficulty and with complete objectivity, and thus the national community (for the two were confused at the time), insofar as their interests coincided with those of the governing class and their vision of the world with that of the bourgeoisie from which it emanated.

Even when they had come from other strata, socialization within the organization led them to adopt the same referent values. Of course, gathering data in order to measure the degree of civil service politicization in the past is impossible. Some strong evidence indicates that such affirmations of neutrality were valid as regards Foreign Affairs and Defense.[4] Besides these two in this *etat-gendarme,* only a couple other departments existed with the purpose of maintaining order in the arena where laissez faire was supposed to regulate the natural course of economic and social affairs. At that time, government could proceed on the basis of a small, manageable set of judicial rules and norms enforced by civil servants relying on a common value system in making decisions.

Up till 1848, Belgian public servants could run for national political offices.[5] A few years later, Unionism, as the expression of the National Union in the king's cabinet, declined then perished as the political elite split into two parties, later three with factions in each one. The rise of the workers' movement brought new values into the social system.[6] Ministerial cabinets, till then nothing but ministers' private secretariats, have been steadily growing since that time. With the politicization of ministerial functions as ministers were held responsible to parliament and became involved in party politics, the size of ministerial cabinets has been increasing and their functions have evolved to include political decision making. These cabinets counterbalanced the traditional bureaucracy committed to the idea of a unique common interest.[7] Bureaucracy itself had become politicized in a definite way. Some observers denounced the sharing of administrative posts between the two parties in power in 1860 and 1915. In the case of appointments as well as examinations, if the latter existed, ministers chose only those candidates recommended by members of parliament. Although generally accepted, patronage was criticized as

a corrupting system which weakened morale since personal interests prevailed over the general interest. Not only recruitment but also promotion suffered because of it.[8]

In highly specialized services, on the other hand, technical-rational expertise was often beyond public servants recruited at the bottom and brought up within the organization. These idiosyncratic Weberian services tended to develop policies based on professional criteria. In a like situation, whenever a minister ran into trouble having his own policy implemented, he relied on his reinforced staff—his personal cabinet. Members of his cabinet shared his political beliefs since he had chosen them from among the most competent for that very reason.

When, after World War I, Socialist ministers first entered the government, they were faced with departments politicized by former patronage, much as Lipset describes in *Agrarian Socialism*. [9] These ministers fell back onto their cabinets. In the meantime, they appointed party activists to key positions. Hence, cabinets have latently helped break down monopolies and introduce pluralism within public bureaucracy. So also did the cabinets bring new professional skills, such as those of economists in the thirties,[10] into public administration. However, these actions generated a vicious circle: The minister, distrusting his own ministry, which he knew had been politicized, increased politicization yet more by appointing and working with people who supported his views. Of course, these latter expected some rewards.

Between 1937 and 1939, a reaction took place with the Camu Reform which established the merit system. An impartial central agency conducts formal examinations as the exclusive grounds for recruitment; and merit has become the primary basis for promotions to positions determined by departments' quantitative and qualitative needs. Civil servants, as well as their positions, are classified according to educational backgrounds and intellectual prerequisites.[11] This system, built on mechanistic principles, is quite Weberian except for its lack of a homogeneous political elite at the top. Although this system continues in force, breaches appeared in its regulations shortly after adoption. In the first place, as a consequence of World War II, the government had to quickly fill an abnormal number of vacancies. Economic recovery necessitated temporary emergency recruitments. These appointments were normalized afterwards. As for higher positions, an article in the reform act makes it possible to recruit competent specialists outside normal procedures if they are not already available within the civil service. Although scarcely applied nowadays, this article was a large gateway for patronage during the decades following the war.

Anyway, the minister decides whom to promote out of the best classified public servants on the list furnished by the board of the department. After selection based on competitive examinations, the king appoints—with the minister's "countersign"—highest level civil servants, whose jobs involve policy making. Once appointed to a position, they stay there. Unlike in France, the next minister cannot put other functionaries in those positions. Appointments have major importance because their implications reach far into the future. By controlling promotions, successive ministers of different parties in coalition governments build a self-regulating mechanism into the system. Aware of political fluctuations, they maintain some sense of proportionality between the three national parties, Neo-Liberal, Socialist, and Christian-Democrat. Such calculations are already evident in semipublic organizations, and they are informally spreading throughout the traditional departments.[12] Within this "sense of proportion," merit can still place good civil servants in the right positions; but personal frustration results whenever qualified individuals are sacrificed to proportionality.

Specific economic, social, cultural, and regional interests mobilize small groups in each of these parties.[13] Furthermore, such groups tend to reach across party boundaries. These interest groups organize joint lobbying actions to attain common objectives. They facilitate negotiations on rational bases without ideological rigidity. Through civil servants, they participate in drawing up policy decisions. Each group exerts pressure within its party in order to legitimate its demands. The outcome is more flexibility and greater margin for maneuvering. Problems not resolvable on the party level can be transferred to underlying structures where pragmatic solutions emerge out of power relationships. These groups politicize, to a certain degree, their own interests within the parties; but at the same time they tend to depoliticize them from within these political subcultures by injecting their own criteria into traditional systems. Moreover, they open bureaucracy to outside ways. Thus do cultural, linguistic, professional, financial, and economic reference groups politicize departments concerned with their spheres of activity.

Trade unions too play an important role. Each union is related to one of the traditional parties. They hold an official monopoly over the representation of civil servant interests. These two obligations create role confusion because unions must both represent the professional interests of their members, that is, civil servants, and participate in the struggle for key bureaucratic positions as part of their own commitment.

At first glance, a fundamental contradiction seems to exist in that recent research in Belgium has found that top civil servants are not thought to be very influential. Confirmation occurs in an analysis of a series of policy developments.[14] However, such findings are debatable because they deal mostly with hot problems, that is, highly politicized ones. The civil servant generally works in a politician's shadow, so his influence can easily be understated.[15]

As for non-civil service public servants, such as those in parastatal organizations, their influence on overall policy making varies. Directors of public enterprises may have broad power over a large spectrum of decisions. However, flexibility is limited because political parties are more or less proportionally represented within these enterprises. Sometimes discrepancies occur between governmental policy and the actions of these parastatals. Such was the case with regard to credit policy in semipublic banks.

As an organized group, top civil servants do not have much influence. Their association is caught between government and trade unions. They lack the solidarity and prestige of a French administrative corps. Foreign Affairs is an exception since, in essence, civil servants draw up foreign policy without political participation. In general, a civil servant's influence depends on his individual personality and his active membership in a political "family" or subculture. He does not exercise influence through normal bureaucratic channels but primarily through participation in ministerial cabinets and party or professional group study commissions. However, these "extracurricular activities" strengthen his intraorganizational influence. He develops power by furnishing politically oriented professional advice, sorting data, weighing information, and proposing policy alternatives in these specialized work groups.

Action is not unidimensional. On the whole, different interacting forces operate within the set of roles that a public servant plays in the above-mentioned subgroups which overlap party boundaries. This phenomenon is becoming more common because it stems from ethical (conservative vs. progressive), economic, cultural, or regional groupings which burst through party dikes and determine policies.[16] All these affiliations make it possible for the public servant to influence the execution of general rules while remaining within the lines laid down by law. For example, within the framework of a regional development program, he can detour public investments or subsidies toward his linguistic community or attract foreign investment to regions with which he has some ties. Similarly, he might influence the laying out of new highways or the establishing of cultural centers and schools. Likewise, he can speed up or retard policy preparation in his particular field. The more a particular policy is technical, the more he can play his own game of power politics in coalition with the interested client groups who are on the ad hoc commission especially if, for instance, they do not agree about some aspect of the government's proposal. All this is so much the easier if everyone belongs to the same political subculture. In some cases, research and policy formulation have taken so long a time that government was paralyzed from moving on to the stage of implementation. A civil servant's motivations can be an expression of power relationships within the party as much as an affirmation of technocratic competence. In educational policy, a civil servant may press for some academic appointment, therefore creating goodwill in the academic world. Consequent to such an appointment, he has more prestige as a public official.

The apex of power is reached by combining personal power within the party's bureaucracy with professional skills and power within governmental bureaucracy. This combination is possible whenever his minister belongs to the same party as himself. The top civil servant who generates more power within his party's bureaucracy and the related political subculture than does his minister who belongs to the same party develops more overall power as the minister becomes dependent. The integration of political and administrative power ensues. If the political constellation changes, the horizon changes. The next minister, if belonging to another party, will rely on his personal cabinet since the civil servant retains his position. This latter will have to withdraw into his department; as a result, he will try expanding his bureaucratic power base. There is little chance that he will resign because he can serve his party only to the extent that he combines political and administrative skills. He could become a national politician, but then he would have to resign from the civil service. Furthermore, by the time his party returns to power over the department, new technology may have developed or party power equations may have changed. These are some reasons that politicized bureaucrats, after arriving at the top, commit themselves to the closed bureaucratic milieu and refrain from change. Thus, those Belgian civil servants promoted partly because of their political involvement tend to become the defenders of bureaucratic rules and goals.[17] Such a stance compensates for their loss of political influence. To be mentioned also is a growing trend towards civil servant participation in personnel and organizational policy within the departments. The unions have somewhat integrated this trend into broader national interests.

On the other hand, some groups of top civil servants, such as specialists in managerial technology, do have increasing influence over policy making. Displacement of goals and the emergence of parallel goals come out of these groups.[18] The centralization of information services and of the specific skills needed for electronic data processing, systems management, forecasting techniques, and linear programming enhance the "profession" of public service and increase civil servant power relative to that of politicians. The former's monopoly over information and its elaboration into policy alternatives[19] occurs since the end-means relationship sprouts up at each branch of the decision tree and asks for a technical as well as political frame of reference so that political finality can include technical rationality. New political goals and other value-oriented choices have been revitalized through the growing consciousness of the scarcity of means as confronted with the quantity of real and artificial needs. Awareness is developing about the problems created by specialists who hold a monopoly over information, managerial skills, and technical know-how as opposed to politicians who only have some of those skills and then by chance. Guidance and control of the latter over the former become very difficult. We may be entering the era of a Weberian bureaucracy which integrates political functions through a new type of *homo politicus:* the bureaucrat-scientist-statesman.[20] Confronted with these problems, the Belgian politico-administrative system is searching for a new synthesis of differing criteria.

Public decision making has to deal in the first place with a political program determined by culture, norms, attitudes, and expectations about what societal goals should be. Only democratic consensus can validate such a program. In the second place, the cost-benefit analysis of present and future actions needed to implement a political program requires empirically validated criteria.

Some observers would like to create a pool of high civil servants from among which ministers could select those who support their political views.[21] Also, the proportionality previously discussed is institutionally controlling the politicization process. Other persons suggest reinforcing cabinets in the realm of policy making so that traditional departments deal with routine operations. Yet another idea advocates equipping parliament with a scientific infrastructure, thus enabling it to weigh options and check whether or not goals are reached by executive power and how so.

Debureaucratizing the civil service and shifting to a matrix organization of project management could possibly provide a solution.[22] Accordingly, civil servants, contracted experts, and political people would be hired for the duration of various projects. Systems management would be applied in the public sphere. Thus could techno-rationality and political goals be integrated by injecting, at each decisional level, a value judgment related to the system's political goals.

NOTES

1. H. H. Gerth, C. Wright Mills, *Max Weber, Essays in Sociology* (New York: Oxford University Press, 1958), p. 198.

2. E. Greyson, *L'administration, ses faits et gestes* (Brussels: Rozez, 1895); E. Ducpetiaux *Mission de l'Etat, ses règles, ses limites* (Brussels: Muquardt, 1871); L. Wodon, *Mémoire sur la réforme administrative* (Brussels: Roneo, 1915).

3. L. Moulin, "The Politicization of the Administration in Belgium," chapter 5 in this volume.

4. A. Molitor, "L'Administration dans la société belge," p. 110 in *Aspects de la société belge,* edited by M. Grégoire (Brussels: Librairie Encyclopédique, 1958).

5. They still can stand for local offices in elections.

6. C. H. Höjer, *Le régime parlementaire belge de 1918 à 1958* (Uppsala, Stockholm: Almquist-Wiksells, 1946); T. Luyckx, *Politieke Geschiedenis van België* (Brussels and Amsterdam: Elsevier, 1964).

7. H. Van Hassel, "Belgian Ministerial Cabinets: Spoils in a Spoiled Merit System," Res Publica 15, no. 2 (1973): 357-369.

8. Greyson, Decpetiaux, and Wodon, in the works cited above.

9. S. M. Lipset, *Agrarian Socialism* (Berkeley: Univ. of California Press, 1967), pp. 255-275.

10. H. Van Hassel, op. cit.

11. L. Camu, *Rechtstoestand van het Rijkspersoneel. Erste verslag inzake de hervorming van het bestuur* (Brussels, 1937).

12. L. Huyse, *Passiviteit, pacificatie en verzuiling in de Belgische politiek* (Anterpen: Standaard, 1970), p. 267.

13. Recent research on top civil servants in Belgium shows that only 11% are of working-class origins but that 33% were born to elitist families. The proportions among Walloons (French-speaking) and Flemish (Dutch-speaking) probably differ. Elitist origins would be more frequent among the francophones because, until the early 1900s, the elite came exclusively from that ethnic group. Cf. R. Depre, "Career Patterns of High Civil Servants in Belgium," Res Publica 15, no. 2 (1973): 261-278.

14. See: W. Dewachter, "La hiérarchie du pouvoir dans la politique belge," Res Publica 15, no. 2 (1973): 279-290; J. Maynaud, J. Ladrière, and F. Perin, *La décision politique en Belgique* (Paris: A. Colin, 1965), p. 370.

15. A. Delperee, "La prise de décision dans l'administration," Res Publica 9, no. 2 (1967): 199-213.

16. A. Vandenbrande, "Elements for a Sociological Analysis of the Impact of the Main Conflicts on Begian Political Life," Res Publica 9, no. 3 (1967): 437-470; also "Voluntary Associations in the Belgian Political System, 1954-1968," in Res Publica 15, no. 2 (1973): 329-356.

17. A. Molitor, "La politisation de l'administration," in Res Publica 13, no. 2 (1971): 219-220.

18. R. K. Merton, "The Unanticipated Consequences of Social Action," pp. 894-904 in American Sociological Review (1936); P. Selznick, "Theory of Organizational Commitments," pp. 194-202 in Reader in Bureaucracy, edited by R. K. Merton (Glencoe, Ill.: Free Press, 1952); A. Gouldner, Patterns of Industrial Bureaucracy (Glencoe, Ill.: Free Press, 1954); M. Crozier, Le phénomène bureaucratique (Paris: Seuil, 1964).

19. R. Dethier, "Informatique et pouvoir," in Res Publica 15, no. 3 (1973).

20. A. Philippart, "Pour un fonctionnaire scientifique," Res Publica 15 (1973).

21. A. Molitor, "La politisation de l'administration," op. cit., pp. 207-208; also by the same, "Les superstructures des administration centrales en Belgiques," in Les superstructures des administrations centrales, edited by J. Siwek-Pouydesseau and others (Paris: Cujas, 1973).

22. D. R. Kingdom, Matrix Organization, Management Information Technologies (London: Tavistock, 1973).

HUGO VAN HASSEL is associate professor in the Faculty of Social Sciences, Catholic University of Louvain. He is also the coordinator of Management Training for Higher Civil Servants (Leuven) and general secretary of the Flemish Section, Belgian Political Science Association.

7

French Ministerial Staffs

JEANNE SIWEK-POUYDESSEAU

Edgar Faure has said that if members of the opposition have the impression that they are not being properly informed as to what is really happening, sometimes members of the majority (and even some ministers) get the same feeling.[1] This is so because the "technostructure" sets options and prepares decisions. By techno-structure, he meant the cabinets of the Prime Minister and the President of the Republic together with directors of the central administrations and ministerial cabinets.[2] Farther on, with regard to "technician-ministers," he declared:

> These are perhaps the men who influence events most. When they have any particular intent of their own, they know how to shape it so that the technostructure will assimilate it; and they will easily find the necessary support within the technostructure because they themselves are part of it.

The relations between French politicians and high civil servants stand thus revealed.

Since the beginning of the Fifth Republic, the existence of such technician-ministers has very acutely posed the problem of the transfer of civil servants into the political world, so acutely that we can speak of the technicians' colonization of political territory. Looking at the composition of a recent government, we find that 37% of the ministers originate from the public services, 37% come from the nonpublic sector, and 26% have purely political back-grounds. However, classification is debatable. Is it very significant to place Chaban-Delmas among treasury inspectors rather than among politicians? Is Debré's service on the State Council more important for purposes of classification than his term in the Senate? In the last example, a positive response is easier to make because the years Debré spent in the public services have no doubt strongly marked his personality. Whatever the case, the fact of having received a technician's training does not mollify a minister's political temperament, whether he is a legislator or not, especially since most of those not belonging to Parliament later do obtain electoral approval, profiting of course from their title of minister. Today, people talk about government by civil servants, but during the Third Republic they did not talk about government by lawyers. At that time, law faculties had educated a good number of ministers. Nowadays, men for these positions tend to graduate from the National School of Administration (ENA), but their political nature is not thus compromised although this change does entail important psychological and behavioral differences. The channels for promotion of political figures have changed, and this change inevitably involves modifications in the style of government.

The characteristics of those holding ministerial portfolios quite obviously influence the recruitment of ministerial staffs. A Radical or Socialist minister with strong provincial ties does not surround himself with the same kind of men as a Gaullist minister belonging to the Parisian bourgeoisie even if, in both instances, their associates do come from the public services.

1. MINISTERIAL CABINET PERSONNEL

The ministerial cabinets, such as we know them today, were formed at the beginning of the Third Republic. A 1911 law and a 1912 decree laid down rules for them. These have fixed the maximum number of assistants that can serve on a minister's cabinet. At that time, these cabinets were criticized because of their overreaching activities and their encroachment on the civil service's fields of competence and, above all, because of the constant rise in the number of their personnel and the primacy given to political factors.

Appointments have always been at the minister's discretion. He chooses and dismisses members of his staff as he sees fit. The number of members is limited to ten for most ministers: a cabinet head, a director, a head of the secretariat, and seven other technical counselors or heads of special missions (or, on occasion, attachés). The lists published in a recent issue of the *Journal Officiel* comprised about thirty assistants for the President and the Prime Minister, seventeen for the Minister of Finances (thirty counting the two state secretaries attached to this ministry), from nine to thirteen for most other ministers, and from four to six for state secretaries.

In fact, these ministerial cabinets include not only official but also a nearly equal number of semiofficial members. Even a third category is distinguishable: the "clandestines" in that they do not always have clearly defined duties. These latter more or less make up an entourage. Where the cabinet proper ends is often difficult to say. Actual numbers vary greatly according to the minister; certain staffs include up to about a hundred persons. In such a case, we can wonder whether this is still a command staff at the minister's disposal or whether it has not become the embryo for a new civil service. In my statistics, I have taken only official personnel into account. Whether the semiofficial has markedly different characteristics is, at first glance, difficult to say; but it does not seem to.

Diverse factors influence appointments. Personal relationships certainly play a very major role, relatively more important than political relationships themselves. In any case, these latter are of prime importance in certain cabinets and for certain positions, such as cabinet head. Some staffs have a very homogeneous composition in the sense that all their members belong to the minister's party. But under the Fourth Republic as under the Fifth, numerous cabinet members have collaborated with ministers wearing various political labels.

Finally, technical aspects are often determinate. Either the minister retains his predecessor's assistants who have the advantage of being familiar with things, or he chooses officials from branches within the civil service, or he wants to attract competent persons belonging to a particular administrative corps. Thus, without any other consideration, he frequently asks the State Council or the Treasury Inspectorate for a technical counselor or an agent to be assigned a specific mission.

This in no way means that such "technical" personnel have no political attachments. Even a more or less notorious member of the opposition collaborated with a cabinet during the Fifth Republic, but no general conclusion can be drawn from this exception. Those serving on the Fifth Republic's cabinets accept the regime although they do not all belong—far from it—to the Gaullist family or do not even consider themselves as tied to parties forming the governmental majority. Quite obviously, some staff members would serve ministers under a government with a clearly different orientation. Civil servants who have no clearly formed political opinions, even though leaning toward the opposition, become very favorably inclined toward the government after spending some time on a cabinet.

For civil servants wishing to obtain higher positions, collaboration with a minister at some point during their careers is indispensable. Others more simply believe that membership on a cabinet possesses a much more superior interest than daily work in the civil service. In particular, the members of inspection and control divisions have the impression that their action is more positive and efficacious within a cabinet. Finally, devotion to the ethics of public service is also a reason for working with a minister.

Quite often however, civil servants loathe appearing too strongly marked in a political sense. During an unstable period such as the beginning of the Fifth Republic, numerous persons waited around awhile for a change in the majority. But when Gaullism seemed quite firmly established, some of them did not want to risk their chances, especially since the years were passing and the channels for promotion corresponded to precise moments for career development. So they decided to silence their political misgivings. General de Gaulle's departure relieved many consciences; there then appeared previous associates with Mendes-France and, in a certain sense in their wake, some newcomers less fearful of being classified as "right wingers." Accordingly, in a large enough number of cases, the politicization of cabinet members is nothing other than accepting a compromise with a politician.

2. SOCIAL AND PROFESSIONAL ORIGINS

There have always been very few women on ministerial cabinets, with the exception of the heads of the private secretariats. Women represent about 8% of the personnel.

The average age of the ministers' assistants is 42; the cabinet directors' is slightly higher, about 45. So staff members are relatively young. These positions require, it is true, strenuous activity and dynamism; but the comparatively young age creates difficulties in relations with branches of the civil service.

Cabinet members quite often hold two diplomas, law and political science, or law and humanities. The representation of law faculties, political science institutes, and ENA is becoming more and more important. In other words, university origins are less and less diversified. In 1968 for instance, 60% of the cabinet members were law graduates; 37%, political science; and 33%, former ENA students as opposed to 47%, 26% and 11%, respectively, in 1958. Graduates in the humanities represented 22% of the 1968 figures as opposed to 19% perviously, and those in the sciences remained unchanged at about 1%. Over the decade, military schools declined from 8% to 3%, whereas engineering schools rose from 3% to 5% and Polytechnic, from 4% to 5%.

Reference to existing studies concerning students in the universities or the most prestigious schools lets us conclude that the great majority of cabinet members spring from the middle or upper bourgeoisie. As for members of the major administrative corps who have gone to ENA, they must pass competitive examinations, but 85% are of bourgeois origin.[3]

Already during the Third Republic, about 60% of staff members were civil servants; today, more than 90% are. Various reasons other than job qualifications explain this phenomenon. Relinquishing a position for an undetermined period of time in the private sector is so very much more difficult than in the civil service where the minister then has the responsibility of finding new places for his helpers. A civil servant has no trouble being reintegrated if he belongs to the State Council, the Audit Office, or the Treasury Inspectorate. Likewise, he will, without much difficulty, be able to return within his ministry's administrative hierarchy; and besides, the minister will find it very easy to locate openings in the civil service or the public sector. Another point, the minister does not have sufficient funds at his disposal to pay staff members fully; hence, a civil servant temporarily assigned to the cabinet will only receive allowances accumulated with his salary. Any way, some civil servants retain their former jobs, thus protecting themselves from the possible fall of their ministers. Such was especially true for subprefects during the Third and Fourth Republics and is still true for many assistant directors in the central administrations. Table 1 presents data of the professional origins of cabinet members. In recent years, the rate of increase in the number of engineers is running at 9%; they now make up 73% of the category "high civil service."

The level of professional qualifications has improved considerably since the Third Republic. At the start of the century, auditors from

TABLE 1

PROFESSIONAL ORIGINS OF CABINET MEMBERS

	1958	Percentages	1970	Percentages
State Council	14 ⎫		16 ⎫	
Audit Office	6 ⎬	13	16 ⎬	15
Treasury Inspectorate	17 ⎭		22 ⎭	
Prefects	8 ⎫		8 ⎫	
Subprefects	22 ⎭	10	41 ⎭	14
Diplomatic Service	12	4	18	5
Overseas Administration	12	4	1	- -
High civil service	95	33	123	35
Other civil servants	18	6	12	3
University	11	4	12	3
Army	19	7	17	5
Cabinet members	18	6	2	1
Legal careers	4	1	14	4
Journalists	15	5	4	1
Secretaries	14	5	9	3
Private sector	1	- -	- -	- -
No information	- -	- -	35	10
Total	286		350	

the Audit Office or members of the State Council were often cabinet heads. Today, State Council rapporteurs, who have generally had long experience, always fill that position.

The distribution of professional qualifications varies according to the cabinet's hierarchy. For instance, the Grand Corps, including the Diplomatic Corps, are well represented among the directors and assistant directors since corpsmen hold a total of three-quarters of such positions. Members of the Prefectoral Corps occupy a good number of positions as cabinet heads; in effect, they are specifically in charge of political relations.

It is interesting to measure the importance of transfers onto ministerial cabinets for each of the Grand Corps. In fact, the percentage of members who have assisted some minister at least once is: Prefectoral Corps, 55%; Treasury Inspectorate, 52%; State Council, 50%; Audit Office, 30%.

3. TERM AND TERMINATION OF SERVICE

Admission onto a ministerial cabinet is often only a stage in a career, hence the high turnover of personnel even when the minister does not change. The average length of service is about three years;

however, some make an actual profession out of their association with ministers: they stay around for more than ten years. In 1968, more than half the members of the directing staffs in the ministries had never before belonged to a cabinet, but more than a quarter had participated in one or several cabinets for over six years. An examination of the cabinets of those ministers who remained in office from 1961 to 1968 reveals very few associates who stayed throughout.

The members of a minister's staff essentially value the cabinet's strategic location at the head of the French Civil Service, especially since positions at the top of the civil service hierarchy are at the government's discretion. During the Third Republic, legislators strongly criticized the practice of "ministerial testaments" and the abuses of favoritism. Consequently, they decided to limit the number of staff members and the funds accredited to the cabinet. Table 2 shows how careers unfold after cabinet service.

Although not complete, these figures clearly indicate that participation on a cabinet is a means for professional advancement. Moreover, the positions most sought after or most easily obtained have changed according to the times. The tour through a Grand Corps is well known; this permits experienced civil servants (who are, besides, favored by a minister) to be appointed to the State Council or Audit Office without making their way up from the start through the traditional system of competitive examinations—today, without passing by way of ENA. Obviously, these positions are quite limited in number. The most significant example of appointment to civil service positions is that of central administration directors because, in effect, half of them have worked with a minister and a third of these just before their appointments.

TABLE 2

POSTCABINET CAREERS (in percentages)

	Fourth Republic	Fifth Republic
Duties with no important change or with normal promotion	8	7
Promotions to civil service jobs at the government's discretion	25	28
Positions in the public or semipublic sectors	19	8
Positions in the private sector	2	5
Parliament	2	2
Ministerial cabinets	10	6
No information	34	44

From 1958 to 1968, the number of deputies having belonged to a cabinet nearly doubled. Today, they represent 14% of the total in Parliament. More and more high civil servants, particularly members of the Grand Corps, are standing for election to seats in the National Assembly. The great majority of those elected have previously served with a minister. Moreover, most of them belong to parties within the majority. A second category, far less important, includes Socialist or Radical legislators who belonged to Fourth Republic cabinets. This phenomenon ties in with the general evolution of the channels for promotion in France. Formerly, the normal procedure for promotion was deeply rooted at the local level. Before entering Parliament, many politicians had previously been town councillors, mayors, or the equivalent of country commissioners. This kind of careerist is still found in the Senate. Nowadays, Gaullism or its successors are sufficiently strong to have candidates elected who have been "parachuted" into regions where they do not or have never lived. As often as not, these men are civil servants who have collaborated with Fifth Republic ministers. The fact that a civil servant has participated in a ministerial cabinet manifests, on his part, a certain taste for politics. That he may afterwards try his chances in a legislative election is understandable, especially since the risk of failure for the majority party is less than for the others. Finally, the system of "substitute parliamentarians" has permitted many cabinet members to enter the National Assembly, whereas their minister successfully carried the election. Thus, whenever the minister assumes a portfolio, his substitute elected at the same time and on the same ticket becomes parliamentarian in his stead and remains so even if the minister loses grace.

4. HOW MINISTERIAL CABINETS FUNCTION

Inordinate increases in the number of staff members led Parliament to limit, in 1911, the sizes of ministerial cabinets. Since 1948, ministers are not supposed to have more than ten assistants, and state secretaries, not more than seven. The official lists reveal that these limits have not always been attained; but in spite of everything, they are often exceeded because of semiofficial assistants. Nevertheless, the importance of the latter must not be overestimated. In 1971 for instance, out of sixteen cabinets, I have been able to count an average per cabinet of two semiofficial assistants with ranks and functions identical to those of technical counselors or heads of mission and two additional aides of a lesser rank. Civil servants from the ministry assist some cabinet officials. Some cabinets have no semiofficial members. On the other hand, the Ministry of the Army has from twenty to two hundred, if decorations, legislative interventions, and similar areas are taken into account.

The total number of cabinet members varies with the number of ministers and state secretaries. The official figures give around 250 to 350. In fact, the increasing competence of the ministers' staff personnel seems to be more important than their increasing number. Furthermore, a progressive standardization of cabinet hierarchies and roles has taken place.

The head of the private secretariat is most often a private secretary. In recent years, he (or she) no longer always figures in a cabinet's official composition. He actually has very little in common with the minister's other assistants. The secretariat principally takes care of the minister's private mail. Although its functions are very important, they are obviously of a relatively minor order.

The cabinet head is mostly responsible for political problems concerning relations with Parliament, the minister's constituency, his party, and the press. He also pays attention to the cabinet's practical and financial problems and to certain matters regarding awards and personnel. Sometimes a head of mission or an attaché is responsible for relations with Parliament. The legislative attaché used to be one of the cabinet's classical figures. Today, this title has fallen into disuse.

The major part of the personnel consists of technical counselors and heads of mission. They study the files and perform the various "technical tasks" involved in relations with government agencies. The division of labor is made either according to the structure of the ministry—the minister's assistant covering one or several branches of the civil service—or according to important problems, for example, the budget, legal matters, or reforms. Technical counselors and heads of mission, in liaison with various offices, examine administrative and technical problems as a whole. They are the ones most likely to organize a hierarchy parallel to the ministry's. Because their functions are rarely of a purely technical nature, these assistants are led to take into consideration political facts, if only because of their contacts with elected members of representatives of professional associations.

The role of cabinet director deserves special emphasis. During the

Third and Fourth Republics, the cabinet did not usually have a good structure. It worked like a military command staff whose relatively independent members had direct contact with the minister, hence the saying that each assistant was the minister's "alter ego" and could act directly in his name. Although this thinking persists, it corresponds less and less with reality. Sometimes there used to be two hierarchies (the word is undoubtedly too strong): on the one hand, the cabinet director, technical counselors, and heads of mission who had direct contacts with the ministerial department; on the other, the cabinet head, attachés, and private secretary, who were familiar with political factors, expecially in the sense of politics, that is, relations with Parliament, and the like. The minister brought about the synthesis.

In most instances today, the cabinet director has become the one most responsible person in the cabinet. Sometimes the cabinet head still preserves a measure of autonomy but in relatively secondary political matters. The director is considered, and considers himself to be, the point through which all business must pass. Most often, he sees all the important mail, and he alone is entitled to sign papers. Of course, in urgent cases or matters of oral procedure, the technical counselors and heads of mission can directly address the minister without going through the intermediary of the cabinet director, but the latter is always kept informed. The cabinet director's usual functions include: texts to be signed by the minister; legislation and regulations; cabinet and ministry organization; relations with the President's and Prime Minister's staffs; the ministry's general political orientation; all urgent, important, secret, or delicate matters; and more generally, political affairs that affect the minister's relations with political figures or that are capable of provoking public opinion. The cabinet director may also be responsible for important appointments and relations with trade union and professional organizations.

Obviously, there are many exceptions, but I have tried to identify what seem to be the principal lines of force and the present trend of developments. In the majority of cases, the cabinet director seems to be the minister's administrative and sometimes political right hand. He is the super-general manager (or secretary-general) of the ministry and the staff's unchallenged head. Given these conditions, the cabinet looks like a well-structured and hierarchized body. So, it is becoming less and less true to say that each staff member is acting individually in the minister's name.

We shall see that the structuring, even the bureaucratizing, of the cabinet goes hand in hand with an ever-increasing grip on the civil service. Also noteworthy is the part played, in parallel, by technical counselors and heads of mission "in the minister's presence." These people generally remain apart from the cabinet's traditional hierarchy. Some of them exercise a kind of power behind the scenes as the minister's political counselor. Others are specially competent in a technical sense, and they follow, for instance, a set of problems particularly difficult to solve. In every case, they are placed in the position of staff director. Do they form the nucleus of a veritable cabinet in its original meaning? They sometimes seem to be an antidote for different drawbacks ascribed to present cabinets. In 1971, we can count one such person attached to the President, three to the Prime Minister, two to the Minister of Finances and one to each of the Ministers of Agriculture, Education, Public Works, Transport, and Construction.

5. THE ROLE OF THE MINISTERIAL CABINETS IN THE POLITICAL-ADMINISTRATIVE SYSTEM

Initially, the existence of cabinets was tied to the idea, widespread in France, that administration—the civil service—must be independent of political factors. To the degree that administration does not deal with political questions (in the sense of politics, but were to trace the boundary between policy and politics?), such problems must be dealt with somewhere. In Great Britain, the civil service has to be neutral; hence, it normally enough collaborates with governments, whatever their tendencies. In France, the civil service is believed to be incapable of this kind of loyalty. In order to protect it from trespassing, an attempt is made to guard it from contact with politics. At least, this is the traditional conception.

Conversely, French civil servants literally dread politics. The fear of taking on any responsibilities reinforces this attitude. In their strategy with regard to the cabinets, central administration directors feel they do not have to be cognizant of political problems.[4] They are thus acting like civil servants integrated into the administrative structure. On the other hand, when questioned without any reference to their struggle against the cabinets, they do not make any fundamental distinction between their activities and the cabinets'. They then react more like members of the political-administrative elite which constitutes a class with common characteristics.

In short, the cabinets' present practices amount to denying that administrative action independent from politics can possibly exist. Their development in France is even a demonstration by means of the absurd that the civil service cannot be kept from political realities.

The development of these cabinets is very much linked to factors pertaining to the civil service. To say that their role has continuously increased is banal. The constant tendency toward centralization, greatly due to superiors' lack of confidence in their subordinates, can only reinforce this movement. Central administrators judge local administrations to be incompetent and so they act in the latter's place; the cabinets judge the central administrations to be incapable and so they duplicate the latter's activities; the Prime Minister's cabinet duplicates the ministerial cabinets and is, in turn, duplicated by the directing staff at the Elysée. Certainly a coordinating body is indispensable at the head of the ministries. The proliferation and stability of these staffs have led to the disappearance of most of the secretaries-general in the ministries, who were few in number. In effect, the existence of secretaries-general is incompatible with that of omnipotent cabinets. But the coordinating body, even when there is no secretary-general, has to be supple if it wants to play a coordinating role. Any increase in managerial tasks can only be made to the detriment of actual coordination since current affairs quickly become all-demanding, regardless of the cabinet's size.

In fact, if cabinet members take up many matters which seem of relatively minor importance, they do so because they wish to find a solution different from the one which the civil service would come up with. They do not take into account only traditions and precedents or even regulations. The reasons are not necessarily of a political nature, anyhow not in the sense of politics. Quite simply, a cabinet has some idea of the solutions to be brought to bear and finds it easier to act directly rather than to have to explain to lower ranks the direction to move in—and why. Perhaps this is one of the principal sources of a cabinet's overreaching activities. To delegate responsibilities and not to raise questions suppose that circumstantiated explanations are given on the policy to be followed and also that this policy will be stuck to for a certain time. To direct branches of the civil service supposes, first of all, what is wanted and why it is are both known. A piecemeal mentality is not applicable within an administrative structure; only directing staffs can implement decisions made bit by bit.

Ministerial cabinets are simultaneously the product and reflection of the French administrative system as a whole. Thus, the "system" of ENA is one of the present factors in their development. In fact, ENA has trained ministerial assistants and even ministers rather than administrators. If it has been unable to produce enough civil service administrators, the reason is that it did not recruit future administrators but future members of the cabinets or the Grand Corps, since the sons of the good Parisian bourgeoisie have never dreamed of becoming civil servants. This system has given us, in spite of everything, talented senior civil servants, some of whom have been and still are great administrators. But the fact remains that the civil service lacks administrators and that those in office find their work uninteresting, the more so since this vicious circle leads the cabinets to profit by constantly dispossessing government agencies.

Therefore the reasoning of most cabinet members is perfectly logical: cabinets are indispensable because the civil service is not the equal of its tasks. But would the function not rapidly create the means if the opposite policy were followed? Reducing cabinet activities would give many administrators already in office a taste for responsibility and would attract valuable recruits into their ranks especially since, on the whole, the argument that cabinet members must palliate the insufficiencies of central administration personnel borders on absurdity. The French Civil Service has many quality civil servants whom it needs, but they are not placed where they ought to be. Many technical counselors or heads of mission, originating from the service or the Grand Corps, would be in better positions as directors or assistant directors in the ministries and would be able to accomplish jobs corresponding to their ranks if they knew how to amply delegate matters to their associates. The latter would rapidly become more competent if they had the impression that they were at least required to do a job they are capable of—and even work permitting them to surpass themselves. The perfectionism of a certain administrative style might suffer, but the working of the total administrative machinery would no doubt gain in efficiency.

The fact remains that ministerial cabinets reflect the civil service's inaptitude in facing up to tasks incumbent upon it. The traditional administrative system lacks speed, "creativity," and the ability to continually adapt to new needs; and above all, its agents refuse to assume real responsibilities. Cabinets very imperfectly make up for these deficiencies. They only avoid total suffocation; and in another way, they greatly contribute to the deterioration of the situation. So, given the actual interrelations between the cabinets and civil service, how could the administration be reformed if the cabinets' role remains unchanged or becomes more important? In conclusion, what is the political influence of ministerial cabinet members? And, above all, do they play a role different from what they could have within the administrative structure? Obviously, the ministers' assistants occupy a choice position in the French government because of the advice they lavish, the decisions they prepare, and the implementation they supervise. Does this mean that ministers are totally enfeoffed to a caste of civil servants and that they do not enjoy complete political freedom? In reality, although these civil servants have in common a particular way of approaching problems, most of them certainly are not activists with clearly defined political intentions. No doubt this is one of the reasons they are so willing to cooperate with the government. Beginning from an easily established consensus as to what must not be changed, the roles of the government and civil service consist of managing national undertakings and avoiding, from day to day, anything which could challenge the established equilibrium. This is true on the general level. With regard to details concerning decisions made, political factors would probably have less influence if the administrative hierarchy normally dealt with affairs.

NOTES

1. An interview with Edgar Faure in L'Expansion (Sept. 1969).

2. In the French system as in the British, the Prime Minister has a Cabinet composed of his ministers; but unlike in the British one, each minister also has a cabinet, that is, a private staff, made up of public officials. This paper is dealing with the latter, referred to either as a ministerial cabinet or staff. Central administration designates a ministry's centralized services in the capital as opposed to field offices.

3. Cf. Jean-François Kesler, "Les anciens élèves de l'Ecole Nationale d'Administration," Revue Française de Science Politique (April 1964): 243-267.

4. Cf. Ezra Suleiman, "Political versus Administrative Roles in the French High Civil Service," a report made to the Eighth World Congress of the International Political Science Association, Sept. 1970.

JEANNE SIWEK-POUYDESSEAU is chargé de recherche, Centre National de la Recherche Scientifique (Paris), and is the author of *Le personnel de direction des ministères* and *Le corps préfectoral*.

8

The Managers of Public Enterprises in France

DANIEL DERIVRY

State intervention in and control over the national economy rejoins a long ago but tenacious tradition: Colbertism of the mercantilist period. After the Liberal, laissez-faire, thinking of the nineteenth century, this tradition resurfaced following World War II.

Although most public enterprises resulted from nationalizations, that is, state expropriation of a private company, the government has directly created some of them. Hence, I will refer to them as public and not nationalized enterprises. The judicial formulas applied to such takeovers or creations vary according to the situation. I will just mention that the enlargement of the public sector occurred during two major periods: under the Popular Front between the two wars, and during the years immediately after the Liberation. In fact, the preamble of the 1946 Constitution ordained that "any wealth or any company whose exploitation has or acquires the characteristics of a national public service or a *de facto* monopoly must become the property of the collectivity."

1. THE PUBLIC SECTOR'S POSITION IN THE ECONOMY

In 1969, the public sector in relation to all nonagricultural enterprises represented 13% of the employees, 29% of investments, and 15% of gross wages and salaries. Public corporations in energy, transportation, and telecommunications alone accounted for 7% of national production and 20% of nonagricultural investments. These figures imperfectly reflect this sector's real importance, first, because of the exclusion of subsidiaries from such accountancy, but also because of the strategic position that public enterprises hold in the industrial process, and finally because of their increasingly important role as "pilot companies."[1]

The public sector's importance derives first of all from its nearness to the sources of the production cycle. Prices in the nationalized sector influence production costs. In some industries, such as coal, gas, electricity, and telecommunications, the public sector has a quasi monopoly. In other areas, for example, aeronautics, armaments, and transportation, it holds a preponderant position. In the transportation field alone, it accounts for 65% of investments.

In the report of the interministerial committee on public enterprises, S. Nora declared:[2]

> For twenty years now, the public sector has played an eminent economic and political role. The hopes and passions surrounding its creation, its importance in the national economy and in the volume of its employment, the magnitude of capital transfers passing through it, the place it has assumed in conducting economic and social policy, all these keep it from being otherwise.

The Nora Report stressed the dual nature of these enterprises: companies of an industrial and commercial type devoted to efficiency but also privileged by subsidies and constrained by the public interest. They are destined to favor the public authorities' economic and social policies. They "pilot" many domains, that is, the government uses them as an essential tool in state planning and as an important testing ground for social and economic reforms. Accordingly, the public sector itself is an important agent in industrial decentralization and regional development programs.

Several examples can be cited of the public sector's role as a promoter or innovator. In 1970, Renault launched the principle of ongoing job training. The 1970 "progressive" contracts, which guaranteed raising wages in keeping with the rate of inflation, at French Electricity (EDF), French Gas (GDF), and the French Railway Authority (SNCF) and in the coal mining industry, introduced an important innovation which subsequently served as a reference mark for other public enterprises such as the Paris Transport Authority (RATP), then for the whole of the public services, and finally even for some major private companies. Generally speaking, the public sector's contract policy is always more advanced.

It is not so easy to distinguish those innovations of governmental inspiration from those which, while they fall within the government's general policy, a company undertakes on its own. Each public enterprise does not enjoy the same degree of autonomy. Those having to face competition usually have the largest elbowroom, not only in the market but also even in internal affairs. A company like Renault is not officially subject to any public service mission. It has to balance its budget and compete in the automobile market; that is all. Yet, it has a sort of moral duty to be in advance from every point of view.[3] As a vanguard, Renault has implemented a number of social measures, not without the public authorities' reticence, such as the third then fourth weeks of paid leave. Such a decision shows what the ambiguous notion of "pilot enterprise" means.[4] Renault is all the more important because it is national and has sufficient autonomy so that its decisions are attributable to it. Anything that happens at Renault is an important test. A minister has even declared, "I'm not exaggerating to say that when Renault sneezes, all of France gets the shivers."[5]

2. MANAGERIAL POWER

Two men head a public enterprise: the president of the board of directors and the general manager. Sometimes the same person assumes both functions like the president-general-manager (PGM) at Renault. These men in power are, first of all, men from Power by virtue of the rules for acceding to such positions. In effect, the government enjoys a quasi absolute control over nominations and appointments.[6]

The president of the board is most often chosen from the board's members. In some cases as at Renault and the National Board of Energy, he can be chosen from outside and then become a board member because of his appointment. The means for making nominations are extremely diverse, but all regulations assure the same control to the public authorities. The government may make appointments, directly or indirectly. Or the board of directors may appoint—in those companies where the state's administrators make up the majority such as North and South Aviation or the National Company for the Study and Construction of Airplane Engines (SNECMA). In the nationalized banks, the board makes appointments but with the consent of the Minister of Economy and Finance.

In the energy sector, the government appoints on the basis of the board's nominations, likewise in the insurance companies and Air France. Nearly all appointments are actually made by Ministerial Council decrees.

As for the general managers, their selection is hardly regulated. Sometimes the plurality of offices—combining president and general manager—is formally forbidden. In other cases, it is statutorily provided for. Exceptionally, there are provisions according to which the general manager must be chosen from "among competent persons proven in the profession." The board of directors very seldom makes appointments, although they do in the insurance companies where the office of general manager is not statutory. Most often, the state appoints on the basis of nominations presented by the board. Sometimes the board itself makes the appointment but subject to the consent of the minister in charge, for example, at SNCF and the National Company of the Rhône. Appointments are generally made by Ministerial Council decree.

Though appointed by the government, do these managers depend on the government? After all, are they not only high civil servants? Public enterprises represent a form of decentralization that permits an advantageous triple specialization: of resources, of methods, and especially of men by distinctly recruiting personnel from the central administrations of the ministries. G. Vedel has gone so far as to say, "Nationalizations are a procedure for selecting directors."[7] The power of appointment is undoubtably both the most discreet and most effective form of tutelage, assuredly more effective than the multiple a priori and a posteriori controls.[8]

Once appointed, these managers do not become puppets. Observers have often remarked that within management-union committees, the appointees are often freer from those who named them than elected representatives are from their electors. The power of appointment is not so almighty as has been asserted. Managers of the public sector enjoy an undisputable freedom of action. Even the boards of directors hardly limit managerial power, this being so because of the educational and "staff/caste" links which generally bind together managers and administrators.

Although government representation usually occurs through the ministries,[9] the grand corps—the major administrative corps in the government—literally hold positions on the boards. At the beginning of 1957, out of 134 state administrators within public enterprises in the fields of energy and transportation and in mechanical industries,

50 were senior civil servants of which 23 were inspectors from the Ministry of Finance and 35, technical corps engineers (17 of the latter were mining engineers).[10] General managers come from among specialists within the relevant field. A mining engineer directs the National Coal Board; aeronautical engineers, the aeronautical companies; and finance inspectors, the financial establishments. These staff links between state administrators and company directors reinforce the latter's power. The president of the board, most often an alumnus of the same school, arbitrates disagreements, as much with the board as with the ministerial authority in charge.

These staff/caste ties are so strong that certain observers, such as P. Bauchet,[11] have wondered whether the influence exercised by the state through its trusteeship is not less important

> because of the close ties between directors and those charged with supervising them: both are alumni of the same major schools, both belong to one of the civil service's major corps, both have similar career patterns.

He concludes with a severe critique of present recruitment:[12]

> Enlarging the appointment privileges of the Finance Inspectorate and Mining Corps will not better enlighten the public interest. What would be necessary is to go so far as to forbid plurality of office holding in public, industrial and commercial, enterprises. This measure must only be one step. It would be insufficient for warding off the attention given by the civil servant tempted with "slippering" into firms where his former schoolmates are ready to make room for him.

On the contrary, A. Delion believes that the control exercised by the major state administrative corps and high public offices is legitimate:[13]

> We can validly maintain that the state's administrators must be civil servants holding positions in the administrative and technical corps of control and management. But to make up for this, their positions as state administrators must be taken into account in order to relieve the appointees of minor activities. Not attributing several administrative jobs to the same official will enable him to better fill the unique office conferred on him.

Knowing he has the solid backing of his board, a manager is also very independent with respect to the public authorities, partly because of the sterility of controls but especially by governmental wish. The sterility of controls results, in the first place, from a collusion between controllers and controlled. There again, corps and school solidarity comes into play. In a recent report, Griotteray wrote:[14]

> Agencies in the technical ministries, generally made up of engineers belonging to same corps as technicians in these enterprises, are hardly equipped for looking at the latter's suggestions with a critical eye. Not really capable of exercising their duties, they are gradually brought down with anemia.

The ineffectiveness of controls also results from their multiplicity since control undoes control, in some cases, from the need for secrecy and nearly always from the inadequate number of government inspectors. Controls are threefold. First is the trusteeship system: technical trusteeship by government commissions and financial trusteeship by state controllers and control missions, such as the interministerial commission on salaries and wages. Next is a system for the verification of accounts with accountancy commissioners and also with the Committee for the Verification of the Accounts of Public Enterprises. P. Bauchet writes:[15]

> Verifying the soundness of the management of 149 companies is a task that surpasses the possible for the 25 members of the Audit Office. Once admitted that this staff cannot possibly be enlarged on account of the corps' quality and prestige . . .

Finally comes parliamentary control which can lead to the setting up of nonpermanent committees of inquiry. Though usually lacking enforcement penalties, these controls nevertheless do not negligibly come to bear on daily administration.

In recent years, public authorities have strained to let managers have more freedom of action in policy making by going from a system of excessive control to a more contractual one. This change fulfills a wish that enterprises themselves expressed for a long time. For instance, in April 1958, the Federation of the Upper Staffs of the Electricity and Gas Corporations publicly declared that under the influence of the ministers and particularly of the Minister of Finance, these two companies had gradually lost the autonomy accorded by law:[16]

> The upper staffs which exercise powers of direction or delegated direction very intensely feel the consequences of the ambiguity in command. Partly deprived of their freedom of action and decision, frequently subjected to external interventions and solicitations, they fear they can no longer accomplish their mission. . . . Irresponsibility and stagnation threaten to

infiltrate every level of the hierarchy. . . . Interventions are becoming too frequent. They emanate from political figures and concern promotions or appointments.

On the outside, a number of experts were also speaking in favor of not burdening the public sector with too many constraints. Again, P. Bauchet:[17]

> The too forceful hold of public power, even if it assures fidelity to the public interest, turns against itself because it is too paralyzing. Enterprises engaged in the production process must be free to maneuver.

As early as 1954, the National Assembly slackened some controls. The author of this proposal, Gazier, a Socialist, declared himself firmly against a priori controls and for managerial responsibility. However, credit for restoring the autonomy necessary for good management falls to the Fifth Republic. An interministerial work group for examining management in public enterprises was set up in 1966 under the direction of S. Nora. Its report presented a series of suggestions.

Since the Nora Report, the ambiguous notion of "public service mission" has undergone profound revision. The principal mission of public enterprises is to satisfy their markets at the least cost to themselves and to the collectivity. The state's mission can, however, lead it to demand special services but under the double condition that the advantage thus procured for the national economy be greater than the costs accruing to the enterprise and that these obligations be the object of clear cost accounting.

The report clearly differentiates the competitive sector, such as Renault, Aerospacial, and the chemical companies, from the domain of public interest. The first amounts to being the "state's private enterprises." Directors are designated for long terms. They must manage their companies as do managers in the private sector. In particular, they must be able to fix salaries, wages, and especially prices. As for the "public interest enterprises," they fall under the principle of profitability not only for themselves but for the nation. Public authorities can utilize them toward cyclical ends, for example, by fixing prices below normal in order to fight inflation. Furthermore, public enterprises appear more and more like a preferred instrument for national economic policy because opening the frontiers has reduced the possibility of traditional forms of economic interventionism.

The Nora Report's proposals for reestablishing public enterprises on the field of competition led the government to take diverse measures aimed at giving managers more freedom in policy making. So the government and certain enterprises have agreed on "program" contracts. The government sets some objectives; the enterprise then commits itself to reach them. In return, the latter obtains the freedom of choosing the means. Thus was applied the Nora Report's suggestion that "each time it is possible, it is better for the state to have done than to do by itself." These program contracts favored the drawing up of progressive contracts between management and employees. External elbowroom was necessary in order to negotiate freely on the inside. Beforehand, the two parties had practised an irrealistic ritual. Discussion between worker representatives and managers-without-power (The latter's power was then in the hands of the Minister of Finance who hid himself from any face-to-face contact.) had only resulted in a kind of dupery.

Although movement toward autonomy is a reality, its scope must not be exaggerated. First of all, it is not the same in every enterprise. In some way, it remains limited by what has been described as a "regime of supervised liberty." There is a fundamental difference between the "public interest enterprises" and those in the competitive sector.

Among the "state's private enterprises," only Renault seems to benefit from real independence. One man, appointed by Ministerial Council decree, manages Renault. He fills the two positions of president and general manager. His responsibilities are comparable to those of a private corporation's PGM. He chooses the other principal directors. There are no state controllers around, perhaps because the need for secrecy is incompatible with the obligation to report to civil service bureaus. A 17-member board of directors assists him. For more than 25 years, the PGM and this board have never conflicted. Statutory autonomy is reinforced by the constantly affirmed will of the directors who, in order to keep their freedom, recall that they do not financially depend on the state. In 1954, Lefaucheux, then in charge at Renault, declared:[18]

> The state created us. It does not nourish us at all and we do not seek to live in its shadow. We consider state control to be the worst evil which could befall Renault.

In his turn, Dreyfus, who succeeded Lefaucheux, stated:[19]

The Minister of Industry chose a man in whom he has confidence, a man who, he thought, would effectively manage this national patrimony which has a very important role in the economy. But once having made his choice, the Minister must let this man be free. Lefaucheux understood things in that way, and he always succeeded in preserving his independence. I hope I will be able to do as much. . . . Renault is an enterprise belonging to the nation, but it is a free enterprise. I think that . . . Renault has oriented the policy of the public authorities rather than the opposite. I do not much believe in subordinating ties between nationalized enterprises and public powers, except in very special cases.

Renault's success is certainly related to the fact that responsibilities have not been scattered about but rather have been conferred on one man, chosen by the government for his strong personality and competence and appointed for a long period. In 26 years, only two PGMs have presided over Renault.

In his already cited study, A. Griotteray declared that public enterprises must no longer escape from political control and that, in particular,[20]

Parliament must play an important role since it represents the totality of citizens who, indirectly, are the proprietors of the public enterprises and because, each year within its budget, it votes considerable subsidies.

He stressed that by transforming a corporation like Havas into a holding company or by multiplying subsidiaries in foreign countries, as Renault has done, a public enterprise can spare itself many disturbing inquiries and can fully enjoy the advantages of its hybrid status which frees it both from shareholder curiosity and from civil service investigations.

3. PORTRAIT OF AN ELITE

How does someone become a director in a public corporation? No written rule lays down the conditions; however, in light of the careers of those appointed to such positions, I can sketch a portrait of the good candidate: (1) he comes from a major school *(les grandes écoles);* (2) he then enters one of the state's major administrative corps *(les grands corps);* (3) between the ages of 45 and 50, he reaches the summit of his civil service career by, for example, serving as assistant to a minister. He who decrees today will manage tomorrow. From the state's service he passes to the state's business. This career pattern seems firmly established.

The positions of director and especially president of the board have often been depicted as easy chairs or rest homes. True, some high officials are seated there at the end of a long civil service career; and some other men, parachuted—transferred from the outside without regard for procedure and promoted in the process—into esteemed and well-paid offices in return for faithful services. But these consecrations, recompenses, or compensations are less numerous than supposed. Although the public sector pays higher salaries than the senior civil service, thus serving as a means for promoting those who have arrived on the last rung of the civil service hierarchy too soon, these easy chairs are not as well padded as believed. Their holders exercise responsibilities.

While the public sector is not a rest home, the recruitment of its managers is quite closed. Whereas Italian public enterprises are "colonies" of certain political parties,[21] both the civil service and its major corps colonize the French public sector. Again we meet up with school/corps ties. A. Griotteray has commented on the similarity to a private game reserve:[22]

I am thus led to question the criteria for selecting members of general staffs in public enterprises. At present, too many managerial positions in these companies are considered as natural outlets for deserving high civil servants who are approaching the end of their careers or as private game-parks for the major corps or sections within the ministries. A rapid examination of the professional origins of the 44 presidents and general managers of the 20 principal national companies suffices to convince anyone of this. Governmental administrative staffs account for 30 of them. Out of these, 23 originate from what are commonly called the grand corps, 15 from administrative corps (10 from the Financial Inspectorate and 5 from the State Council) and 8 from technical corps (4 from Mines and 4 from Bridges and Highways).

Certainly no one can doubt the value and devotion of these highly placed public servants for whom passage via a managerial position within a public enterprise constitutes a necessary stage and often the ultimate one in a brilliant career. What is criticizable and worrisome is not the itinerary followed by So-and-so but rather the automation and regularity of the mechanisms which decide that if someone has not belonged to certain very narrow categories of governmental employees, if he has not occupied a precise position in a given branch of the Ministry of Finance, then he will not have access to jobs which, in any case, require an experience totally foreign to what he has acquired in the civil service. The paradox is that the strict application of these nonwritten rules places a judge at the head of French Radio and Television (ORTF), a diplomat in the presidency of the Mining and Chemical Company and a State Council member flanked by a prefect on the management of Havas. After all, this colonization of public enterprises by high civil servants is not limited to general managerial positions. Thus, there are no less than 15 former students of the National

School of Administration (ENA) who hold various positions in Elf-Erap; there are 14 at ORTF and 11 at Renault.

This purely administrative conception of career development, a conception not involving any rupture when transferring from the civil service into the public sector, consequently dilutes responsibilities and lessens the possibility of applying penalties. The general manager who has not succeeded can be removed then given the same position in another company and often under the same conditions as one whose management has brought good results.

I regret that other conceptions have not been retained and that appeals have not been made to political figures or to specialists from the private sector, depending on the situation. Certain corporations which manage monopolies and employ some tens of thousands of employees should be headed by persons who have the habit of treating business from a perspective larger than a strictly technical viewpoint. These could be, for example, state secretaries held responsible for public explanations before parliament. In still other cases, successful men from the private sector could be recruited and asked to bring their experiences to bear on the reorganization of a given enterprise or group of enterprises. This is the way the British government has again and again "enticed" the heads of private industrial groups. It has offered them interesting contracts in order to ask them to take in hand the coal mines or the railways. Such diversity would contrast with the present uniformity and would give new breath to the public sector which tends to inherit the indispositions and, all too soon, the paralysis of the civil service.

Since 1945, a threefold development has characterized the recruitment of managers for the public sector: first, a few major schools have laid claim to fiefs; second, the number of administrators has grown to the detriment of technicians; and third, among the latter is an increasing number of managers with a mixed education. If, overall, the public sector resembles a private game park, yet each school has tried to set up its own domain therein. Thus, railroads and electricity seem to belong more to Polytechnic than to the nation, because Polytechnicians find a comfortable setting for pursuing an easy career among alumni. Although the scientific educational establishments, such as Polytechnic, Central, Mines, Sup-Aero, and Sup-Elec, used to monopolize most managerial positions, administrators mainly from ENA have been entering the public sector for several years. This process is not proceeding without difficulty. Many technicians think that management of a public enterprise has to be a trade. H. Ziegler, former general manager of Air France, declared:[23]

Little difference as to the enterprise, the essential thing is to be of the trade. . . . I distrust the business schools which claim to be able to educate managers capable of succeeding in whatever sector.

Ziegler is the very example of a technician "of the trade." A graduate of Polytechnic and Sup-Aero, he was a pilot, then test pilot before World War II. Nevertheless, a mixed educational background characterizes a growing proportion of these managers. Nearly half of the two-thirds who have graduated from a scientific educational establishment have also received a juridico-administrative education.

Belonging to one of the state's major administrative corps also favors access to these managerial positions. If a man belongs to such a corps, he most often does nothing more than to pass on, just having the time to ensure himself with useful relationships. Hence, success for a member of the Financial Inspectorate is to quit the Inspectorate.

Has the base of recruitment widened? Debate on this point is certainly not over. Obviously, the selection of directors becomes more and more important as autonomy accrues. In Great Britain, where property was transferred to the public sector not so much in order to nationalize it but rather in order to put it in more competent hands, supervising the selection of directors has gotten more attention than supervising the directors themselves.

4. TYPES OF MANAGERS

Although recruitment proceeds along well-determined lines —school, corps, secretaryship in the ministries, or directorship on ministerial cabinets—appointments to a command post within a public enterprise takes on diverse meanings. Not all careers unfold in an identical manner. Even though appointment as director always contains a promotional quality, promotions do not always have the same finality. In any hierarchy, promotion can consecrate a competent subordinate or push aside a man who has pretentions to political functions that others do not wish to see him take on.

The directors of the public sector fall into three categories: (1) those who have made their careers within public enterprises; (2) those who are only passing by, for whom the public sector is a springboard, a testing ground, or a waiting room; and (3) those who end up there, that is, appointment as coronation. The cleavage between technicians and administrators comes in on top of these three. Two major species coexist: politicians who are the exceptions and civil servants who are the rule. The last cleavage seems to me to be the most significant.

There are few political figures among managers of the public sector because governments of the Fourth and Fifth Republics have seldom used these positions to place political friends. This is not a sign of probity but rather shows that such positions cannot be filled in any old way. Definite skills and qualifications are requisite. Appointment by kindness, when it occurs, is as president of the board rather than as director on the board. The latter has to be a technician. Such duties hardly allow public sector officials enough time to simultaneously participate in politics. The few politicians met up with most often alternate political activities with managerial responsibilities; they rarely combine the two. Also rare are those who managed public enterprises and then definitively quit the public sector in order to enter politics. Managers generally have their political experiences before coming into the public sector. Their political background serves as a springboard. Itineraries are quite diverse. Often, such a man has left a ministerial cabinet in order to finally receive a charge within the public sector.

Generally speaking, managerial positions in the public sector are either exits or waiting rooms for politicians. They are exits for those beaten in elections, evicted from the government, or disappointed by political events. Thus, Chenot, a former minister, transferred into the insurance field; and Grandval, former Minister of Labor, entered Maritime Shipping. They are waiting rooms for those who leave the public services to look for a political career and who, because of a reverse in circumstances or during the time until election year, quite naturally find that the public sector helps prepare a future. When Lelong, a member of the then Prime Minister Pompidou's cabinet, was beaten in the 1967 elections, he became president of a public enterprise until elected deputy the next year. So also for Papon, former prefect of policy in Paris: he was president of the corporation grouping together North and South Aviation until elected deputy. There are not so many politicians. Without a doubt, they will be even fewer in number as autonomy increases. Politicians placed by their parties were most numerous at the time of nationalization during the 1950s.

The majority of directors in the public sector come from the senior civil service. Their appointment is either a transition toward the private sector, a coronation, a springboard, or a testing ground. For those on their way toward the private sector, managerial positions in a nationalized company can serve as waiting rooms. But this does not happen often because men educated in the spirit of the public services feel like, and are felt to be, foreigners in the "private" world. More often, such positions are a hommage for services rendered. A man has attained the summit of his corps and takes over a managerial position until his near retirement. Hence, Benedetti, Prefect of the Seine, served as PGM of the National Coal Board for three years. Saltes, finance inspector and vice-president of the Bank of France, was president of National Credit for some time. Also, Lauré, income tax director, is director of Compagnie Generale. However, a coronation sometimes amounts to a sidetrack. For instance, Massé, quitting the Plan, took over the presidency of EDF for three years and was replaced by Delouvrier, former prefect of the Parisian region. The same for Bloch-Lainé who, after Savings and Deposit Association, entered Lyon Credit. For all these eminent personalities, the ends of their careers were in sight.

Entirely different is the situation of a cabinet member or an undersecretary in a ministry, aged thirty or forty, who enters the public sector. Here is the case of a real or imaginary springboard. Thus, Mayoux who left Debré's cabinet was put at the head of Agricultural Credit in 1963. Dupont-Fauville, cabinet director for Debré then in the Ministry of Finance, was appointed at the head of National Credit. So also, Saint-Geours changed from being the director of Financial Forecasting in the Ministry of Finance to hold the same position at Lyon Credit. Galichon, upon leaving General de Gaulle's cabinet, took over the presidency of Air France.

The public sector is also a means of making a career by displaying special abilities. It is often said that the fact of not being subject to the same economic imperatives as private companies, that is, maximization of profits, has slowed down the public sector's expansion. What is forgotten is that, partly freed from commercial concerns, a manager often finds a testing ground in public corporations where he can realize technocratic ambitions. These technocrats are usually very mobile.

5. CONCLUSION

Although often thought to be top civil servants, the directors of French public enterprises are not mere executives but literal decision makers. With respect to the public authorities and even through the latter's will, they have benefited from an autonomy which has not stopped growing during these last years. Because of the corps spirit already described, they enjoy a large freedom of action within their enterprises. Full-fledged bosses, these men hold, by the nature of things and even by reason of both the qualitative and quantitative importance of the economic spheres they control, an incontestable political power. Although the existence of this power is undoubtable, the means through which it is exercised are not well known.

This power is certainly not basically different from that of a major director in the private sector, but it probably reveals itself in a different way. The strong ties which bind the directors of public enterprises to the high civil service (from which they usually come) and the permanent contacts that they entertain with the government allow privileged channels through which to exercise their political power. But saying more than this is difficult. Their action is assuredly less "public" than that of directors in the private sector. If they make up a distinct category in the country's high administration, they nevertheless respect certain requirements of neutrality and discretion. They seldom appear in consultative bodies, rarely in clubs. Only exceptionally do they become involved in politics.

NOTES

1. Moreover, these estimates include only nonfinancial institutions. Because of this, they need to be raised by about 20%.

2. Simon Nora, "Rapport sur les entreprises publiques," in La Documentation Française (April 1967), p. 13.

3. See Bardou, Brachet, Levy, and Naville, L'Etat entrepreneur (Paris: Anthropos, 1971).

4. See Jean-Luc Bodiguel, La réduction du temps de travail, enjeu de la lutte sociale (Editions Ouvrières, 1969).

5. Maurice Bokanowski during the debate on the 1963 budget in the National Assembly, Journal Officiel: Débats (An, Jan. 10, 1963), p. 422.

6. For a detailed account, see Philippe Pondaven, "Les organes dirigeants des Entreprises Publiques," Revue Française de l'Energie 20, no. 212 (June 1969): 420-431.

7. Georges Vedel during the Law Faculties' Second Colloquy (Dalloz, 1956), p. 166.

8. A. G. Delion confirms this judgment. According to him, appointment constitutes the essential control: power over acts is meaningless if the directors are not competent, superfluous if they fulfill their duties. See Berger Levrault, Le statut des entreprises publiques (1963).

9. The number of ministries varies from six at Renault to two at Basin Colleries.

10. See A. Delion, L'Etat et les entreprises publiques (Sirey, 1959).

11. Pierre Bauchet, Propriété publique et planification (Cujas, 1962), p. 262.

12. Ibid., p. 266.

13. A. Delion, op. cit., p. 159.

14. A. Griotteray during the National Assembly's first ordinary session, 1971-72, "Rapport sur les entreprises nationales" (Document no. 2010), p. 13.

15. P. Bauchet, op. cit., p. 309.
16. See Le Parisien, April 3, 1958.
17. P. Bauchet, op. cit.
18. Le Monde, March 10, 1954.
19. *La grande entreprise et l'économie moderne* (Paris: Les Echos), quoted by J. Bodiguel, op. cit., p. 90.
20. A. Griotteray, op. cit.
21. J. Meynaud, "Les catégories dirigeante en Italie," Revue Française de Science Politique 14, no. 4 (Aug. 1964): 639-674.
22. A. Griotteray, op. cit., pp. 14-15.
23. Entreprise, March 22, 1969.

DANIEL DERIVRY is attaché de recherche, Centre National de la Recherche Scientifique (Paris), and lecturer at Descartes University.

9

The Ordinary and Special Bureaucracies in Italy

STEFANO PASSIGLI

1. THE POLITICAL CONTEXT

Whether conceived in broad or narrow terms, the political role of a bureaucracy can be defined by three main factors: (1) the systemic environment, that is, the structural features of the political system and the attitudes of other actors vis-à-vis the bureaucracy; (2) the attitudes of the bureaucratic elite; and (3) the nature of demands made on the political system. Thus, any attempt to assess the political role of the Italian bureaucracy first calls for a brief comment on the overall functioning of the Italian political system.

The standard assessment depicts the Italian polity as a system of polarized politics. According to this view, an alienated and irreconcilable opposition confronts a center coalition weakened by internal dissent reflecting traditional cleavages in a country still searching for integration. This assessment also holds that, because the opposition is antisystem, it offers no possible government alternative.[1] Although no clear consensus exists among scholars about whether the trend of the system is centrifugal or centripetal, the opposition certainly holds significant power. Most agree that the outcome of this unhealthy relationship between government and opposition is a distorted and excessively prolonged policy making process which results in inadequate output.[2]

More recently, some scholars have challenged this established view. They argue that the main opposition party (the PCI), far from being alienated and antisystem, has in reality filled a positive role by integrating into the parliamentary system some significant fringe

[226]

groups which would otherwise have turned to more militant tactics.[3] This description might represent an extreme view of the opposition's functional role; however, one could plausibly argue that if a system characterized by such great polarization and conflict has not broken down entirely, but on the contrary shows some encouraging signs of depolarization,[4] then some compensatory mechanisms must be at work. By providing the opposition with an actual and significant role in legislation, Parliament may serve as a meaningful arena for reconciliation.[5] Local politics, with its flexible coalitions, offers a similar example, as does the labor movement where the present drive toward unity testifies to yet another breaking down of the rigid barriers between the democratic center majority and the opposition.[6] Whether or not these developments point toward a healthier political system remains debatable.

Whatever the differences of interpretation, no one would deny that the main feature of the political system is still its inadequacy in responding to societal needs. Output falls pitifully short of demands. While unfortunately true in many areas (housing, health care, education, transportation, etc.), this state of affairs has come about because of the absence of a legislative answer to growing demands. But, the absence of major legislation does not, by itself, prove the absence of any policy making. Indeed, a close look at how the Italian polity works will discern two quite distinct policy areas. The first includes fields already covered by legislation, where innovation calls for additional laws. The decisional impasse arising out of the party system blocks this area. On the other hand, there is a second area where bureaucratic organizations not dependent on legislative action regularly make important, even vital, decisions. The first area devoid of significant output includes social services where most political demands focus. The second area covers economic policy, in particular public enterprises, where major decisions deeply affecting the allocation of national resources are made. So while the Italian system shows a marked tendency toward legislative inaction bordering on paralysis, it also evidences a high degree of bureaucratic activism, especially in matters of governmental intervention in the economy.

Lest this assertion seem too radical, I will substantiate it with a few examples. Spurred by an accelerated process of industrialization and economic development, Italian society underwent in the fifties and sixties rapid demographic and cultural changes, epitomized by the massive transfer of working population from the primary to the secondary sector of the economy and the consequent extensive internal migration both from the countryside to the cities and from the South to the North. These changes have, in turn, caused deep structural problems such as severe shortages in housing and urban social services, and a total disruption of the precarious financial conditions of local governments. In addition, the disappearance of the extended family, typical of a traditional agricultural society, has increased the need for new welfare and social security legislation.

While these changes have been gaining momentum, legislation aimed at coping with consequent structural problems has lingered for years in Parliament. Political conflict has not been the only reason for this inability to produce much needed output in social services. Whereas excessive conflict did occur in some cases (e.g., educational reform and housing legislation), in yet others, lack of adequate financial resources was a primary consideration (as in the case of all proposals for raising pensions), or played an important role along with political disputes (as in projects for a national health care system). Even though output has been lacking in social services, public enterprises have tapped huge financial resources and made decisions about direct economic investments, as in the case of the postwar decision to proceed with the reconstruction and expansion of IRI's steel interests (The Instituto di Riconstruzione Industriale now accounts for almost 60% of the country's production) or in the case of the creation of Ente Nazionale Idrocarburi (ENI). Later examples include the building, as part of the IRI empire, of a vast network of highways, perhaps unparalleled throughout Western Europe in terms of the percentage of GNP absorbed; or the progressive move of ENI from its original monopoly over oil and natural gas drilling into petrochemicals, and above all its later attempt to gain control of Montedison (Italy's largest chemical concern and second largest corporation), the controlling interest of which is now shared fifty-fifty between private and public shareholders.

Whereas output paralysis and a relative scarcity of resources for social investments have undoubtably characterized the decisional area managed by the elective political elite and the civil service, aggressive activism and the availability of vast resources for direct economic investments have been the rule in the decisional area presided over by bureaucratic elites in public enterprises.

These two phenomena might not be unrelated. First of all, capital investment by public enterprises has fostered much of the Italian "economic miracle" of the fifties. Second, this rapid economic development has caused many of the structural problems the country now faces. Hence, some observers assert that by choosing to direct financial resources to special agencies in charge of the public sector or by leaving these agencies free to meet their needs by syphoning funds off the financial market—funds that could otherwise, through taxation or more simply through direct Treasury indebtedness, have been put to use on structural problems—Italian political elites were indeed choosing (or not preventing) a certain pattern of economic development and decision making. The alternative between economic development and social services is a classical dilemma. As in Italy, resolving it has traditionally been in favor of initial economic investment in directly productive areas. What might be surprising is the peculiarity seen in this country where two parts of the political and even of the bureaucratic elites have been in charge of different decisional areas, and where the expansion of the public sector seems to have arisen more out of the impasse in one decisional area than out of an open positive choice made by all the elites concerned.

2. THE SPECIAL ADMINISTRATION

Different bureaucratic organizations represent these two decisional areas. Next to the "ordinary administration" (i.e., the established ministries which perform the traditional functions of government and are subject to all the controls and detailed procedures of continental administrative law), a group of special agencies have grown up in recent decades. Primarily engaged in a variety of economic functions, these agencies are substantially freer in procedure and scope of action. This "special administration" began to develop in the early thirties under Fascism.[7] It responded to the new economic demands that the industrial crisis and the progressive collapse of the banking system placed upon the government.[8] After the war, it continued growing when new agencies, such as the Fund for the South and ENI, joined already existing institutions like IRI and Instituto Mobiliare Italiano (IMI). These additional agencies undertook the ever more pressing task of fostering economic development, particularly in the South.

How much economic development is still in the hands of these special agencies becomes evident in view that the entire public sector is basically under the control of three financial holdings, two of which are ENI and IRI; that IMI and Mediobanca raise much of the long-term capital needs of both public and private industry; that a host of other agencies play vital roles in securing adequate financing for ventures in least developed areas. Some simple figures very clearly illustrate the situation. Whereas the total earmarked for investments in the 1973 National Budget was just over 2,500 billion lire, ENI alone spent—in 1971—469 billion lire on new fixed investments alone. For its part, during the same period, IRI spend 393 billion lire on fixed investments. Most of this sum was raised through the issuance of bonds, whose total amount stood at 537 billion lire at the end of 1972. IRI's operating subsidiaries spent additional amounts also financed through bonds. Obviously, these sums greatly exceed budget allocations to the ordinary bureaucracy for investment expenditures. Moreover, these loans have come about through widespread reliance on long-term indebtedness.[9] Do not overlook the magnitude of this phenomenon. The global amount of bonds in issue at the end of August 1972 exceeded 42,000 billion lire, of which Treasury indebtedness accounted for approximately one-third and public expenditures for well over 60%.[10] Given that the Italian GNP for the same year stood at 68,000 billion lire, this indebtedness could easily be considered one of the most salient features of the Italian economy and one of the most interesting developments in the Italian administrative system. Someone could argue that, in the course of the past decade, significant readjustments have taken place in the formulation of economic policy with the focus shifting farther and farther from traditional economic minis- tries to special agencies. Because he who pays the piper picks the tune, the substantial financial independence of public enterprises has considerably strengthened their role at the expense of planning organizations and the Ministry of the Budget.[11] Only the Treasury and Bank of Italy, in their functions as supreme arbiters of monetary policy, form an effective counterpart for planning both the alloca- tion of national financial resources and the overall lines of economic policy.[12] Although not all agencies in the special administration deal with economic affairs, this administration tends to be closely identified with economic policy making.

3. COMPARISON OF THE TWO BUREAUCRACIES

The main differentiation between the ordinary and special administrations does not stem from their functional roles but rests rather on some important structural and attitudinal features which emerge clearly upon closer comparison. The most important difference consists in structural and procedural factors. The very origin of the special bureaucracy and the nature of its tasks have necessitated that it be free from most of the limitations that bind the traditional administrative system. For instance, some of the classical controls, such as those exercised by the Court of Accounts, do not apply to some agencies in the special administration because their subsidiaries are legally set up in the form of corporations and thus fall under private law.[13] On the other hand, the slow procedures and formalistic requirements of nineteenth-century administrative law, where the concept of administrative responsibility reduces to accountability rather than responsiveness, encumber the ordinary administration. Whereas the special administration can be free and timely in its interventions,[14] the structure of the institutional system slows down the ordinary administration.

The institutional statuses of the ordinary and special administrations are perhaps their single most important difference, but other important ones occur at the bureaucratic level. Very few studies have been made about bureaucratic elites, except for a few on the ordinary civil servant[15] and some biographies, usually of exceptional figures in the special administration.[16] Even on the basis of this scant information, differences are impressive. Many features common to all classical, Weberian bureaucracies characterize the ordinary administration: entry through competitive examination; promotion on the basis of merit and seniority (but essentially the latter); tenure of office; and so on. In addition, the Italian ordinary bureaucracy displays some traits all its own. Most of its staff come from the South[17] and hold degrees in law or related fields. Career advancement is very slow so that they reach top positions at an advanced age.[18] Finally, not only is lateral entry practically unknown and mobility to and from private employment extremely limited, but also no transfers take place between different branches within the administration.[19] As for attitudes, available research indicates that top civil servants, though aware and resentful of their declining social status, lack achievement orientation and feel alienated from politics and politicians.[20]

No attitudinal study nor, for that matter, adequate sociological data exist on bureaucrats in the special administration. From a cursory review of what is available, the opposite may be true on practically all accounts.[21] No particular geographical pattern is discernible in their recruitment; their average age, much lower; their educational backgrounds, much more varied with scientific and economic degrees making up the majority. Also, advancement is by merit, whatever the criterion for judging it; and lateral entry is quite frequent, if not the rule. Mobility rates are high, especially from one public enterprise to another. As for attitudes, because of the total absence of any data, I can only suggest that top bureaucrats are achievement-oriented and more closely resemble members of the elective political elite than do their counterparts in the ordinary administration.

This last point deserves further comment. On the basis of his penetrating research on the attitudes of British, German, and Italian top civil servants, R. Putnam has formulated two models, the classical bureaucrat and the political bureaucrat.[22] Italian bureaucrats in the ordinary administration typify the first. The second model seems to fit the special administration, if the only choice is between these two models. However, other models are conceivable. For instance, the "technocrat," hinted at by Putnam, would be definitely problem-oriented and would not hold procedure in high esteem—unlike the classical bureaucrat.[23] Unlike the political bureaucrat, he would believe in technical objectivity, the possibility of finding "best" solutions and the bureaucracy's duty to actively search for them. He would be an activist who tends to believe in administrative neutrality provided that it not be defined as readiness to cooperate with any legitimate government. He would replace the classical definition by one stressing the bureaucracy's right to remain autonomous in its judgments and stay above political conflict. As a result, he would regard elective political elites with ambivalence: on the one hand, with diffidence and superiority as he considers them to be unprepared persons who can disrupt his work; on the other, with envy and inferiority because he recognizes that they alone often have the power to realize his plans. Out of this psychological predicament arises, in extreme cases, the temptation to bypass the elective elite and seek formal power directly or more commonly to escape from any political control. As this happens more and more often in many Italian special agencies, I would advance the proposition that the "technocratic" model best fits the special administration.

4. POLITICAL ROLES

Let me sum up comparisons by resorting to the three criteria initially selected for judging the bureaucracy's political role. In Italy, the special administration undoubtably plays a more important role than does the ordinary bureaucracy in bringing about whatever outputs the system produces. It is structurally privileged, since its procedures leave it freer to operate and more independent in setting goals and raising the necessary financial means for achieving them without getting trapped in the decisional impasse of the party system. Attitudewise, it is prone toward activism and intervention. What is more important, the other actors expect it to be so. In short, the Weberian ethos does not apply to it and no one expects it to. Finally, this administration mostly deals with one problem, economic development, which is the least controversial of all even though specific policies might not be. So, a relatively young, well-trained, and problem-oriented bureaucracy presides over the state's economic activities.

In contrast, a second bureaucracy, old and formalistic, lacks modern technical skills, is entangled in its own procedures, doubts its own efficacy, and vainly attempts to fill in for the defects of the party system. It desperately tries to correct many structural problems, such as migration, housing, health care, education, and transportation, which the very efforts of the special administration to promote economic growth have helped bring about. Lacking a political elite capable of arbitrating effectively between the two bureaucracies and of regulating the pace of economic expansion in order to reconcile it with the societal changes thus rendered necessary, Italian society has seen its structural imbalances and shortcomings worsen. Turning again to the political role of the Italian bureaucracy, one is forced to recognize, at least *prima facie,* a simple dichotomy: in terms of policy output, one bureaucracy is highly effective whereas the other is definitely ineffective.

But is policy output the only criterion by which to judge a bureaucracy's political role? From the point of view of the wider systematic functions that a bureaucracy can undertake, even the performance of the special administration is not satisfactory. None of the many other crucial functions expected of a bureaucracy is adequately carried out. The special administration fails, for instance, to provide an effective means for recruitment of a political elite. If anything, the flow of personnel is the other way around, from politics into lucrative top jobs in certain special agencies.[24] Nor does the special administration significantly foster social integration. Indeed, it has actually contributed to dissatisfaction and social conflict because, being a major source of economic and social changes, it has consequently raised the need for outputs and helped create the conditions for increased conflict. Although present changes might contribute to national integration in the long run, they have, at present, underscored all the latent conflicts in Italian society.

Moreover, the Italian special administration is not a significant arena for political reconciliation, at least in the sense of providing a subsystem where national politics is progressively depolarized and where majority and opposition are not permanently confined to uncompromising roles.

Finally, even from the angle of policy making, the special administration's performance might seem less than impressive. When one's attention shifts from output to the entire policy making process, he will see that the special administration does not provide an adequate channel for the transmission of political demands. In other words, the input phase is wanting. Impressive as outputs may be, many critics do not consider them to be related to real needs. Whatever the substantive merits of their argument, the potential role of the special administration is considerably jeopardized as a consequence. In a system where the prevailing sense of legitimacy still prizes responsiveness to political demands, and where the need for recruiting an effective political elite remains critical, the failure to perform these two crucial functions severely limits the overall political role of the special administration.

In conclusion, while those institutions traditionally invested with legitimacy have failed to provide a much needed response to the growing needs of Italian society, those noted for their output capacity—even though only in economic matters—have equally failed to perform some crucial functions. Consequently, neither can fill a larger political role. The paradox is thus reached of a system where legitimacy and output capacity rarely occur together. This damages not only political efficacy but also, in the long run, the system's capacity to survive without major changes in the present relationships between subsystems.

NOTES

1. See J. LaPalombara, *Interest Groups in Italian Politics* (Princeton: Princeton Univ. Press, 1964); by the same author, "Italy: Fragmentation, Isolation and Alienation," in *Political Culture and Political Development,* edited by L. W. Pye and S. Verba (Princeton: Princeton Univ. Press, 1965); G. Sartori, "European Political Parties: The Case of Polarized Pluralism," in *Political Parties and Political Development,* edited by J. LaPalombara and M. Weiner (Princeton: Princeton Univ. Press, 1966); S. H. Barnes, "Opposition on Left, Right and Center," in *Political Oppositions in Western Democracies,* edited by R. A. Dahl (New Haven: Yale Univ. Press, 1966); and D. Germino and S. Passigli, *The Government and Politics of Contemporary Italy* (New York: Harper and Row, 1967), pp. 127-132.

2. G. Galli, *Il bipartitismo imperfetto* (Bologna: Il Mulino, 1966).

3. S. G. Tarrow, *Peasant Communism in Southern Italy* (New Haven: Yale Univ. Press, 1967); G. Galli, *Il difficile governo* (Bologna: Il Mulino, 1972).

4. See, for instance, the results of recent research on the attitudes of Italian MPs: R. D. Putnam, *The Belief of Politicians* (New Haven: Yale Univ. Press, 1973).

5. F. Cazzola, "Consenso e opposizione nel Parlamento italiano: Il ruolo del PCI dalla I alla IV legislatura," Rivista Italiana di Scienza Politica, no. 1 (1972): 71-96; A. Predieri, "Aspetti del processo legislativo in Italia" in *Studi in memoria di Carlo Esposito* (Padova: Cedam, 1970) and more extensively in *Il processo legislativo nel Parlamento italiano* (Milano: Giuffré, forthcoming).

6. No comprehensive study of local politics has yet appeared. On the labor movement and its progressive independence from the party system, see A. Pizzorno, "I sindacati nel sistema politico italiano," Rivista Trimestrale di Diritoo Pubblico 25 (1971); G. Baglioni, *Sindacalismo e Protesta Operaia* (Milano: Franco Angeli, 1973).

7. In reality, special agencies had begun developing well before Fascism as one of the innovations in Giolitti's cabinets around the turn of the century. Early examples include the creation of a monopoly over life insurance and the adoption of special provisions in favor of Naples which paved the way for later forms of economic intervention. However, most special institutions did arise under Fascism. The best account in English of the growth of the special administration is M. Posner's and S. Woolf's *Italian Public Enterprises* (London: G. Duckworth, 1967). In Italian, see the works of S. Cassese: *Partecipazioni pubbliche ed enti di gestione* (Milano: Communità, 1962) and "Aspetti di storia delle instituzioni" in the second volume of *Lo sviluppo economico in Italia,* edited by G. Fuà (Milano: Franco Angeli, 1969).

8. For the impact of the economic crisis on the rise of the special administration, see F. Forte, "Le imprese pubbliche in Italia dalla prima guerra mondiale al 1957" (Milano: CIRIEC, 1957), mimeographed. The author convincingly argues that resorting to special agencies was due to the collapse of the industrial and banking systems more than to the ideology of the Fascist regime.

9. Four or five agencies account for over half of the total amount of outstanding bonds. The fact that approximately 44% of these are subscribed to by the banking system shows the degree to which public enterprises have drained savings accounts.

10. According to *Data cumulativi di 655 società italiane 1968-1972* (Milano: Mediobanca, 1973), the private sector does not account for more than 1%, or at the very most 2%, of outstanding bonds.

11. Worth noting is that the relatively new Ministry of Public Enterprises has seldom been able to perform its assigned role of promoting coordination in the public sector. Indeed, often this Ministry has not even succeeded in avoiding open warfare among competing agencies, as in the case of the showdown between ENI, IHI, and the Montedison management over control of the latter.

12. In view that the banking system subscribes 44% of all bonds and that the Treasury holds a predominant position in the Comitato per il Credito e il Risparmio, it is easy to see how the Treasury and Bank of Italy can be the only effective counterparts to public enterprises. Quite understandably, they are the actual focus of governmental policy making in the economic sphere.

13. The Court of Accounts has tried to step up its controls. In its periodic reports to Parliament, the Court has often denounced specific wrongdoings or lamented its lack of power to pursue investigations further. The fact that the Court's actions have remained *vox clamantis in deserto* clearly indicates the unwillingness of the elective political elite to modify the special administration's role. Whether this also indicates the real attitudes of the political vis-à-vis the special administration or only signals the latter's power and financial connections with the party system is a different question. It is common knowledge that some of the major agencies have played an important role in financing certain major parties. On the more recent behavior of the Court, see D. Serrani, "Il risveglio della Corte dei Conti," *Politica del Diritto*, vol. 1 (1970), pp. 269-283.

14. This is not always so. Whenever the special agencies must interact with the ordinary administration, the ills of the latter spread to the former. Cf. G. Pescatore, *L'intervento straordinario nel Mezzogiorno d'Italia* (Milano: Giuffré, 1962).

15. The main works are: F. Demarchi, *L'ideologia del funzionario* (Milano: Giuffré, 1969); L. Cappelletti, *Burocrazia e società* (Milano: Giuffré, 1968); and the collective volume *Il burocrate di fronte alla burocrazia* (Milano: Giuffré, 1969).

16. Typical of these journalistic but sometimes useful accounts is P. Frankel's *Mattei: Oil and Power Politics* (London: Faber and Faber, 1966).

17. P. Ammassari, "L'estrazione sociale dei funzionari dello Stato e degli enti locali," in *Il burocrate di fronte alla burocrazia* (Milano: Giuffré, 1969). See also A. Spreafico, *L'amministrazione e il cittadino* (Milano: Communità, 1965), pp. 150-155; A. Taradel, "La burocrazia italiana: provenienza e collocazione dei direttori generali," Tempi Moderni 6, no. 12 (1963): 9-18.

18. Concerning gerontocracy in the high civil service, see: L. Cappelletti, "Burocrazia, potere politico e programmazione," Tempi Moderni 6, no. 12 (1963); F. Garzoni Dell'Orto "I funzionari e la carriera," in *Il burocrate di fronte alla burocrazia* (Milano: Giuffré, 1969); and R. D. Putnam's chapter in the present volume.

19. Only during three periods of Italian history, and then only in some ministries such as the Interior and Foreign Affairs, was lateral entry at all significant: the 1860s, the years following the advent of Fascism, and the years immediately after World War II. In short, lateral entry has been thought of only as a political remedy of ensuring loyalty in crucial times of change. For some data on lateral entry in the prefectoral corps, see R. Fried, *The Italian Prefects* (New Haven: Yale Univ. Press, 1963).

20. F. Demarchi, op. cit.

21. My seminar on public administration held at the University of Florence in 1972-73 attempted to systematically review available information. Much to my surprise, many influential figures in the special administration did not even appear in the pages of the various *Who's Who*s. The general theme of the seminar and its conclusions are in F. Rizzi, *Il ruolo politico della burocrazia italiana* (Firenze: Cooperativa Libraria, 1973). This book provides a comprehensive summary of developments in the Italian administrative system.

22. Cf. R. D. Putnam, chapter 3 in the present volume.

23. These three models do not exhaust all possibilities. What about, for instance, bureaucrats in a one-party system where bureaucracy becomes so intertwined with the totalitarian or hegemonic party and so imbued with ideology (be it nationalism or other) but is often so deprived of technical skills? Is not a fourth model necessary for the "bureaucrat in arms" who, as guardian of ideological orthodoxy, always formulates policy alternatives for the advancement of his cause, alternatives that are in harmony with directives coming from the party or charismatic leader? Do the bureaucracies of so many

new nations, still deeply oriented toward tribalism or clientelism, not necessitate additional models?

24. This is especially true of influential politicians who have failed to gain reelection. In general, transfers from the civil service into the special administration are rare, as rare as the interchange between the civil service and politics. A top civil service position does not serve as a passport into a political career. Finally, *pantouflage*–transfer from the civil service into private industry–has been rare so far.

STEFANO PASSIGLI, who is professor of political science at the University of Florence, is the author of *L'Analisi della Politica* and *Emigrazione e Comportamento Politico* and co-author of *The Government and Politics of Contemporary Italy.*

10

The Political Influence of Senior Civil Servants in Switzerland

ROLAND RUFFIEUX

The Swiss civil service, compared to those in neighboring countries, has evolved in a converging manner. Having started from a very different base, it has, by adding modern traits to its primitive character, thus giving it a highly composite structure, ended up with a similar status.[1] Indeed, when examining the bureaucratic phenomenon in the Swiss public sector, do not forget that the federal state appeared quite late and that its development by no means suppressed the more or less advanced cantonal and communal administrations. Much to the contrary, the development of the federal bureaucracy provoked a considerable extension, sometimes a modernization, of cantonal and communal offices.[2] Still more, the vigor of democratic feelings imposes a rather nonhierarchical organization at all levels of public administration. Switzerland has experienced neither Prussian bureaucratic castes nor French grands corps. A sense of equality amply permeates everything concerning the recruitment, status, and promotion of civil servants. This results in an identification, in the broadest sense of the word, between the citizen and government employee because of the phenomenon, frequent in Switzerland, of "plurality of roles" which tends to somewhat mask the importance of the bureaucratic milieu.

In fact, the democratic aspect of public administration is much less evident when analysis of its political role is approached solely from the angle of relationships with other partners in the political

AUTHOR'S NOTE: I thank Dr. R. Germann who helped me gather the necessary information for this paper.

game. From 1848 to 1891, the widely representative character of the Swiss political regime combined with the Radical Party's monopoly on the central government gave a clearly partisan tint to the federal administration, which thus incurred the hostility of Catholic and Socialist minorities. The 1918 introduction of proportional representation for National Council elections did not immediately bring about proportionalization of the government. This permitted limiting for a still longer period the access of minority party supporters to posts in the senior civil service.[3]

Nevertheless, the latter's evolution toward political pluralism was accelerated by other causes. The extension of popular rights at the end of the nineteenth century, with the introduction of the constitutional initiative and the legislative referendum, had, among other goals, that of combatting the bureaucracy's influence by submitting its powers to sovereign control. On the other hand, the custom of consulting economic and social circles when drafting an important law,[4] a custom introduced at the beginning of the federal state, put the administration in contact with competing elites.

Thus, applying the term "mandarins" to Swiss civil servants is possible with certain qualifications. In consideration of the disciplined character of the Swiss people, for whom the state of law merits respect, Max Weber's definition of bureaucratic domination applies to the high administration of our country. Not provided with any particular social status, higher-up employees nevertheless benefit from the respect which public opinion has for rules and "that which is written."[5] The increasing intervention of the Confederation in every domain of social life, by the practice of subsidies jointly made with the cantons and communes and by the systematic attribution of competence in all new matters to the federal government, has considerably augmented the power of the civil service. But the latter has not stopped exercising its powers jointly with economic and political circles and, last but not least, the people. The result is that the senior civil service has real political power at its disposal but that the methods by which it exercises this power are peculiar.

1. MAJOR CHARACTERISTICS OF THE SENIOR CIVIL SERVICE

In a study published in 1925, F. Fleiner characterized the Swiss political system then in force by recourse to the paired concepts of bureaucratic/popular state *(Beamtenstaat/Volksstaat)*. Accordingly, the cantons belong to the second category where administrative duties are, to a large degree, assumed voluntarily, officeholders rebecoming ordinary citizens at the expiration of their mandates. On the contrary, the Confederation appeared to him to be an attenuated form of the bureaucratic state. Appointed by the executive power and not elected by the people, its officials are officials by profession and their mandates generally extend until retirement age.[6] This distinction is hardly valid any more. The difference between the administrations of the federal government and of the heavily industrialized, hence rich, cantons is, above all, of a quantitative order.[7] The popular state system with its quasi honorary offices does not subsist any longer except in the small, economically backward cantons and in small communes.

If the federal high administration meets the general criteria of a modern bureaucratic state with respect to the requirements posed from the point of view of its structure and level of competence, it significantly deviates from these criteria when looked at from the angles of recruitment and influence. The country's federalist structure causes this deviation. The major characteristics of the present Swiss senior civil service, the product of a shorter historical evolution than in the case of the large European nations, result from certain given facts: the absence of a privileged social status, conformity to the rules of proportional representation, and employment stability.

ABSENCE OF A PRIVILEGED STATUS

From 1848 on, Switzerland began imitating the United States in the field of administrative recruitment as in many others. Holding a large majority in both houses of the Federal Assembly plus all seats on the Federal Council, the Radical Party openly practiced the spoils system. Even if it is impossible to evaluate the certainly quite small number of senior officials between 1848 and 1945 who had no declared party affiliations, I can affirm with assurance that no Conservative/Catholic before 1919 and no Socialist before 1945 ever entered the federal high administration. This exclusivity corresponded to the ruling party's claim that it was imposing a government whose values were identified with the Radical platform: progressive centralization, standardization of law, secularism hardly tolerant of confessional pluralism, respect for free enterprise, and self-realization of the individual by enlarging his personal rights.

However, the slow growth of the federal high administration, explained by the Confederation's modest financial resources and the cantons' will to limit the weight of this superstructure, brought about a major consequence: high offices continued to be held by notables whose social level and means of livelihood were above average. This situation was particularly evident in the Diplomatic Service where old families belonging to the aristocracy or the business bourgeoisie monopolized posts because they were familiar with international relations through the Foreign Service, exterior commerce, and commercial banks.[8] Similarly, the political class of those cantons ruled by the Radical Party furnished most recruits in other administrative branches through a kind of osmosis between public cantonal magistratures and the federal high administration.

CONFORMITY TO PROPORTIONAL REPRESENTATION

The absence of a privileged social status, perceptible before all else in the lack of a definite educational background among senior staff members, has facilitated the progressive proportionalization of the federal civil service. The social sequels of both World Wars and the Depression considerably accelerated this process. The "decolonization" of federal departments and major public administrative systems was undertaken at the expense of the Radical Party and to the profit of minority parties, the Socialists coming in last. This occurred more slowly in upper than subaltern ranks where all kinds of minorities had already been admitted since the nineteenth century.

The 1927 Civil Service Statute did not directly approach the problem of representation of linguistic, confessional, and political minorities. Such a development has resulted from practical considerations. Under pressure from disadvantaged groups, the federal government has become sensitive to arguments demanding a more just redistribution of higher offices, as well as to the interest it has in giving a chance to worthy candidates not belonging to any party. The Federal Council's directives on this subject have brought about a relatively satisfactory situation in the public services, especially from the viewpoint of linguistic groups.[9]

Religious confession is another domain where proportional representation is applied in the federal civil service, so much the more since, for a long time, Catholics have rightly believed that they did not have equal opportunity. This accusation is no longer true for the federal administration as a whole where they represent 42% for a contingent of 41% in the resident population. But this advantage gradually disappears nearer the center of power: their share is no more than 16% in the central administration, that is, the actual ministries in the capital as opposed to field offices.[10]. As for the Jews, to take another confessional minority as example, they have not, so to speak, entered the higher heavens of public administration.

The even more obvious discrimination toward the feminine sex is certainly tied to the tardy concession of voting rights to women (1971). Whereas they represented 29% of the country's active population in 1960, their proportion in the federal administration was only 14%, with marked preference for the under-30 age group which naturally fills the lower positions.

Spoils system practices have disappeared with the loss, in 1919, of the absolute majority held by the Radical Party and because of the adoption, in 1927, of a civil service statute guaranteeing freedom of opinion and employment stability. But traces of former domination by the "Grand Old Party" still exist as do traces of its colonization of several major public corporations. Conversely, other sectors carry the marks of efforts made by Catholic and trade-union groups hoping to break this monopoly.

Admitted that, for the most part, political proportionalization is rather high, its exact measure within the senior service is difficult to assess. The attribution of a political tendency to a senior employee relies on criteria of very unequal value: affiliation with particular political formations, sympathies acknowledged in a more or less discreet manner, but also the simple "color" assigned by his origins or past activities. A French Swiss periodical of Socialist inspiration has published statistics based on some 80 high federal appointees. These statistics give rise to estimates shown in Table 1.[11]

TABLE 1

	Percent of the Total	
Parties	Positions	Seats in the 1967 National Council
Radical	35	25.5
Christian-Social-Conservative	20	24
Peasants, Artisans, and Burghers	5	11
Liberal	2.5	3
Socialist	2.5	26.5
Remainder	35 (unknown)	10 (other parties)

This still incomplete proportionalism in the administrative sector is, quite obviously, only one consequence among others of a much more general tendency. The introduction of proportional representation into parliament's National Council,[12] the Swiss equivalent of the U.S. House of Representatives, after a long struggle which had challenged the very essence of the representative regime installed in 1848, has brought about a proportionalization of the Federal Executive, progressively realized between 1919 and 1959, and even of the Supreme Judiciary. The most complex proportionalization was introduced during the Federal Chancellory's reorganization in 1968. The former chancellor, assisted by a vice-chancellor without any definite power, has been replaced by a "troika" with well-assigned tasks: a German Swiss Conservative chancellor, a Socialist vice-chancellor from a linguistically mixed canton, and a francophone Radical vice-chancellor. Expansion of translation services met Ticino Region demands. We can ask if the "fourth power's" evolution has not favored the advent of a "partitarian" state while simultaneously enfeebling older forms of opposition.

EMPLOYMENT STABILITY

The attenuation of political struggles, formerly involving—especially in the cantons—practices originating in the spoils system, and the development of administrative law have resulted in guaranteeing employment stability to senior as well as to other civil servants. At the beginning of this century, Swiss jurists did not yet agree on the status of the federal public services. For some, this relationship was an ordinary contract under private law analogous to contracts existing between employer and employee in the industrial sector; but others considered it to be a mixed system containing elements of public law. Shortly after World War I, the Federal Tribunal's jurisprudence was modified so as to entirely place this category of worker relations under public law.

The adoption in 1927 of a statute concerning federal employees confirmed this new orientation; however, directors fall only partially under this law because special regulations defining their functions, particularly in commercial establishments and public corporations, also govern their positions. Nevertheless, high officials have indisputably profited from these guarantees. Although work schedules are also imperative for senior employees, employment stability has been assured so that they now have every chance of terminating their careers in the service of the Confederation—if they do not voluntarily quit or seriously fail to fulfill their duties.

For a long time, careers progressed along several well-determined lines.[13] For lack of having imposed an education specialized in terms of definite responsibilities, as in France or Germany, three main lines give access into high public offices: legal adviser to the administration, engineer or administrative technician, and career civil servant. Entry is achieved along these three lines, generally at a low level of the high administration after completion of university studies or before the age of thirty. Step by step, careers progress through a series of promotions dispensed in accordance with merit as well as seniority.

The legal adviser's career is typical in traditional departments; it represents the bureaucratic mentality defined by Max Weber. The administrative engineer and, more recently, the pure scientist recruited as such compel recognition in numerous branches within the Departments of Interior and of Energy and Communications, likewise in large public enterprises. To the number of officials whose careers have followed special paths, we can add professional military officers who make double progress, within the military hierarchy and on the administrative ladder with frequent passages from one to the other, and diplomats who also advance by passing from the central government to foreign posts and vice versa.

2. THE HIGH ADMINISTRATION'S POLITICAL INFLUENCE

In every industrial country, some general factors inherent in contemporary political developments determine the influence of high officials within their domains. On the one hand is increasing state control and the complexity of its tasks. On the other, we have to reckon with administrative directors' often-unavowed-but-real pre-occupation with contributing to policy formulation just as effectively as the leaders of the executive power and of parliament. In Switzerland, these general tendencies run through classical institutional channels and even more through recent developments in the political system which appreciably diverge from the constitutional model on certain important points.

The civil service's role in ordinary legislative processes is long-standing. However, the development of consultative procedures and of a generalized recourse to experts have given it much greater weight than during the nineteenth century. In the second place, the significance of the initiative and referendum,[14] originally conceived in order to optimize popular participation, has altered so as to have become a complex decision-making mechanism where the civil service intervenes with powerful methods, thereby lending support to the thesis of a technocratic peril. Finally, dependent on the first two, the third aspect—the service's self-will to forge the country's political future in accordance with its own vision of democracy—poses the problem of bureaucracy as the defender of public interests.

IN ORDINARY LEGISLATION AND MANAGEMENT

Every year, the Swiss Federal Administration prepares legislative texts, the budget, and the traditional management report. In this complex process, the civil service plays a determinate role; and high officials can amply exercise their powers of initiative, arbitration, and even decision-making concerning the arrangements for applying policies in fields allotted to them.

The priming of the preparliamentary, also called administrative, phase of a legislative bill can be undertaken in many ways.[15] The impulse most often comes from the outside: popular initiatives, petitions from citizens or associations, and especially, parliamentary motions—certain of which are inspired by administrative bureaus thanks to relationships existing between parliamentarians and senior officials. When it comes to bills that the administration has made up its mind to propose, senior officials play an even more influential role in drafting them, setting deadlines, and orienting their content. For this reason numerous drafts enter the legislative circuit, each under the name of the divisional head responsible for its elaboration.[16]

This means that every senior official worthy of his title sets himself a program to be realized in order to mark his passage to the head of the administrative branch devolved on him. In virtue of a new constitutional principle adopted by the people, these officials are sometimes chosen to carry out the remaking of laws on organization or on the infliction of penalties. Perceptible since the 1968 reform of the Federal Chancellory, recent trends toward the planning of legislative work limit the individual freedom of action of high administrative officials. But, the coordination thus accruing within each department gives them, in return, a collective influence because the Federal Council's directives are prepared within staff councils where, consequently, division heads collect around the responsible federal councillors. What the senior civil servant has lost in personal influence at his divisional level, he largely regains in the form of collective responsibility on the departmental level.

The role of high officials is not less important in the work of committees charged with examining administration proposals. Although the Federal Council appoints the experts—representatives of the cantons, of various interests, of science—in order to form these ad hoc committees, the very delicate process of the selection of persons to serve falls on these very same senior civil servants, in accordance with the 1950 directives concerning consultation with associations and designation of committee members. At this point, the professional origins, personal relations, or political affiliations of high officials can orient the choice, even if strict enough criteria are set up for balancing various groups, regions, languages, and religions. These officials naturally try to compose their request so as not to imperil the conception they have of the project to be studied. In case unforeseen resistances pop up, the high administration can incline the Federal Council, the Executive Branch of the government in Switzerland, toward delaying outside consultation, limiting such consultation, or even reshuffling the committee.[17]

On the working level, the relationships between high civil servants and the "political cabinets" which often make up these ad hoc committees are even more complicated. As a general rule, the experts do not hesitate to propose far-reaching modifications of the draft prepared beforehand and defended in their presence by the civil service. This confrontation takes place behind closed doors, a procedure giving rise to criticism. Consultation is often enlarged by appeal to other administrative requests or by recourse to one or another of the more than two hundred permanent specialized committees at the Federal Council's disposal and on which the high administration has seats. If no agreement is reached, it is up to the Federal Council to clinch the matter. Admittably, it does not do so without having heard the advice of the divisional chief(s) concerned.

Oral consultation allows senior employees to exercise their influence to the full. As for written consultation, it produces a mass of advice which the administration tallies up in order to produce an overall picture. As this is not a matter of simple recapitulation, the high administration can again bring up contested issues although arbitration is reserved for departmental heads. This very delicate phase, which oils the way for passing from consultation to decision-making, has given rise to numerous criticisms of administrative power which is thought to be too discretionary.

High officials are reproached for practicing the politics of calculated risk by preparing a bill so as to satisfy as many people as possible, to clear the parliamentary cape, and finally, to avoid the sand bar of the referendum. Although we cannot speak of a lobbyist dictatorship, the civil service apparently avoids running afoul of them, just as it refuses to brave political parties and public opinion, neither of which are very affectionate in case of failure. Senior officials play an important part in negotiating compromises, a major characteristic of the present Swiss political system.

The high administration is responsible for the recent change concerning giving information on the consultative phase. Formerly, a blackout was imposed as a result of an ethic of responsibility without the need for immediate justification. A desire to improve the civil service's public relations has effected a noticeable change. The high administration now strains to inform the public about its intentions and about the state of bills in progress but without going so far as to reveal the content of received advice.[18]

While the consultative procedure remains largely marked by its empiricism, the phase immediately preceding the Federal Council's decisions was regulated in 1914 by a law on organization which established interdepartmental cooperation. Since 1968, some directives have imperatively determined consultation by relation to the problems posed. The Ministry of Finances must be consulted on a proposed measure's financial effects; the Personnel Office, about augmenting personnel; the Justice Division, on bills modifying legislation or the Constitution; the Secretariat of the Federal Department of Foreign Policy, on questions of international law or foreign policy; the Central Administration, on questions of organization if the administrative structure must be modified. These are, of course, minimal requirements since a bill or even one of its articles might be submitted for appraisal to fifteen or so divisions.[19] This means that internal consultation proceeds in accordance with a hierarchy existing within the administration itself and that senior officials have very unequal holds on the elaboration of general policy. Divergences are resolved by special appeal to the Internal Conciliation Conference.

At the level of actual management, the role of high officials is not less obvious. Besides directing public corporations and large governmental offices, certain of which, such as the military, include thousands of persons, the high administration has decisive responsibility in the management of current affairs. Its monopoly is more evident in matters of internal than of external policy. To be aware of this, all we need do is analyze the activities of the Federal Office for Arts and Crafts, Industry and Labor, and those of agencies concerned with international economic organizations. In the latter, we witness a form of quasi institutionalized cooperation between the senior civil service and the business world. Indeed, almost every two weeks, the Permanent Economic Delegation (Ständige Wirtschaftsdelegation) meets. It is made up of high civil servants from qualified branches of the federal service, as well as representatives from *Vorort,* the Swiss Farmers' Union, the Swiss Trade-Union Congress, and the Swiss Union of Arts and Crafts. In this domain where the Confederation has kept the habit of close collaboration with economic circles, whether in matters of statistics or in actual diplomatic activity through the formation of mixed delegations, senior public officials undertake action jointly with the leaders of economic lobby groups. A handling of public affairs, rather different from habitual ways, results. This can give rise to resistance within the Federal Assembly or even within public opinion.[20]

IN SWISS SEMIDIRECT DEMOCRACY

An exhaustive analysis of the role of senior civil servants in drafting major laws should be made by beginning with case studies, so great is personal influence on this process as seen when a bill opposes an initiative or when recourse to the referendum brings unexpected results. Historical literature, abundant enough on the question of referendums at the turn of the century, barely stresses the role of the high administration. A more "excavated" analysis of several major sequences of referendums between the two wars—adhesion to the League of Nations, introduction of proportional representation, the draft of a monopoly on cereals, tentatives toward a law on old-age and survivers' insurance—has permitted bringing to light the very great diversity of the high administration's methods of influence, especially when the process extends over several years, thus giving it time to maneuver.[21]

The civil service's intervention in our semidirect democracy's processes rather largely depends upon circumstances proper to each case, as well as the personality of the senior official(s) most directly concerned. Although a stricter regulation of consultative procedures has recently limited the senior civil service's margin for political maneuvering, its influence remains important in the parliamentary phase and during popular campaigns. With respect to work in the houses of the Federal Assembly, what is worthy of note is that senior servants in office are subject to rules on incompatibilities and that access to the Assembly is possible only for the middle level staffs of federal corporations and for certain members of cantonal administrations, such as prefects. The civil service's influence at this stage remains indirect and very limited; however, the impact of economic and social circles represented in the Assembly tends to increase, to judge by the number of elected members who also have seats on boards of directors. In 1968, 83% of the Federal Assembly's members held at least one such position, against 69% in 1944 and 58% in 1920. The average varies according to the party.[22]

As to high officials' influence during popular ballotting, it also tends to follow the recent evolution which places campaigns less under the sign of direct means—rallies, oral propaganda by personal contact—than in the orbit of the mass media. For the time being, the mass media favor elections over initiatives and referendums, hence limited the channels through which the upper administration can have its arguments passed to the public at decisive moments. A special aspect of this question resides in what has been called "citizen's information by the authorities." In federal matters, the Houses have, on several occasions, been beset by proposals suggesting that bills submitted to the people be accompanied by an explanatory text drawn up by the authorities. After a trial effort in 1950 which confirmed that the senior civil service, which had certainly prepared the commentary, and the Federal Council could not avoid lapsing into official propaganda, the revision of the 1874 popular ballotting law was abandoned. As it then became apparent that informing the public principally fell upon political parties and the press, what was suggested was to multiply the number of press conferences and to make better known the authorities' viewpoint and the content of parliamentary debates. The fear of unwarantable meddling by the civil service in public opinion won out.[23]

3. CONCLUSION

Experiences up to now have shown that possibilities for control over senior officials, although increased, still remain too weak because of the Federal Council's political composition. This laxity also comes from the fact that the Federal Assembly is still a parliament made up of "militia troops" from different political parties. At the very most, public opinion is now more sensitive to the possible connections between the Federal Council and the business world.[24] This awareness may incline the government to be even more cautious in certain activities. Any reason for hoping that high officials remain the defenders of public interests is to be sought within the human dimension of their civic comportment. They must often be so under difficult circumstances because the magnitude of powers delegated to "economic and social partners" risks causing the civil service to "disperse itself into a series of guild-like fiefs."[25] Given the actual state of things, if the Confederation's senior servants appear to be mandarins of a political system undergoing complete mutation, the reason for this is that they have the responsibility—in the absence of clearly defined norms—of finding a conception of public interest which satisfies the requirements of a democracy and of a postindustrial society. More than ever, their duties toward the state merge with their duties as citizens.[26]

NOTES

1. H. Nawiaski, "Die grossen Entwicklungslinien des Personalwesens in der Schweiz," in *Das Personalwesen der öffentlichen Verwaltung* (Veröffentlichungen der Schweizerischen Verwaltungskurse, Bd. XIX, Einsiedeln, 1958), p. 19.

2. Most studies of the Swiss Civil Service take into account federal, cantonal, and communal levels all at the same time. In particular, see: C. Friedrich and T. Cole, *Responsible Bureaucracy: A Study of the Swiss Civil Service* (Cambridge, 1932); O. Leimgruber, "L'administration suisse," Revue administrative (May-June 1948); the 90th session organized by the Institut suisse de cours administratifs, *Le Personnel des administrations publiques* (Montreux, 1956).

3. For the political periods of the federal state's first century of existence, see E. Gruner, *Die Parteien in der Schweiz* (Bern, 1969), pp. 49-55.

4. Cf. L. Neidhart, *Plebiszit und Pluralitäre Demokratie* (Bern, 1970).

5. In addition to Max Weber's views on the "traditional" ideal type, I would like to point out A. Köttgen's analysis, *Das deutsche Berufsbeamtentum und die parlamentarische Domokratie* (Berlin, 1928).

6. F. Fleiner, "Beamtenstaat und Volksstaat," in *Ausgewählte Schriften und Reden* (Zurich, 1941).

7. This is the reason that, from the viewpoint of administrative development, hardly any qualitative difference exists between the federal civil service and the administration of a large canton, such as Zurich whose population is near a million.

8. *Neue Zürcher Zeitung*, (Dec. 3, 1967).

9. For data on linguistic proportionalism, see: "Eidgenössiches Personalamt" in

Personalerhebung (Tabelle 40, 1965); U. Klöti, "Die Chefbeamten der Schweizerischen Bundesverwaltung–Ein Forschungsbericht," Annuaire suisse de science politique 11 (1971).

The latter is the first exhaustive study of the senior civil service in Switzerland; the author's complete results were published in a book under the same title (Bern, Francke, 1972).

10. The Catholic magazine Civitas (no. 3/4) investigated this phenomenon in 1968.

11. Domaine Public, no. 35 (1965).

12. For some years now, the State Council (roughly equivalent to the U.S. Senate) whose manner of election is left to the cantons, has also been the object of demands for augmenting the number of Socialists in it. At present, they hold only three of the forty-four seats.

13. U. Klöti, op. cit.: pp. 121-131.

14. Two means of linking the legislative process to the electorate. The initiative is a proposal coming up from the grass roots into parliament for discussion. The referendum is the converse, that is, the passing down of a proposal from parliament to the voters for approval or rejection.

15. Cf. W. Buser, "Le rôle de l'administration et des groupes dans le processus de décision en Suisse," Annuaire suisse de science politique 9 (1969): 121-135.

16. A bill enters the popular phase with the designation *lex* accompanied by the name of the federal councillor who defended it in the Assembly. This accounts for certain resignations after failure at the polls.

17. W. Buser (op. cit., p. 123) correctly points out that these reshufflings generally result in expansions, although the civil service is wary of committees so large as to risk paralyzing their activity.

18. See F. Hummler, "Les 'public relations' des autorités," *Informations de la Banque populaire suisse*, no. 43 (1963); W. Buser, op. cit., pp. 131-132.

19. Cf. W. Buser, op. cit., p. 134.

20. Cf. D. Sidjanski, "Les groupes de pression et la politique étrangère de la Suisse," Annuaire suisse de science politique 6 (1966): 36-44.

21. R. Ruffieux, with the collaboration of R. Natsch, H. Mesmer, and A. Lasserre, presents a detailed study of these four cases in *La démocratie référendaire en Suisse dans l'entre-deux guerres: Die Schweizerische Referendumsdemokratie zwischen den beiden Weltkriegen*, vol. 1 (Fribourg, 1971).

22. Cf. E. Gruner et al., *L'assemblée fédérale suisse 1920-68: Die Schweizerische Bundesversammlung 1920-68* (Bern, 1970), pp. 50-60.

23. Cf. J. Castella, "L'exercice du droit de vote," Rapports et Communications de la Société suisse des juristes 93, no. 4 (1959): 609a-612a.

24. Such awareness was particularly manifested in July 1970 when Schaffner, who had just quit his post as head of the Public Economy Department, had to refuse the presidency of the board of directors of Brown Boveri Company, Inc., one of the most important firms in Swiss industrial exportation.

25. Meynaud, *Les organisations professionnelles en Suisse* (Lausanne, 1963), p. 313.

26. See A. Muggli, "Bürger und Verwaltung," Landwirtschaftliches Jahrbuch der Schweiz 1 (1955): 20-23; and W. Von Greyerz, *Verwaltung und Oeffentlichkeit* (Magglingen, 1957).

Term of achievement: July 1971.

ROLAND RUFFIEUX is professor of contemporary history, University of Fribourg, and of political science at the University of Lausanne. He is the author of *La Suisse entre les deux guerres* and *La démocratie référendaire en Suisse*.

11

Top Civil Servants and the
National Budget in Norway

JOHN HIGLEY
KARL ERIK BROFOSS
KNUT GROHOLT

1. *The civil service elite*

2. *The civil service elite in the elite system*

3. *The national budget: a case study in civil service influence*

4. *Implications for elite theory*

A major theme in writing on civil service elites is the competition, tension, and conflict that allegedly characterize their relations with other elite groups, especially political elites. The general image is of encroachment by one elite on the sphere of the other, an image most often picturing politicians as slowly losing out. In this as in many other areas of political analysis, the emphasis is on imbalance, dysfunction, conflict. Little attention is paid to the more peaceful and harmonious aspects of relations between civil servants and politicians. Analysts of politics tend to be less interested in political stability, how groups with different and conflicting interests and positions actually cooperate fairly well over reasonably long periods of time.

These comments are appropriate to an examination of the relation between civil service and political elites in postwar Norway, for there are numerous indications that this relation has been characterized more by cooperation and a mutually satisfactory division of labor than by conflict and encroachment on one another's domain. When asked in 1969 by two of the present authors to name sets of groups between which there occurs the largest conflict of interests in Norway, only 1 of 41 members of the political elite and none of 22 civil service elite persons singled out conflicts between themselves. Another question asked the same respondents to comment specifically on the extent of conflict between civil servants and politicians in Norway. In their responses, 13 of the civil servants and 14 of the political leaders denied the existence of conflicts, while another 7 of the former and 15 of the latter said that what conflicts do exist are merely natural and expected products of the two groups' division of labor. Only 2 civil service and 11 political leaders exhibited less complacency and satisfaction by asserting that there is real conflict between the groups, although less than a handful thought this a really worrisome problem. That extant dissatisfaction and conflict are not thought to be very serious by either group was further demonstrated by responses to a request to characterize current relations between the civil service and the government. All who responded in the civil service elite and all but 2 in the political elite characterized existing relations as either excellent or satisfactory.

These data indicate that the persons who lead the civil service and political sectors of Norwegian society perceive little mutual antagonism. The behavior of top-ranking civil servants and political leaders further supports this description. During the postwar period political harrassment of the civil service in the form of parliamentary or special investigatory bodies aimed at uncovering bureaucratic blunders and inefficiences have, with the single exception of an investigation into a coal mine disaster in the state-owned King's Bay Co. in 1963, been conspicuous by their absence. Again with the single exception of a dispute over policies governing the military back in 1949, there have been no resignations-in-protest by influential and visible civil servants. Likewise, sabotaging political programs and policies through such tried and true techniques as the strategic leaking of plans and secrets to the press by discontented civil servants is virtually unknown.[1] In short, while there is in Norway as elsewhere considerable rhetoric about the "struggle" between civil service technocrats and politicians in modern society, there is not much attitudinal or behavioral evidence to suggest that those presumably most involved in this struggle are much discontented with the current state of affairs. Indeed, the evidence we have been able to uncover points to the opposite conclusion: by and large members of the civil service and political elites maintain a system of interaction that is mutually satisfactory and devoid of substantial rivalries and tensions.

Why is this so? In sociological terms, what is it about the structure of power and interaction between civil service and political elites that has produced this era of good feelings? How stable and institutionalized is this structure, and what are the underlying trends? Further, what propositions of theoretical significance does the Norwegian situation illustrate? We will attempt to answer these and related questions first by combining biographical and interview data to describe structural aspects of the interaction between civil service and other elites. Second, we will describe some of the dynamics in this interaction by summarizing a detailed study of the decision-making process leading to the formulation of the national budget for 1970. Third, we will reflect briefly on how the Norwegian case might be generalized in terms of elite theory.

1. THE CIVIL SERVICE ELITE

The core of the Norwegian state apparatus today are the 14 departments and Prime Minister's Office which make up the Central Administration. Each of these units has a political leadership consisting of the cabinet minister and his undersecretary. All other persons below this thin layer of politicians, however, are civil servants.[2] In 1970 there were 2,212 of them located in 77 Divisions which in turn contained 231 Offices. The critical positions in the departments are those of Department Counsel, the highest-ranking civil servant in each department, and the Division Chiefs immediately below the Counsel. Both Department Counsels and Division Chiefs report directly to the cabinet minister and his undersecretary. Below these 89 persons the chain of command in the Central Administration follows standard principles of bureaucratic hierarchy. In addition, a number of civil servants equivalent in importance to Department Counsels and Division Chiefs are located in the numerous independent and semi-independent state agencies which flank the Central Administration.

Insofar as one wishes to speak of a civil service elite, then, it consists of those persons occupying the two uppermost types of positions, Department Counsel and Division Chief and their equivalents, in the numerous departments and agencies comprising the state apparatus. We identified 135 such persons located in the Central Administration and in ten independent and semi-independent agencies plus the four largest state-owned industrial units. To find out about the social composition of this elite, two of the present authors coded virtually all available biographical material for them as of 1967. These materials proved to be uniform for 109 of the 135, and it is on this segment of the elite that the following analysis centers. In addition, the authors interviewed 22 of these 109 civil servants in 1969 at the same time they interviewed 112 members of other principal Norwegian elites.[3] The analysis in the remainder of this and the following section combines these biographical and interview data.

It has been a common research finding that in spite of efforts to ensure equality of opportunity in the recruitment and promotion of civil servants, in Western societies those who occupy the highest civil service positions tend to be quite unrepresentative of the populations over which they preside. By classifying the occupational and organizational positions held by 104 fathers of the 109 civil servants studied, we found that the Norwegian civil service elite does not differ greatly from civil service elites in other countries in this regard. Thus 12% of the civil service elite in 1967 had fathers who themselves occupied one or another national elite position. Another 62% were offspring of fathers clearly located in the upper middle class and holding select, but probably not elite positions in the legal, military, academic, and civil service professions, as well as in political, business, and shipping units of some importance. Listings in Who's Who? and participation in various cultural and service organizations suggested that many of these fathers probably belonged to local elites, and within the boundaries of such localities their sons presumably enjoyed privileged status. Thus only about a quarter of the elite originated in middle and lower status categories, the last-named category, in which paternal occupational titles were "worker," "farmer," "fisherman," "sailor," and so on, producing but 10% of the elite. These data indicate that for top echelons in the civil service the substantial efforts toward equalization of opportunity which Norway made under a thirty-year span of social democratic governments had by 1967 resulted in nothing like an elite recruited from a cross-section of the society.

As in other Western societies, high educational attainment is virtually a precondition for careers leading to elite status in the Norwegian civil service. Thus it is no surprise that, with 93% of its members holding university degrees, the civil service elite is the best educated of the several major elites.[4] Traditionally, lawyers have been the dominant professional group in the civil service. Throughout the second half of the nineteenth century they enjoyed a near monopoly of positions, and as late as 1914, 86% of higher civil servants in the Central Administration were lawyers (Hovden, 1969). Since then, however, and particularly since World War II, other professionals, especially economists, have entered the state administration in growing numbers. Thus the proportion of lawyers among all newly recruited civil servants declined from 60% before 1945 to 48% in the period 1957-1965. Meanwhile, the proportion of economists among new recruits increased from 6 to 10% during the same period (Donjem, 1969). This change in the balance of professional types was even more marked in the higher echelons. Among Office Heads and still more senior personnel, the proportion of lawyers declined from 72 to 38% and that of economists increased from 5 to 29% (Donjem, 1969). Similarly, our data for 1967 show that at the elite level the proportion of lawyers decreases with decreasing age while that of economists increases with decreasing age. Thus 71% of the elite who were 61 years or older in 1967 were lawyers while this was true of 38% of those under 50 years. Conversely, 3% of the elderly group were economists, while 31% of the younger group were. These differences indicate that, while law remains the classical administrative education, economics has been established firmly as the modern administrative education.

This postwar accession of economists to top civil service positions probably enhanced cooperation between the political and civil service elites. In large measure the economists have been oriented toward macro-economic planning. Consequently, they have tended to favor an expansion of the state sector and its ability to control the economy, a disposition that has placed many of them on the left in the political spectrum. The centrality and political preferences of these civil servants meant, in turn, that the governing Labor Party's programs were probably more sympathetically received and implemented than they would have been had the civil service elite continued to consist almost entirely of lawyers. Indeed, the suspicion of excessive ideological compatibility between some top civil servants and the Labor Party underlay the efforts of the bourgeois coalition government which took power in 1965 to broaden and strengthen political control of the civil service.

An analysis of careers leading to elite status in the civil service reveals that professionalism is a hallmark of this elite. Eighty-four percent of the elite had by 1967 spent more than two-thirds of their work lives in the state apparatus, and only 9% spent less than half their work lives there. The modal career of a member of the civil service elite in 1967 began with his graduation from the University of Oslo Faculty of Law in 1933 at the age of 24. He then spent three years in the typical apprentice positions for law graduates such as deputy judge, deputy attorney, or assistant lawyer in a private firm before entering the state apparatus as a secretary. There followed gradual advancement in the bureaucratic hierarchy, during which there was one transfer of departments or agencies, until elite status was achieved 20 years later at the age of 48. Thus by 1967 the typical member of the elite had spent the last four-fifths of his work life in the civil service, the last 10 years of which were at the elite level. This modal career describes almost exactly the actual careers of 35 of the 109 persons studied. But this number jumps to 59 if the 24 persons who spent no time in apprentice positions but spent their entire work lives in the civil service are added. Thus the wholly professional core of the elite consists of more than half its members.

By mixing positions in the state apparatus with positions elsewhere, the remaining 50 careers studied deviated in some degree from the modal professional one. Of greatest interest here are the frequent indications of a more general public sector career type that interlocks with the strictly professional civil service career. Thus 18 of the persons who joined the civil service after substantial outside careers came from the public sector (the judiciary, politics, other public institutions, education, an international organization), and 24 of those who left the civil service for interim positions elsewhere went to other areas of the public sector. It appears that the boundary between the civil service narrowly defined and the larger public sector is relatively permeable in Norway, while the boundary with the strictly private sector is crossed much less frequently. One can thus speak of an elite composed largely of professional civil servants and professional *public* servants, the latter appearing with sufficient frequency to permit speculation about the existence of a kind of "state elite" that has jurisdiction over the entire spectrum of official functions in the society.

This career linkage between the state apparatus and the larger public sector probably lends added attraction to civil service careers, for they are seen to offer many more possibilities than the proverbial bureaucratic long crawl. The prospective civil servant is able more plausibly to anticipate playing a considerable role in the making of broad choices between directions the society will follow in a large number of diverse positions. Moreover, this aspect of civil service careers should be viewed in the context of postwar labor market conditions governing recruitment to elite positions in the society as a whole. In large measure the labor market for top positions favored the seller. Rapid postwar expansion created a surplus of top positions and a shortage of persons qualified formally to fill them (Torgersen, 1967). This meant that, to attract and retain qualified personnel in top civil service positions, the "servant" aspects of such positions had to be played down while giving to able recruits considerable latitude for mobility, choice, and influence. The postwar seller's market, in short, contributed to an expansion in the scope of careers based in the civil service concomitant with the expansion of the civil service elite's power position vis-à-vis other elites.

2. THE CIVIL SERVICE ELITE IN THE ELITE SYSTEM

We have said that the economic situation and developmental needs of Norway after the last war facilitated a restoration of higher civil servants to a position of considerable prestige and influence, but there are few indications that this seriously jeopardized top civil servants' relations with the political and other elites in the society. Support for this assertion can be found in data describing the interaction that occurs between the civil service elite and these other elites. To anticipate these data, they indicate a differentiated elite structure characterized by relatively limited interaction that occurs for the most part within institutionally defined channels. The civil service elite is clearly an important component in this structure, although the data by no means show it to be dominant. In general, it enjoys good access to each of the other elites without being inextricably meshed with any of them.

To take this last point first, we can begin by asking about the occurrence of positional interchange between the civil service and other elites. Frequent movements from elite positions in one sector to similar positions in another negate the notion of a structure consisting of elites differentiated from each other by function and specialized in terms of value and instrumental norms (Keller, 1963; Porter, 1965). Frequent interchange is more consistent with the notion of a power elite in which the group cohesion of the powerful is manifested, in part, by the ease and frequency with which they trade positions across sectors (Mills, 1956; Bottomore, 1963).

When we looked for positional interchange in the careers of 649 members of the Norwegian business, labor union, political, and civil service elites, we found that only 27 or 4% of these persons had held positions in elites other than the one in which they were located in 1967.[5] All four elites experienced some loss of members to other elites, and all but the labor union elite recruited members from other elites. The civil service elite most frequently supplied recruits to other elites (10 persons), while the political elite ranked second (7 persons) in this regard. In fact, traffic between these two elites alone accounts for 41% of the elite interchanges identified. Thus 3 persons moved from elite positions in the civil service to elite positions in politics, while 7 persons traveled in the opposite direction. But 4 of the 7 persons who went from the political to the civil service elite were in fact merely returning home: they had been recruited originally from subelite positions in the civil service to elite positions in politics. In reality, then, 7 of the 10 persons involved in interchanges between the political and civil service elites were professional civil servants, the only variation among them being the point in their civil service careers at which they were recruited for a stint in politics. To complete this picture, the 3 persons recruited from elite positions in the civil service to elite positions in politics eventually returned to their civil service positions as well.

A separate examination of careers leading to membership in the political elite turned up additional instances in which persons were recruited from subelite positions in the civil service to elite positions in politics without as yet having returned to elite positions in the civil service. Thus 45 persons occupied cabinet positions in the four governments constituted during the period 1960-1967. Four of these cabinet ministers had held positions previously as Chief of Bureau in the civil service. Similarly, 7 of the 27 persons who were appointed undersecretary between 1960 and 1967 came from subelite positions in the civil service. Altogether, 15 of the 72 persons who held top government positions in Norway during this period were recruited from the civil service, and 13 of them returned to the civil service after serving in political office.

In individual cases this process of interchange between the two elites entails virtually shuttling back and forth between the two sectors as governments come and go or as persons are needed in one area or another. What we may infer is that in a minority of cases the distinction between the civil service and political elites is as much a matter of political convenience and fortune as of formal institutional autonomy. As we noted earlier, for a number of persons, political and civil service careers merge in such a way as to suggest the existence of a "state elite" whose members spend their working lives in the public sector.

Nevertheless, our data show that, for the large majority of top civil servants, interaction with the political and other elites occurs in the institutionally defined channels and networks surrounding their particular positions. In other words, our data give relatively few indications of interaction between top civil servants and other elites more inclusive than those arising from and necessary to the performance of occupational roles. Two sets of data indicate this limited aspect of the civil service elite's interaction with other elites.

The first of these is data on the extent to which leaders of the civil service are also active leaders of the voluntary cultural, charitable, educational, humanitarian, sport, and other associations which crowd any map of social structure. Usually cognate to primary elite positions, leadership positions in voluntary associations comprise networks in which those who are influential in the occupational world interact more informally, often while wielding influence in the general processes of nonelite opinion formation. Examination of biographical materials for the civil service elite reveals quite modest participation in such networks, however. Only 14% of the civil servants studied occupied national posts in such associations during the period 1960-1967. This compares with similar incumbencies by 41% of the political elite, 16% of the business elite, and 8% of the labor union elite.[6]

A second indication that interaction between top civil servants and other elites is restricted largely to institutional contexts can be found in responses to our request of 17 of the 22 civil servants we interviewed to name the leaders of other elite sectors with whom they interact most often. Although responses were sometimes incomplete with respect to one or another sector, these respondents designated 87 members of the political, business, and labor union elites as frequent interaction partners. To begin with, 13 of the respondents named 55 politicians with whom they interact. These politicians were named a total of 85 times. An analysis of their positions shows that civil service interaction with politicians is limited largely to government members, first and foremost to the political leaders of the respondent's own department. Thus 28 of the 55 politicians named held government positions during the 1960s, 23 as cabinet ministers and 5 as undersecretaries. Moreover, these 28 government members captured 54 of the 85 designations our respondents gave. Twenty-five of the remaining 27 politicians named were members of parliament. But these parliamentarians hardly comprised a cross-section of that body: 6 of them were parliamentary party leaders, 3 sat in the parliament's key president and vice-president positions, and 14 more were either chairmen, vice-chairmen, or secretaries in one of parliament's 13 standing committees. Only 2 belonged to the parliamentary rank and file. Thus our data show that top civil servants interact most frequently with the more prominent and high-ranking members of the political elite, but primarily along departmental lines. Interaction is most frequent with their immeidate political bosses, a pattern that accords with the formal structure of political and administrative authority. Insofar as they interact with parliamentary representatives, the latter tend to be the leaders who schedule and control parliament's processing of matters in the preparation of which civil servants have been active.

Regarding interaction with the business elite, only 8 of our respondents named 36 business leaders a total of 43 times, thereby indicating less frequent interaction with this elite. All the business leaders named were pominent in their elite, 9 of them occupying full-time executive positions in the largest business interest organizations. Five others were or had recently been the elected presidents of these organizations. The explicit task of these leaders is to represent the interests of the business sector in negotiations with the state. Likewise, the remaining 22 businessmen named were leaders of major companies who with few exceptions were active in branch organizations and in various consultative bodies bridging the private and public sectors. As with the political elite, then, the civil service elite's interaction with the business elite follows expectable institutional lines. Those formally delegated to represent business interests to the state are most often those who civil servants name as interaction partners.

Interaction between top civil servants and the labor union elite is even more limited. Thus 11 of our respondents named but 9 union leaders a total of 23 times. Six of these leaders sat at the top of the central administration in the Federation of Trade Unions and accounted for 20 of the 23 designations. The 3 remaining leaders were trade union presidents, two of whose unions organize public employees.

These two sets of data describe a pattern of interaction centering on the institutional location and tasks of top civil servants. Yet, there are also indications that this institutionally oriented interaction is patterned so as to make the civil service elite a linchpin in the national elite structure. Two additional sets of data support this assessment.

The first pertains to the role of the civil service elite in Norway's pervasive system of government-appointed consultative committees, boards, and councils. In 1970 there existed slightly more than 1,000 such bodies to which some 6,000 persons had been appointed (Hallenstvedt and Hoven, 1971: 1). Sitting in 679 of these bodies were representatives of 240 of the approximately 1,000 voluntary associations and interest groups having national scope. About a third of these representatives came from the Federation of Trade Unions and its constituent unions, while another third were from the employers' associations and other large business organizations. Representation in these consultative bodies gives interest groups direct access to administration and policy-making at the national level. A recent investigation, for example, asked leaders of all nationally organized associations to indicate the contacts most important for them in trying to influence governmental policy. The responses showed that 95% of their contacts are with the higher civil service (Hallenstvedt, 1972), and it is a fair guess that many of these occur through the mechanism of consultative bodies. At the same time, these bodies provide higher civil servants and government officials with opportunities for sounding out the big interests on controversial issues. Meeting behind closed doors and in a constitutional vacuum (Rokkan, 1966: 108), they serve as an input channel to the state, as an arena for nonpublic articulation and aggregation of interests, and as a mechanism for coordinating the society's major institutional sectors (Fivelsdal and Higley, 1970: 202).

Civil servants participate extensively in this system. One study shows that in 1966, when there were 954 committees, boards, and the like, 272 higher civil servants held 623 positions in 351 different committees (Hoven, 1969: 23). Our own study showed that in 1967, 78% of the civil service elite occupied 272 positions on these committees, an average of 3.2 positions each. All but 5 of these elite persons sat on at least one permanent committee, and half of them sat as chairman or vice-chairman of at least one committee. That there is here an important context for interaction among the elites is shown by our additional finding that, at the same time, 52% of the political elite held 108 positions in these bodies, 72% of the labor union elite held 115 positions, and 24% of the business elite held 124 positions. It is important to stress that the extensive participation of so many top civil servants in consultative bodies, often as their appointed leaders, does not merely allow for the registration of differing interest positions with the public administrators. It also provides opportunities for civil servants to steer the process wherein divergent points of view are reconciled or mediated so that policy proposals are "cleared" for presentation to democratically representative organs like the cabinet and the parliament.

The civil service elite's centrality among Norwegian elites and the intensity of its interaction with the other elites is best described, however, by the data reported in Table 1. In interviews with 134 members of the four major elites, we asked each respondent to indicate on a check-off list how well he was acquainted with each of 24 persons who occupied what we took to be the most prominent positions in the four elites in 1969. The respondent was asked to choose one of five characterizations of his acquaintance with each of the 24 individuals on the list: "know him personally well," "know him pretty well," "have had contact with him," "have heard of him," or "have never heard of him." By giving the last characterization a score of 0 and the first a score of 4, the average intensity of interaction both within and among the four elites was computed.[7] Thus the rows in Table 1 present the average scores each of the four elites assigned to their own top members and to the top members of the other elites on the list, and the columns in the table present the average scores that each group of top elite persons on the list received from other elites. On the assumption that the politicians associated with the then governing bourgeois party coalition and those associated with the Labor Party opposition comprised two relatively distinct groups, the political elite is divided into two components. Further, *intra*-elite scores are enclosed in brackets to indicate that they are excluded from computation of average *inter*-elite scores in column 6 and row 6.

The first observation to make is that *intra*-elite interaction is more intensive than *inter*-elite interaction for all five groups. This suggests that the balance between elite integration and autonomy is tipped in the direction of autonomy, as much of the theoretical writing on modern elites leads us to anticipate. A second observation is that intra-elite interaction is least intensive among civil servants, although it is still greater therein than the interaction between any two elite groups save that between labor union leaders and Labor Party politicians who have long formed a substantially monolithic labor "movement" in Norwegian society. This comparatively lower interaction among members of the civil service elite reflects the dispersal of the elite in formally autonomous departments and agencies in which the flow of communication is primarily vertical.

Turning to *inter*-elite interaction, members of the civil service elite report interaction of moderate intensity with all the other elites.

TABLE 1

INTENSITY OF INTERACTION AMONG CROSS-SECTION OF
NORWEGIAN ELITES, 1969

Elite Groups	Trade Unions	Business	Civil Service	Coalition Politicians	Labor Party Politicians	Average Interaction	N
Trade Unions	(3.9)	1.3	0.8	1.5	3.3 ·	1.6	29
Business	1.7	(3.2)	2.1	2.5	2.1	2.1	42
Civil Service	1.9	1.6	(2.8)	2.1	2.5	1.9	22
Coalition Politicians	1.8	1.7	2.0	(3.4)	2.6	1.9	29
Labor Party Politicians	3.7	1.5	1.4	2.6	(3.9)	2.2	12
Average Interaction	2.0	1.5	1.7	2.1	2.6	1.9	–
N	4	7	4	6	3	–	24/134

They report interacting more intensively with labor union leaders
(average score of 1.9) than do the coalition politicians (1.8) or
business leaders (1.6). They report interacting more intensively with
the business elite (1.6) than do either the labor union leaders (1.3) or
the Labor Party politicians (1.5). They interact more intensively with
the coalition politicians (2.1) than do union leaders (1.5). Finally,
they in effect rank themselves third (2.5) after union leaders (3.3)
and coalition politicians (2.6) in their interaction with Labor Party
politicians. This intermediate position in the overall pattern of
inter-elite interaction is further reflected in the civil servants' total
average interaction ranking of 1.9, a ranking which situates them
above the labor union elite, equal to the coalition politician elite, and
below the business elite and Labor Party politicians.

These and the other data we have presented show that the civil
service elite enjoys a central but not preeminent place in Norwegian
elite structure. Anything but merely subordinate functionaries, they
are quite visible and active in the society's several interrelated spheres
of power and influence. But our data indicate quite strongly that
their place in the elite structure builds directly on their institutionally defined jurisdictions and prerogatives. This is as far as data on
elite structure can take us in assessing the role of top civil servants in
Norwegian policy-making, however. A further assessment of this role
requires a case-by-case analysis of the *content* of the interactions

outlined by our structural data, for it is possible that most of these interactions are merely occasions for receiving instructions and orders from those who really command, in this case probably the politicians. Conversely, it is just as conceivable that in most of these interactions the power of expertise and detailed bureaucratic preparation enable civil service leaders to ride roughshod over amateur and ill-prepared politicians. In the following section, therefore, we assess the content of interactions between top civil servants and leading politicians in a decision-making process of considerable importance to the society: the annual formulation and adoption of Norway's national budget.

3. THE NATIONAL BUDGET: A CASE STUDY
IN CIVIL SERVICE INFLUENCE

Fundamental to Norwegian economic policy since the war has been the use of the national budget as a set of parameters within which major choices of sector priorities and allocations are made (Bjerve, 1959; 1965). The national budget conceptualizes relationships between principal components of the economy mathematically in the form of a model, currently called MODIS III, which spells out the probable consequences of various policy options. It is a kind of navigational fixing of position and plotting of economic course for the good ship Norway.

The formulation of the national budget begins in May of each year when civil servants in the Department of Finance circulate to civil servants in other departments and agencies an estimate of the following year's international economic situation and the likely demand and production tendencies in Norway. On the basis of this forecast, departments and agencies are asked to make more detailed estimates of economic tendencies in the sectors with which they are concerned. For example, in the Department of Commerce and Shipping, the division for foreign trade estimates the likely balance between imports and exports for the following year, the division for monetary affairs estimates the likely availability and movement of capital, and the division for shipping estimates tendencies in that branch. Very often these estimates are made only after consulting with economic specialists employed by interest organizations in each sector.

The detailed estimates are sent to the Office for the National

Budget in the Department of Finance which reworks and submits them to a preliminary mathematical analysis using the MODIS III model. On the bais of this analysis, the Economics Division of the department writes and submits for further modification a draft of the National Budget to the 8 top civil servants who comprise the Working Committee for the National Budget. As modified by these persons, the draft budget is then presented to the government which is asked to approve or disapprove the major budgetary projections.

On the basis of the government's reaction, a more detailed budget is drafted and processed a second time through MODIS III. The revised budget is scrutinized once again by the Working Committee early in September, and the government receives a stenciled draft by the second week of that month. With whatever further modifications the government then chooses to make the national budget is submitted, along with the state budget, to the parliament in the first week of October. The parliament's Finance Committee reviews the national budget and publishes a report on it, commenting on both its general and its sector-specific implications. But unlike the state budget, the national budget is not brought to a formal vote in the parliament. Its status is that of a set of instructions to various departments and agencies which has received formal parliamentary acknowledgement.

Even this brief summary indicates that this is a process entailing complex and extensive interaction among civil servants, politicians, and representatives of various economic sectors on a matter of critical importance to the year-by-year development of the society. It tests rigorously the capacity of civil servants and politicians to reconcile technical requirements with political necessities and desires. All things considered, it is an example *par excellence* of technocratic influence in the making of public policy. The discussion which follows summarizes some of the principal conclusions of an investigation of this process undertaken by one of the authors in 1969 (Brofoss, 1971). The data supporting these conclusions were gathered both from firsthand observation of how the national budget was formulated that year and from detailed interviews with 34 higher civil servants and 14 members of the parliament's Finance Committee responsible for the preparation and assessment, respectively, of the budget.

It is in the nature of the process that the choices of the civil servants who collect and analyze the mass of data from which the national budget is constructed are of fundamental importance to the outcome. This is so because the civil servants have a virtual monopoly of the technical knowledge necessary to the process and because the process gives the initiative to them throughout. Because only the civil servants understand the workings of MODIS III, they alone determine the areas in which decisions by higher authorities are to be made. It is symptomatic, for example, that while successive Ministers of Finance have all been sufficiently erudite in economics to be regarded de facto by civil servants in that department as professional economists, none of these ministers has brought about changes in the model used for the budget. Further, by allocating to them the prerogative of asking the questions that need to be answered politically, the process enables civil servants to control the directions in which the government's attention moves. Only in a very limited degree do members of the government have the time and motivation to consider areas of the budget about which no questions have been asked. Moreover, many of the communications from civil servants to the government take the adversary form: civil servants tell the government how the national budget *should* be composed. Thus not only do they control the general framework in which decisions are made, but they also define the important questions, influence the direction of politicians' attention, and argue for their proposed solutions with the help of esoteric knowledge that is difficult to refute.

Inherent in the process, then, is an irreducible amount of civil service influence that is in fact quite large. But it does not necessarily follow that the making of the national budget is an example of technocracy run rampant. In theory at least, both parliament and the government possess means for checking civil service influence in this as in other areas. Two questions present themselves in this regard: (1) How effective are these means? and (2) How motivated are Norwegian politicians to use them?

Although the Constitution gives to it final authority on all matters pertaining to the operation of the state, the parliament appears not to act as a serious check on the influence of civil servants in the national budget process. The most important reason is that parliament stands in a very uneven relation to the civil service as regards technical expertise. For example, the staff of parliament's Finance Committee consists in its entirety of one economist. Two other committees have one staff member each, but these persons are civil servants temporarily on loan to the parliament. A total of 10 other aides can be found, but these are employed by party groups within parliament, not by the committees themselves. It comes as no surprise, therefore, that, when questioned about the attention they give to the national budget, members of the Finance Committee tended to answer that they lack sufficient knowledge of the conceptualizations behind the national budget to be able to evaluate it seriously. Their basic view is that, in order to make desired changes, one must first bring to bear expertise in theoretical economics. Nevertheless, proposals made in recent years to expand parliament's professional staff have been opposed successfully on the ground that this would lead to a duplication of work already being done by the civil service. The unspoken assumption seems to be that the work done by civil servants is essentially neutral and objective.

Of course, at any given time, parliament's lack of expertise is a problem only for those members who are in opposition to the government, for the governing party or parties, using the assembled expertise of the civil service, present the national budget as the *only* course of action, and it is up to the opposition to suggest alternatives. The opposition's predicament is illustrated by the recent unprecedented effort of the Labor Party to build up its own battery of experts with which to counter programs of the four-party coalition government that replaced the Labor Party beginning in 1965. During the two previous decades when Labor was in power, it had little need for its own expert apparatus: it had the civil service instead. But the party was deprived of this advantage after the 1965 elections, and it began to build up a professional staff under the leadership, from 1967, of an experienced economist. This effort was a clear expression of the felt need among Norwegian opposition groups to counter the expertise of the civil service as used by governing forces. Although Labor's innovation bore fruit in 1969 when it managed to set forth its own state budget as an alternative to the governing coalition's budget proposal, the party nevertheless dissolved its staff of experts in 1971 when it regained power.

Lacking the necessary expertise both inside parliament's walls and back at party headquarters, the parliamentary opposition seems little able to counteract civil service expertise as manifested in items like the national budget. In interviews, for example, 13 of 14 members of the Finance Committee expressed varying degrees of discontent with the process as it now exists, but admitted that their efforts to effect changes have so far misfired. Not a single respondent could point to any change in the macro-economic model used for the national budget resulting from their discontent. For their own part, top civil servants were obviously aware of parliamentary complaints against the process, but they described these as too general and vague to be of any use in the technical preparation of the budget.

If there are effective political means for checking civil service influence, then, they are to be found in the government itself. But while members of the government have both the opportunity and the responsibility to examine critically the intra- and inter-departmental evaluations and comments of civil servants who work on the budget, investigation showed that they seldom do so. As a rule they content themselves with the notes and comments provided them by the civil servants. Items not expressly addressed to them normally escape their attention. The exceptions occur when powerful interest groups direct ministers' attention to matters not brought up by the civil servants. But this happens very seldom because the national budget is not seen by interest groups as directly affecting them. Their perception seems rather to be that the budget has only broad relevance to the society in general, and interest groups seldom feel themselves sufficiently endangered by it to exert pressure on the government. The overall tendency is toward civil service freedom to select the factors that precipitate cabinet decisions concerning the budget.

There is thus reason to believe that, like the parliament, the government normally plays a passive role in the process. Examination of archives containing communications between various government members and civil servants during the entire period, 1947 to 1969, revealed that the government's discussion and reply to preliminary budgets delivered by the civil service has always been meager. It was impossible to uncover any sizable number of written comments or directives from the government concerning the preliminary budget. The absence of these was confirmed by interviews with the responsible parties on both sides in 1969. There were some broad comments transmitted verbally from the Minister of Finance to his highest ranking civil servant, but this was the extent of the political control exerted at that point.

Nevertheless, an unusual development in 1969 prevents a conclusion pointing to civil service hegemony in this process. The national budget devised by civil servants that year was a strongly contractive one because they feared that the change to a value-added tax system on January 1, 1970, with a consequent reduction in personal income taxes, might overheat the economy. In the summer of 1969 the government simply rejected this contractive budget outright because it was politically inopportune. Civil servants were required to discard the proposed budget and make a new one more consistent with political needs. Although many of them disagreed fundamentally with this demand, and although subsequent high inflation rates partly vindicated their judgment, they followed orders. Thus where there is deep disagreement between the civil service and the government, the latter has on at least one occasion had the motivation and power to step in and control the process in accordance with its own wishes. Yet, such a conflict is very much more the exception than the rule. The normal situation is one of political passivity in the face of civil service expertise and initiative.

The national budget is, we think, a clear example of the substantial latitude and influence enjoyed by the civil service elite in Norway. It is probably the area in which its influence has the most far-reaching effects on the society, and the area in which it enjoys the most unfettered access to the making of decisions that are of fundamental importance. But we do not think this illustrates a losing struggle by political and other elites to contain technocracy. Quite the contrary, the explanation for the substantial influence of the civil service in the Norwegian case lies in a broad consensus that has been shared by all elites about the utility of civil service expertise and initiatives as we have described it here. This is to say that in the current period political and other elites are *not motivated* to limit in greater degree than they have the influence of civil servants.

To understand why this is so it is necessary to recall that after the last war Norway confronted a colossal task of reconstruction. As a consequence the need was great for investment capital and for techniques by which an efficient allocation of capital between diverse sectors could be made. The principal solution to the need for capital was to give to the shipping sector, the only sector that could quickly bring large amounts of foreign capital to Norway, very favorable tax and other concessions. The principal solution to the need for techniques with which to allocate capital efficiently was to use macro-economic models of the sort devised for the national budget as the basis for economic policy-making. The paradoxical effect was to strengthen some sectors of private enterprise at the same time one moved in the direction of a planned economy. This sleight of hand was possible only because there was broad agreement among most influential persons about the necessity for a rational allocation of resources if reconstruction was to be accomplished. From the standpoint of the state, reconstruction became essentially a problem of resource allocation that could be dealt with satisfactorily without assuming direct control of the economy's producing units. In this way political conflict of potentially large proportions gave way to widespread cooperation and agreement among the major power groups.[8]

Important to the continuation of this essentially accidental symbiosis of private enterprise and a planned economy was the success of the techniques used. Norway enjoyed consistently high growth rates during the 1950s and 1960s. It was inevitable that under these circumstances the influence and power of those most closely identified with the techniques responsible for the success of the planned economy, the civil service elite, increased substantially. So long as the techniques work and so long as agreement on the desirability of maximum growth and related goals persists, political and other elites are little motivated to take a more critical stance toward the influence and centrality of leading civil servants.

4. IMPLICATIONS FOR ELITE THEORY

In this analysis we have tried to show what lay behind the relatively placid relations between Norwegian civil service and political elites at the end of the 1960s. Treating historical, structural, and processual factors, we described a civil service elite with considerable power and influence in the society but one that is not perceived by other elites to be a threat to their own positions. We interpreted the prominence of top civil servants to depend in the final analysis on a continuation of the consensus about socio-economic ends and means which has pervaded Norwegian elites during the postwar period.

If we now ask how the situation we have described might be generalized in terms of elite theory, we confront immediately the question of whether this situation is a historical happenstance of limited duration, for we emphasized throughout that accidental factors such as the war and the mid-century ascendency of the Labor Party in Norwegian politics had much to do with creating the consensus under which civil service power grew to its present proportions. May we not expect, in the changed circumstances of the 1970s, to witness an erosion of this consensus with consequently greater conflict over the influence of top civil servants in Norwegian society? We can of course give no conclusive answer to this question, yet merely posing it focuses attention on one or two points of relevance to elite theory.

In the bitter debate over whether Norway should join the European Common Market in 1972—a debate which culminated in a national referendum that went against membership in the EEC—allegations that top civil servants were using their status to influence the outcome in one direction or the other were numerous and heated. Along with other components of the postwar consensus the one concerning the neutrality of the powerful civil service elite seemed to be eroding as the fight over Norway's relations with the EEC progressed. Yet we think it most prudent to see this tumult over civil servants' (and other elites') activities in 1972 as essentially superficial and without serious consequences for the rather harmonious relations between the civil service and other elites described by our 1969 data.

The reason is that, while the original postwar consensus over socioeconomic ends and means may well have been adventitious, it somewhat paradoxically enabled Norwegian elites to build a structure of mutual interaction and access in the making of important decisions that gives every indication of being *reliably self-perpetuating,* barring some future external intervention similar to that of World War II. In Norway, and probably in a handful of other Western societies as well, influential persons and groups like top civil servants appear to be held in check less by fear of sanctions that other influential persons and groups might apply against them than by satisfaction with an organization of power in which all these persons and groups are able to exert substantial individual and collective influence without entering into open conflict. Apparently, most or all these power-wielders find in the elite structure and decision processes enough reliable options and alternatives for making their positions on issues count so that they need not constantly maneuver against each other in order to retain their influence.

Our suggestion is that an elite structure allowing for mutual interaction and access along the lines of the Norwegian model gives to influential persons and groups a feeling of safety in the exercise of their influence. It allows effective individual and group self-assertion when and where this appears rational in the policy circumstances. It is a structure, in short, that does not require elites to assert themselves constantly merely to avoid ruin. Where this kind of elite structure is once created, as we think it has been in postwar Norway, those who are influential tend to be interested in preserving it, in making it continue to work. Their calculation is that they have more to lose than to gain in pushing unilaterally for substantial alterations. This acceptance of an individually *and* mutually beneficial organization of power is probably capable of more or less permanently sustaining itself.

But it is necessary to remember, as in fact the histories of most societies show, that this is rarely the inclination of powerful persons not basically satisfied (that is, not possessing sufficient access to decision-making) with the extant elite structure. When such persons are not satisfied, as they normally are not in most societies, they routinely produce a fairly high degree of conflict. In Norway they have not been doing this for several decades, and according to our analysis of the relations between civil servants and other powerful groups in the society, they are not likely to start doing so in the foreseeable future.

NOTES

1. In a curious reversal of this practice that must have few precedents elsewhere, in February 1971 the Prime Minister, Per Borten, leaked *civil service* communications concerning Norway's negotiations to enter the Common Market to an influential opponent of Common Market membership. In the resulting furor there was much dismay that such a tactic could be used, and the Borten coalition government fell in March 1971. It was replaced by a minority Labor Party government which in turn resigned when a national referendum in September 1972 went against Common Market membership. Its replacement was a three-party minority coalition government consisting of Common Market opponents.

2. In the past few years departmental political leadership has been enlarged by adding "political" or "personal" secretaries to the cabinet ministers in some departments. There is also discussion of appointing additional undersecretaries in the largest departments.

3. A detailed report of this interview research may be found in Groholt and Higley (1972). Of the 22 members of the civil service elite interviewed, 10 were Department Counsels and 12 were Division Chiefs in all but 2 of the 14 departments.

4. The corresponding figure for the business elite in 1967 was 70% and for the political elite 53%.

5. For purposes of measurement, the political elite was defined as all those who held cabinet, undersecretary, or party executive committee positions during the entire period, 1960-1967.

6. Fivelsdal and Higley (1970: 204) interpret the infrequent assumption of cognate leadership roles outside the labor movement by labor union leaders as supporting the image of the labor union elite as a relatively closed corporate structure, an image not without relevance to the civil service elite as well.

7. Although semantic ambiguity and the possibility of biased responses might seem to undermine the reliability of this method, by interviewing 18 of the 24 persons on the list itself, and by cross-checking how each of them characterized his acquaintance with the 17 others, we found the data to be quite reliable. Thus in 94 of the 153 possible reciprocal relationships between these 18 persons, identical characterizations of the relationships were

chosen by both parties to them. In another 53 there was a difference of one degree, while in 6 cases there was a difference of two degrees.

8. For evidence that this consensus extended to many other aspects of postwar Norwegian society as well, see Field and Higley (1972).

REFERENCES

BJERVE, P. J. (1968) Trends in Quantitative Economic Planning in Norway. Oslo: Statistisk Sentralbyra. Artikkel 21.
――― (1959) Planning in Norway. Amsterdam.
BOTTOMORE, T. H. (1964) Elites and Society. New York: Basic Books.
BROFOSS, K. E. (1971) "Nasjonalbudsjettet: en analyse av et beslutningssystem." Dissertation, Univ. of Oslo.
DONJEM, H. (1969) "Rekrutteringen til departementene, 1945-65." Dissertation, Univ. of Oslo.
FIELD, G. L. and J. HIGLEY (1972) Elites in Developed Societies: Theoretical Reflections on the First Stage in Norway. Beverly Hills and London: Sage Publications. Sage Professional Paper in Comparative politics, vol. 1, series no. 01-033. 45 pages.
FIVELSDAL, E. and J. HIGLEY (1970) The Labor Union Elite in Norway. Scandinavian Political Studies V. Oslo: Universitetsforlaget. pp. 165-209.
GROHOLT, K. and J. HIGLEY (1972) "National Elite Surveys: Some Experience From Norway." Acta Sociologica 15: 168-183.
HALLENSTVEDT, A. (1972) Dagbladet, no. 9-10 (1972).
――― and J. HOVEN (1971) "Den Kollegiale Administrasjon." Unpublished paper, Institute for Political Science, Univ. of Oslo.
HOVDEN, J. M. (1969) "Rekrutteringen til departementene i tiden." Dissertation, Univ. of Oslo.
HOVEN, F. H. (1969) "Deltagere i en kommunikasjonsstruktur: en analyse av departementenes representasjon i offentlige utvalg og rad." Dissertation, Univ of. Oslo.
KELLER, S. (1963) Beyond the Ruling Class: Strategic Elites in Modern Society. New York: Random House.
MILLS, C. W. (1956) The Power Elite. New York: Oxford Univ. Press.
PORTER, J. (1965) The Vertical Mosaic. Toronto: Univ. of Toronto Press.
ROKKAN, S. (1966) "Norway: Numerical Democracy and Corporate Pluralism," in R. A. Dahl (ed.) Political Oppositions in Western Democracies. New Haven: Yale Univ. Press.
TORGERSEN, U. (1967) The Market of Professional Manpower in Norway. Oslo: Institute for Social Research, mimeographed.

JOHN HIGLEY is associate professor of sociology at the University of Texas (Austin); he spent the 1974-1975 academic year as senior research fellow at the Australian National University in Canberra.

KARL ERIK BROFOSS is research fellow at the Oslo Institute of Political Science.

KNUT GROHOLT is director of the Research Division on Industrial Democracy, Norwegian Ministry of Local Government and Labor.

12

The Political Role of
Nonpolitical Bureaucrats
in Denmark

ERIK DAMGAARD

In Danish democratic thought, the executive branch derives its legitimacy from the legislature by virtue of a parliamentary system, that is, cabinet responsibility to the majority in the Folketing. In practical terms, parliamentary party leaders determine the composition of governments. Before the establishment of a parliamentary system in 1901, ministers were appointed at the king's discretion; and they were under the influence of a conservative, quasi aristocratic upper chamber, the Landsting.[1] Except for the change that no law could be passed without majority backing in the Folketing,[2] executive domination characterized Danish politics throughout the nineteenth century. In a quite different way, much the same has also become true about politics in the present century.

1. THE DEVELOPMENT OF EXECUTIVE DOMINATION

The subtitle given to this section may seem paradoxical because constitutional developments at the turn of the century established the Folketing's supremacy. The paradox is easily resolved. Specific constitutional provisions do not explain the executive's dominant position which, in fact, developed as a consequence of profound economic and social changes in the twentieth century. In the past hundred years, the scope of governmental activity has expanded enormously. The story about industrialization, urbanization, economic development, the increasing need for international cooperation, and the demands from new masses of mobilized voters concerning economic and social security, education, government regulation, and intervention in a variety of economic and social affairs, and the like is, of course, not peculiar to Denmark. Nonetheless, it is quite important to realize how dramatic this expansion of governmental activity really is because it has completely changed the conditions for political leadership.

Around the turn of the century, public expenditures accounted for about 10% of the national income. They increased to about 17% at the end of the interwar period, and then they accelerated after World War II: from about 20% in 1950 to 25% in 1960, and no less than 45% in 1971. Experts estimate that the percentage may well reach 58% in 1985.[3]

Another indicator of increasing government activity is the quantity of output, defined as laws and statutes. A comparison in pages of the official publications for 1911 and 1971 shows that this output increased about tenfold within the last sixty years. It has actually grown more than that since the rules for publication of statutory instruments have changed with the times to the effect that less is published today.

Thirdly, whereas from 1870 to 1901 parliament had, on an average, 60 bills for consideration each year, it had 164 in the latest decade. Not only has the government increased the number of bills for parliamentary consideration but the roles of individual members and opposition parties in law making have been substantially reduced. During the previous century, private members proposed almost one-fourth of all bills; today, only about one-tenth. Similarly at that time, 10% of bills enacted came from private members whereas today only around 1% come from this source.

This simple quantitative analysis indicates that the government's legislative role has been significantly enlarged during this century. Two considerations can amplify this interpretation. In the first place, numbers conceal the fact that the scope of a law in recent years often encompasses what would have previously been enacted in several different bills. In the second place, legislation today is qualitatively different from yesteryear's. Much more is now left for the executive branch to determine within guidelines laid down by laws.

Approximately the same number of parliamentarians still have to do the legislative work although the workload has become much heavier in quantitative terms as well as more complex in a qualitative sense. Parliament responded to rising demands mainly by extending its time in session and by relying more on committee work. Evidently, these actions have not been sufficient for countering the development of executive domination. Like so many other parliaments, the Danish one remains poorly staffed, and it still has very limited information facilities of its own. It did not adjust to what has been called the information revolution; and this is the reason that, more than ever before, many tasks normally labeled legislative in character have become executive in locus, as has been said even about the United States.[4] The most important way in which the Folketing can influence legislation is the indirect one of determining who—which parties—are to form the government. Without overstating the case, the Danish parliament, in terms of its organization, basically reflects the demands perceived in the previous century. However, the crux of the matter is that the executive administration of 1849 does not exist today. "Bureaucratizing" processes have enabled the administration to respond to economic and social transformations and to the information revolution.

Around 1848, the central administration—the actual ministries in the capital with their centralized services—was reshaped according to the common European ministerial system that Napoleon introduced in France. Seven ministries were set up following that model.[5] By 1910 the number had grown to twelve, by 1948 to sixteen, while today there are twenty. In addition, a large number of specialized, subordinate "directorates" have been organized since then.[6] Although specific reasons may account for the setting up of a new ministry from time to time, the more fundamental explanation of this proliferation is an attempt to cope with new demands arising from economic, technological, and social development.[7] Likewise, the number of civil servants has grown almost explosively following World War II. A 1962 report lists 2,240 academically educated civil servants out of a total of 8,810 persons engaged in administrative work within the central administration.[8] These numbers have increased significantly within the past decade. Probably a good estimate is that the number of university trained civil servants is about 3,000 today. Compare this to 184 in 1850 or 644 in 1946. In 1850, parliament confronted seven ministers and two hundred high civil servants in the law making process. In 1972, the Folketing, with inadequate staff and limited resources, confronts twenty ministers supported by about three thousand high civil servants. This shows the importance of studying who these civil servants are and what roles they play in the political process.

2. TOP CIVIL SERVANTS IN THE ADMINISTRATIVE SYSTEM

Two key characteristics show the basic features of Danish administrative organization. First, the central administration is divided into several ministries each of which has responsibility for a broadly defined policy area. Next, a politically appointed minister, most often but not always a member of the Folketing, heads the ministry. Immediately below the minister are one or more permanent top civil servants—the heads of departments or directors general, henceforth referred to as permanent secretaries—depending on how many departments a ministry is subdivided into. Thus, the minister is the only politically appointed official in the system. He has no politically appointed parliamentary secretary or junior minister at his side.

A ministry's departments are hierarchically organized so that each civil servant has a fixed position on the chain of command originating from the minister.[9] Appointments to the civil service follow a merit system. Because, as a rule, promotions occur only within the ministry where the civil servant was appointed, a civil servant's whole career typically takes place within the fairly limited context of one ministry.

A civil servant is normally described as a nonpolitical, impartial, and loyal servant of the government in power. P. Meyer has emphasized the importance of the continental tradition which regards public administration as the application of legal rules just like judicial decision making.[10] A recent study shows that 80% of civil servants in the generalist grade are jurists while 17% are economists.[11] Thus, mostly jurists serve as general administrators in Denmark even though the study of law leads towards a career as judge or lawyer. There are, of course, civil servants with educational backgrounds in fields other than law or economics, for example, engineering, architecture, medicine, or liberal arts; but these persons are typically found in the directorates which are subordinate to the departments and have specialized functions.

Whatever education a civil servant has received, he normally enters the central administration without prior administrative training. As time goes on, he acquires practical skills and experiences in the department. At the same time, he slowly moves up the hierarchy, automatically to a certain level, thereafter only competitively for top positions.

The career pattern of the ordinary top administrator is as follows.

He (no women hold top jobs) has a middle or upper class background. Near the age of 25, he completes a university degree in law or economics. Then he immediately gets a position in the central administration. For about 21 years he is on his way moving up his ministry's hierarchical ladder. At the age of 47 he is appointed to the top position, which he can then hold for another 20 years before retiring with a comfortable pension. At any moment, the average age of a top civil servant is about 58, and he has had his top position for about ten years. This describes the career of the modal top civil servant. A few permanent secretaries leave their jobs at the age of 60 in order to become heads of local administrations. Two recent developments complete this picture. There appear to be more frequent movements from one ministry into another than formerly; and a recent permanent secretary was appointed for a limited term only.

3. THE DECLINE OF OVERT PUBLIC INVOLVEMENT

The political role played by top civil servants has at least two aspects. One is the overt, easily observable participation in party politics, especially in parliament or the cabinet. The other is the much less visible role they play in the preparation and execution of policy decisions. Although their political activities in the first sense have virtually vanished, their political role in the latter sense has assumed increasing importance.

Probably the most significant way a civil servant can participate in politics is by becoming a cabinet member and thereby also the political head of a ministry. An interesting question is to what extent civil servants move from administrative into political jobs.

During the first fifteen years of constitutional democracy, roughly speaking, three competing groups were on the Danish political scene: first, a group of Conservative civil servants remained loyal to the king as they had been throughout the absolutist era; second, a National Liberal group had been especially active in the successful attempt to end royal absolutism and to establish the new constitutional regime; and finally, there was an agrarian party. Before the advent of constitutional politics, power had resided in the hands of the king and a narrow circle of leading civil servants. The most important short-term consequences of the new regime seem rather to have been to legitimatize an institutionalized political opposition to the dominant Conservative elite and to have somewhat broadened the basis for recruitment of ministers without changing it completely, since the constitution did not give the parliamentary majority the right to force ministers to resign.

From 1848 to 1864, about 50% of the ministers held a position in the central administration at the time of their appointments to the cabinet.[12] This picture is refined by breaking data down into a mainly Conservative period, 1848-1856, and a mainly National Liberal one, 1856-1864. In the first, no less than two-thirds of the ministers had been civil servants in the old absolutist central administration, as opposed to only one-third in the latter period. Also worth mentioning is that all ministers who came from other positions during the first period were, in fact, also civil servants, albeit not in the central administration. Because all members of the king's cabinet before 1848 were recruited from the central administration, the new system did produce changes but not dramatic shifts in recruitment patterns. Most civil servants appointed during the absolutist era continued their work after the 1848 reshaping of political and administrative systems; and an impressive number of former senior civil servants served as political ministers under the new conditions.

Following the collapse of the National Liberal government's foreign policy in 1864 after the disastrous war against Bismarck's Prussia, a war that resulted in severe territorial losses, the revised constitution of 1866 placed preponderant power in the hands of a new Conservative elite until 1901. Landowners led this elite which also attracted former National Liberals. The opposition also re-aligned. Around 1870, two main antagonists occupied the political scene: the Conservative right and a left composed of agrarians and liberal intellectuals. Each group, being very heterogeneous, was far from united. During the last third of the nineteenth century, 1865-1901, about 15% of the ministers came from the central administration; but the largest number definitely came from the outside. About 45% of these ministers were landowners. Civil service power was yielding to landowners' power; however, the two groups shared some strong social and intellectual ties. For instance, half of the landowner-ministers had a university degree in law or economics.

The period in question was one of bitter constitutional conflict when the left demanded universal suffrage and cabinet responsibility to the Folketing while the right defended property privileges, equal power for the upper chamber, and the king's freedom of choice in appointing ministers. The left used all possible political means to accomplish its desired goals, including refusal to pass legislation in the lower chamber. This tactic had severe effects on the civil service thus denied salary increases and new jobs. In addition, politicians on the left generally had a very hostile attitude toward civil servants whom they regarded as a closed upper class circle pursuing its own interests. Their leading spokesmen repeatedly proclaimed that they did not trust top officials in the central administration. In particular, they doubted that civil servants would be loyal to a future government formed by the left. Therefore, they even proposed replacing permanent secretaries by politically appointed general secretaries whom the ministers could rely on. On the other hand, Conservative governments demanded complete obedience from civil servants throughout this political struggle. In this heated conflict, civil servants had only two options: to overtly support a Conservative government, thereby exposing themselves to attacks from the left, or to stay out of politics altogether as neutral, nonpolitical administrators.

The situation changed at the turn of the century. After a humiliating Conservative defeat at the polls in 1901, the principle of cabinet responsibility to parliament was finally acknowledged; and the first Agrarian-Liberal government was appointed. Radical-Liberal as well as Social Democratic governments have followed. The strong tendency observed in the last part of the previous century—the tendency of civil servants to withdraw from politics—has completed itself in the first half of the twentieth century. Whereas during the first decades of constitutional government many civil servants regarded an appointment to the cabinet as the culmination of their administrative careers, they no longer take this step. The key to understanding this development is the parliamentary system and changes in the party system. Although many different cabinets were formed during the previous century, they were all Conservative, dominated by upper class or upper middle class representatives, which civil servants with the same social background and political philosophy could more easily join than was true afterward. The twentieth century brought new classes to power, first the farmers and then members of the labor movement. Furthermore, sudden shifts in party strength now often lead to changes of government, adding a new element of uncertainty for civil servants who might aspire to fill top political positions. Nevertheless, some civil servants have joined cabinets during this century, so far a total of fifteen, less than 8% of the total ministers. Of these, as many as six were diplomats serving as foreign ministers. As for the remaining, they were notedly not recruited from the central administration's top echelon.

What about other forms of public participation in politics? The constitution explicitly allows civil servants to enter parliament. Nevertheless, in no period have more than 3.5% of parliamentarians in the Folketing held positions in the central administration at the time of their election; no more than 3% of the parliamentarians in the Landsting have held such positions.[13]

We thus arrive at the conclusion that, because nowadays there is virtually no movement from top positions in the central administration into government or parliament, the political influence that top civil servants might have cannot possibly derive from their public involvement in politics.

4. INFLUENCE ON POLITICAL DECISION MAKING

If influence is defined as a relationship between minister and civil servant whereby the civil servant induces a behavior on the part of the minister—a behavior he would not otherwise have displayed— then the civil servant obviously exerts tremendous influence. There are probably only a few instances where a minister would have chosen exactly the same course of action had he not been advised by civil servants or had no civil servant participated in the decision making process, if for no other reason than lack of time, information, and expertise.[14] However, the real question goes further than that. The following phrases it more appropriately. If the minister personally had all the different kinds and quantities of information available in the central administration as a collective body, would he then have chosen a different alternative, that is, have made another decision or not have made a decision at all, both with respect to decisions which actually involve him and to those in which he had no part although he is ultimately responsible?

Indeed, this is a difficult question that interests students of politics although they seldom really know about it. At least in Denmark, this question seems to be the concern of a few well-informed insiders, those with the know-all smiles on their faces. They may give some hints now and then, but they never publicly report knowledge or findings. I hesitate to speculate about the reasons for that. Maybe the findings would run counter to accepted democratic ideology? Maybe civil servants exert no influence to speak of? Or maybe their influence varies according to personalities and issues? Because the question is far too important to leave with these silent insiders, I will proceed by utilizing the scarce material available.

R. Dahl discusses four main methods used to study manifest influence, all of which have some merit but also distinct drawbacks: the position method, the well-placed judge method, the participation method, and the weighing of participation method.[15] The first of these is of very little use in this connection because, of course, ministers are placed at the top of the hierarchy and top civil servants immediately below, but we are interested in learning about the possible influence of top civil servants on ministers' behavior. However, one variant of the method seems relevant. Presumably of some importance in a minister's ability to effectively control the work in his ministry is how much experience he has had in office. I could hypothesize that, all other things being equal, his ability to control and direct the ministry increases with length of time in office, at least up to some point. Alternatively formulated, frequent cabinet changes and reshuffles tend to decrease the ministers' control over their ministries. I do not have appropriate data for testing these hypotheses, but I can give at least some basic information about ministerial turnover.

Denmark is often described as a "stable" or "working" multiparty system where cabinet changes do not occur as often as in certain other European countries. How often do such changes take place? In twenty-one years, from October 1950 to September 1971, Denmark had six different cabinets, each with an average lifetime of three and a half years. Since politicians are often in charge of the same ministry in different cabinets, the expected total number of ministers in charge of the same ministry would be less than six; however, this is not true. The number of ministers heading the same ministry among the fifteen ministries existing throughout the period under discussion varies from four to nine with an average of six, median also six. During this period, a minister remained in charge of the same ministry for an average of three years and four months.

Another approach to the problem is to look at the total number of years of ministerial experience a person has at the time of his appointment. The cabinet of former Prime Minister Krag, appointed in October 1971, had nineteen ministers, of which eleven did not have previous ministerial experience. As for the remaining, seven had between two and a half and four and a half years of experience, while one—Krag—had been a minister for seventeen years. The previous cabinet of Hilmar Baunsgaard, formed in 1968, had seventeen members, of which thirteen had no earlier experience while four had from about three to four years of ministerial experience.

Viewed in this perspective, politicians are at a relative disadvantage because of their coming and going while the typical top civil servant has spent all his life within the ministry. I chose this twenty-one year period deliberately: it is roughly equal to the average number of years a permanent secretary occupies his post. Some of the current permanent secretaries have seen eight different ministers come and go since 1950. Earlier I said that, due to the renewal process, a permanent secretary has on the average occupied his top administrative position for ten years at any given moment and that, before arriving at the top, he has occupied lower level positions within the same ministry for more than twenty years.

Comparing ministers and civil servants in terms of time in office is, of course, to take a very narrow view of their relationships. Each minister has some kind of background relevant to his job. As a rule, ministers are recruited from the Folketing—sixteen out of nineteen in Krag's cabinet, fourteen out of seventeen in Baunsgaard's—where they have specialized in certain policy areas through committee work, party spokesmanship, and the like. A few of the ministers were civil servants in the central administration, two in Krag's cabinet and three in Baunsgaard's; and several had professional backgrounds relevant to their ministerial jobs. Furthermore, an impressive number of ministers were university educated academics, ten in Krag's cabinet, eleven in Baunsgaard's.

Thus, although ministers come and go relatively frequently, an appointed minister is always prepared, in some way, for taking over his job, be it by his legislative, professional, or educational background, or a combination thereof. However, while a minister's experience in office and his relevant background vis-à-vis the civil servant are important variables, they tell nothing about the degree to which the minister actually determines departmental policies of controls departmental activities.

Ideally I would like to apply Dahl's third and fourth methods to the investigation of this problem; but since I have no data relating to participation in ministerial decision making, all I can do at this juncture is to rely on various statements by people who, in some way, may be considered well-placed judges. What follows by no means approaches an exhaustive description of what well-placed judges think. The primary reason for this is that ministers and top civil servants, probably the two best sources of information, traditionally never disclose what goes on behind their closed doors. As prescribed by Danish parliamentary and administrative norms, they always give the appearance of forming a united ministerial front.

Probably the most widespread view is that the civil servant is absolutely loyal to his minister. Before they came to power, Agrarian-Liberals and Social Democrats were extremely suspicious of the bureaucracy. They feared that it could not possibly be loyal to other than Conservative cabinets since Conservatives had monopolized power throughout the nineteenth century. After some experience in office, however, they changed their minds. The bureaucracy proved capable of adjusting to new types of political leadership.[16] A recent textbook on Danish public administration mentions that, although some people have regarded some civil service appointments as partially motivated by political considerations, it is remarkable "that despite such appointments, we have a civil service which, according to concurrent testimonies from successive governments, is most loyal—working with new political premises is simply not perceived of as a problem by civil servants."[17]

While all authors basically agree that civil servants obey ministers in office, traditional-legal and more modern-realistic descriptions are distinguishable. The traditional description absolutely differentiates administration and politics, and it conceives of the relationship between ministers and civil servants as being almost static.

> From the civil servant is demanded . . . loyalty, competence, personal honesty and integrity. He shall not . . . attempt to appeal to the political powerholder of the moment. On the basis of existing rules—like the judge who follows the law, whether he likes it or not—he has to do what is objectively right, what law and sensible interpretation say. The civil servant has done this not only during the hundred years of constitutional democracy; the tradition goes back to the time of absolutism when the relation between the king as holder of state power and the bureaucracy was exactly parallel to today's relation between the government and administrative bodies.[18]

The administrative philosophy underlying these remarks continues to shape civil servants' attitudes toward politics. A former permanent secretary delimits two general functions a civil servant has when cooperating with his minister. The first derives from political initiatives undertaken by the minister, for example, preparation of new legislation, which, our informant comments, "needs no special explanation. Here the task is simply to assist the minister by word and by deed, to bring to light all relevant information and points of view and to promote work in the best possible way."[19] The second function consists of processing current business and making decisions. In this respect, our former top civil servant maintains that work has to be carried out "objectively and nonpolitically," which in practice is facilitated by the fact that political parties are in agreement more often than is assumed. He also explains that the areas of current business, where divergent political views may arise, are very restricted but that not even they create major difficulties. The personality of politicians is said to be more important than their party label. In sum, this informant, whom I have picked to represent the traditional-legal point of view, bypasses problems involved in carrying out the first function and denies that difficulties are associated with the second. Instead, he poses two questions which the civil servant must ask about his minister:

(1) Can he be trusted in collaboration or does cooperation become uncertain and difficult because of promises and commitments made which he has told no one about?

(2) Does he have influence within the government and the Folketing and can he use it for the interests of his ministry?

"If these two questions are answered affirmatively," the former permanent secretary adds, "the civil servant will usually feel that he has a good minister and he will willingly undertake hard work and difficult tasks." For our purposes, an interesting point to note is that the top civil servant wants a political boss who is strong in dealing with his cabinet colleagues and who uses his influence to promote the "interests of his ministry."

A current permanent secretary gives a more subtle, modern-realistic account of the relationship between ministers and civil servants.[20] He starts out by defining three functions: political, administrative, and scientific. Corresponding to these functions, he lists three types of persons, the politician, the administrator, and the expert, although, in his discussion, telling experts and administrators apart is often impossible. He notes that experts have become increasingly indispensable in the policy making process; therefore, he argues, there is also a need for a summarizing evaluation of various experts' contributions. And here appears a crucial linkage function that top civil servants should perform: "it becomes the responsibility of permanent secretaries to present the results of experts' work to the relevant ministers in a comprehensible and justifiable form." In other words, top civil servants are bridging the gap between experts and politicians.

This bridge is not a "neutral" one, however, because senior civil servants are expected not only to call attention to different alternatives but also to "weigh them against each other and to present a recommendation about which one is preferable." This leads our author right to the question of the basis civil servants have for selecting among different possibilities. From the civil servant's standpoint, a major difficulty is that political guidelines are often vague, unclear, or even contradictory. In departmental work, a remedy for these deficiencies is to constantly consult politicians; but at earlier stages of the process, experts often have to help themselves by making judgments about probable political reactions.

The author then proceeds to a more fundamental aspect, namely, the influence of personal evaluations upon the analyses of social problems. He denies that party political judgments intrude; rather, the product is "an evaluation in which the expert's feelings and philosophy of life—and possibly his ambitions—may play a major role." Finally, he explicitly states that situations inevitably occur where experts and politicians become antagonistically involved. For such situations, he prescribes that those civil servants who work directly with the minister should renounce their freedom of speech if the minister demands and if the command is not illegal or grossly improper.

The author just cited differs from many other civil servants by clearly indicating his awareness of a much more complex interrelationship between politics and administration than older conceptions assumed. This more subtle interplay points out the important questions of whether civil servants can act neutrally or nonpolitically at all and which practical implications ought to follow from a negative answer. In the static society of a century ago, when governmental activity was fairly limited, old conceptions were perhaps more plausible; but today, when legislation has become a device for changing society, how can civil servants be neutral or impartial in their dealings with politicians?

In trying to describe civil servants' political influence, a tempting procedure is to look for signs of disagreement between ministers and civil servants. But this is an all too narrow avenue of inquiry in order to gauge influences. Open disagreements or conflicts do not necessarily accompany influence relationships. Influence can occur in a much broader sense. All departments have, over time, developed ways of doing things, established "departmental views," and the like, which presumably affect policies to some degree. Departments have a life of their own. The civil servant identifies with his department, he wants to promote the perceived interests of his organization, he wishes to expand its power and prestige, he cares about promotional opportunities, and so on. All this is commonplace, but ensuing policy consequences are not sufficiently known.

Anyway, the important point is that the central administration is not simply a passive tool at the ministers' disposal as former writings allege. The civil servant's behavior is, to some extent, determined by his normative frame of reference as shaped by socialization experiences before (e.g., his social and educational background) and after entering the central administration. The former permanent secretary already quoted gives an illustrative example of the latter when he insists that an important quality of a good minister is that he uses his influence in the "interests of his ministry." From a purely normative perspective, democratic theory leaves no room for such a thing as the "interests of the ministry." Nevertheless, this phenomenon is a motivational reality for civil servants, though in the absence of relevant empirical studies, I cannot tell exactly what it implies. All I can say is that politicians today are much more dependent on administrators and experts than ever before and, therefore, the implications of this phenomenon for political leadership are graver than ever before.

During the past ten years, a number of recommendations have been made for reforming the central administration, which, as regards its basic structure, has not changed since 1848. These proposals are usually formulated in terms of the means to achieve greater administrative efficiency; but they also deal, directly or indirectly, with the question of a minister's ability to lead and control his ministry's work.

So far, most discussions have centered on the report of a committee on administration set up in 1960.[21] Its leading idea was that departmental activities ought to be restricted within each minister's personal secretariat by delegating other tasks to subordinate bodies. This would presumably increase the minister's possibilities for playing a controlling and leading role.[22] This idea materialized during the ensuing decade in the reorganization of some ministries. However, the most recent report on reorganization of the central administration is dealing with very much the same problem. The report distinguishes between two main functions of the central administration, "(a) formulating new ideas and points of view, i.e., what could be called legislative and administrative policy, and (b) managing and steering on the basis of determined principles."[23] The report finds that the first function in particular requires the ministers' participation and that ministers often lack sufficient assistance for performing it. Its recommendations basically follow the lines suggested by the former committee.

While some reorganization has taken place, the basic structure of the central administration still has not been affected. Why? One reason sometimes mentioned is that civil servants have resisted changes because one effect might be that many of them would have to move from their departments into lower level directorates, which are supposed to concentrate on routine types of tasks while the new departments take on responsibility of preparing legislation, central planning, and the like.[24] Another explanation goes much farther. E. Koch, for instance, argues that the existing administrative organization has to be understood as a political power structure. To change such a structure is a question not only of administrative efficiency but also of the political goals built into it: "The administrative apparatus is, in fact, a mirror of all the different purposes existing in society."[25] Therefore, any attempt to reorganize it will disturb the actual balance. Here, he is thinking of the connections that link together various ministries and different interests like business, agriculture, and fishery. Some ministries were even established to promote particular interests.[26] Koch also argues that the practice of a civil servant's staying within the same ministry all his life reinforces conflicts among various interests because the civil servant comes to identify with the purpose of his organization. He will never be able to look at a matter from different points of view.

A number of other reform proposals have been made, for example, to broaden the educational basis for recruitment, to establish postentry training programs, or to appoint civil servants for limited terms. Here I only want to mention one proposal which is very old but continues to come up, namely, to place politically appointed secretaries at the top level to assist the minister. Danish politicians and also civil servants apparently think that such positions are not necessary, although they would presumably strengthen ministerial initiative and control. P. Meyer emphasizes another aspect of this problem. After having stated that civil servants are loyal to their ministers, he comments that, in a way, it is remarkable that this is possible since one of the most urgent problems Danish ministers have is to find sufficient assistance in the area where traditional administrative work mixes with "political" work in a narrow sense. Politically appointed secretaries could perform that task. He then writes the following caveat:[27]

> These assistants must of course resign with the government, but positions of this nature are considered a warranty against politicization of the civil service proper. Such positions do not exist in this country; and if they are not created, the civil service cannot very likely maintain its "nonpolitical" character. Danish political parties do not seem to realize that exceedingly important societal values are in jeopardy.

If this diagnosis is correct, then why have none of the civil servants on the most recent administrative reform committee—five out of the seven members—endorsed the idea of introducing politically appointed secretaries?[28]

5. CONCLUSION

Although top civil servants do not publicly engage in politics as they did during the previous century, available evidence suggests that they play a significant role in political decision making. The complexity of modern society and the expanded scope of governmental activity partly explain this; but it is also related to the fact that political leaders have not concerned themselves with ways of strengthening their own positions so as to counter the inertia built up by old administrative structures, civil service recruitment, and career patterns.

If no attempts are made to strengthen political leadership, bureaucratic influence will likely increase in the future. For one thing, there are no signs that the societal developments that have led to bureaucratic influence will come to a halt. A second point that buttresses this argument is the fact that membership in the European Community has added a new dimension to Danish politics and a large number of positions and roles to perform in the central administration. Third, though everybody agrees that planning has become essential in modern times, the odds are that politicians will display reluctance when faced with basic political decisions which are a prerequisite for all planning. But why do politicians hesitate when asked to set priorities about allocating resources? One possible key for understanding this is that even if Danish society is fairly homogeneous as compared to society in several other countries, it is also segmented in a certain sense. Most ministries have well-organized clientele such as farmers, workers, businessmen, students, teachers, or retired people. The overall political function involves making decisions affecting these groups' diverse interests. In carrying out this function, politicians get only a little help from their civil servants because the latter usually identify with a certain section of society or, at least, do not want any trouble with the groups in question. With the possible exceptions of the Ministries of Finance and of Economy, which do not have a particular clientele, the administrative structure is linked to societal sectors. Setting priorities according to given political goals is, under such conditions, close to being impossible;[29] therefore, what we actually find is not rational policy making but "segmented incrementalism" in terms of the allocation of resources and services. But incidentally, perhaps that is how a pluralist democracy really works.

NOTES

1. For a general introduction to Danish politics, consult Kenneth Miller, *Government and Politics in Denmark* (Boston: Houghton-Mifflin, 1968).

2. During the period of constitutional conflict, the government issued provisional laws.

3. *Perspektivplanlaegning 1970-85: Redegorelse fra den af regeringen i november 1968 nedsatte arbejdsgruppe* (Copenhagen, 1971), p. 23.

4. Roger Davidson, "Congress in the American Political System" p. 136 in *Legislatures in Developmental Perspective,* edited by Allan Kornberg and Lloyd Musolf (Durham, N.C.: Duke Univ. Press, 1970).

5. Kai Hammerich, "Systemskiftet i 1848. Overgangen fra kollegium til ministerium," pp. 395-509 in *Den danske Centraladministration* (Copenhagen, 1921).

6. Niels Petersen, "Oversigt over centraladministrationens udvikling siden 1848," pp. 68-80 in *Administrationsudvalget af 1960,* vol. 2, no. 320 (1962).

7. Ibid., p. 61. Also: Poul Meyer, *Offentlig forvaltning* (Copenhagen: Nyt Nordisk Forlag, 1970), pp. 235-242.

8. Efteruddannelse af statens og kommunernes administrative personale, Betaenkning no. 311 (1962): 20-21.

9. According to one top civil servant, a tendency toward greater flexibility in

departmental structure is now developing by the means of frequently regrouping civil servants according to shifting tasks.

10. Poul Meyer, "Die Ausbildung der dänischen Verwaltungsbeamten," Verwaltungs-archiv 55, no. 3 (1964): 196.

11. "Undersogelse af departementernes og udenrigsministeriets personaleopbygning inden for jurist−og okonomonradet," Juristen, 28 (Dec. 1970): 286.

12. For the study from which historical data on ministers is drawn, see Ebba Waaben, "Traek of embedsstandens stilling 1848-1948," p. 130 in Centraladministrationen 1848-1948 (Copenhagen, 1948). In addition, data from Mogens Pedersen, Archives of Danish Politicians (Aarhus: Institute of Political Science, 1972) were kindly made available to the author.

13. These conclusions are drawn on the basis of Mogens Pedersen's data, cf. note 12.

14. While this reasoning is probably valid for most decisions, perhaps it should be qualified to take into account that there are a few significant instances where ministers do not rely on civil servants. A recent example is a draft proposal for "economic democracy."

15. Robert Dahl, Modern Political Analysis (2nd ed.; Englewood Cliffs, N.J.: Prentice-Hall, 1970), pp. 26-28.

16. Waaben, op. cit., pp. 134, 142.

17. Meyer, Offentlig, p. 332.

18. Stig Iuul, Alf Ross and Jorgen Trolle, Indledning til retsstudiet (Copenhagen: Nyt Nordisk Forlag, 1967), p. 55.

19. E. Dige, Politisk Revy (Copenhagen: GEC Gads Forlag, 1964), pp. 31-33.

20. Quotations in the following paragraph come from Erik Schmidt, Offentlig administration og planlaegning (Copenhagen: Gyldendal, 1968), pp. 85-105.

21. Administrationsudvalget af 1960, vol. 1, no. 301 (1962).

22. Cf. Meyer, Offentlig, pp. 62-68.

23. Redegorelse fra arbejdsgruppen verdrorende centraladministrationens organisation, Betaenkning no. 629 (1971), p. 16.

24. Cf. Meyer, Offentlig, p. 64.

25. Eiler Koch, "Modarbejder administrationen Administrationsradets forslag til forenkling af arbejdsgangen?" p. 35 in Notat F, edited by Holger Sorensen (Aarhus: Danmarks Journalisthojskole, n.d.).

26. Cf. Meyer, Offentlig, pp. 235-242.

27. Ibid., p. 332.

28. Redegorelse, p. 20.

29. See the account given by P. Nyboe Andersen, Minister of the Economy from 1968 to 1971, in "Den politiske beslutningsproces," Berlingske Tidende's kronik, (Aug. 17, 1972).

ERIK DAMGAARD is associate professor of political science at the University of Aarhus; he is the author of several studies on Danish legislative politics.

13

Rotation Among Top
Government Officials
in Yugoslavia

RADOMIR LUKIC

The Yugoslavian Constitution provides that certain high civil servants must be appointed for limited periods, normally four years. At the end of their terms, they must relinquish their posts. This is the principle of rotation. Exceptionally, a civil servant may be appointed for a second term on condition that the decision be justified in detail.

Appointed officials to whom the rule of rotation applies are: members of the Executive Council (which assumes the role of government in the British sense), the state secretaries responsible for principal government services, and other important civil servants in charge of other administrative branches. The Constitution allows that laws may enlarge this list to include other positions. Rotation applies to federal civil servants and also to those of the federated republics and autonomous provinces, as well as to some municipal officials and in certain self-managed enterprises or other organizations, in accordance with their respective statutes. Note that this rule also applies to deputies in the legislatures.

In practice, the rule is rather strictly applied. A civil servant is rarely appointed to the same post for a successive term. In spite of certain political and practical difficulties, application is proceeding successfully and appears to be definitively accepted.

The purpose of this rule is evident: the struggle against bureaucracy and for the development of democracy. It is intended to prevent the perpetuation of a man in the same position for such a long time that he finally considers it his own and goes so far as to exercise duties according to his own will and personal interests, no longer taking into account the majority's opinions and interests. The main goal is to prevent the formation of a new "bureaucratic class." Because Yugoslavia is not a multiparty state and there is no alternation between government and opposition, this rotation has to ensure the renewal of political and technical senior government employees. The end sought is a democratic government where high civil servants, chosen from among the workers, are elected or appointed for terms of four years. Then, they return to their former professions, others take their places, and so forth. Therefore, to quote Lenin, "Each one would be a little bureaucratic but no one would really be so."

Rotation raises a very delicate but real problem. In effect, the Revolution and the period during the construction of Socialism caused a large number of politically responsible persons to appear. For twenty and sometimes thirty years, staff members of the Party and other political organizations have never ceased occupying important political positions as well as responsible posts within the state apparatus or in other executive organizations. Having entered the political struggle during their youth, they often lack professional qualifications. They are either former workers who gave up their professions or former students who did not finish their studies. They are professional political figures, often called "political workers." A few of them have completed studies during their political careers. So beginning in 1953, the institution of the rotation system has seriously limited the possibility of furnishing each of them with a position as high as before.

However, their political merits before and after the Revolution, their proven capacity for assuming responsibility, and their long experience made it impossible to keep them out of high offices entirely. Some of them have retired; others have filled less important positions exempt from rotation; however, the greater part have been maintained among high personnel subject to this principle but so as to continue holding important positions. Hence, rotation could not be totally implemented. As a general rule, after four years in a position subject to rotation, an official can move into another position also subject to rotation on condition that the new one is not of the same kind nor at the same level as the preceding one. For instance, after being a member of the Federal Executive Council, he can become a member of the Executive Council of the Republic, then director of a major institution or union leader. Such possibilities simplify the problem but do not solve it entirely. Difficulties persist until resolved by a natural process.

The problem of the relations between high civil servants and politicians in Yugoslavia at the present time arises within this sociopolitical framework. This problem has never been studied in detail; and the lack of precise data, especially statistical, prevents giving an exact explanation. For this reason, I cannot do much more here than to supply certain indications regarding the definition of the terms "high civil servant" and "politician," recruitment of the one and the other, their types of careers, transfer from one category to the other, relations maintained between the two in the fulfillment of their duties, their respective importance, and their foreseeable relations in the future.

1. DEFINITIONS

Let us endeavor to define both statuses, high civil servant and politician. Theoretical and practical definitions can be given. So far, I have used the term "high civil servant" in the sense of a "political figure at a high level"; but I will now avoid prolonging this ambiguity.

From a theoretical approach, a politician is a man having political duties, and a high civil servant, someone exercising important nonpolitical responsibilities, which I shall call "technical." Without attempting to define what are political or important nonpolitical functions, I will only say that behind a political function, we see the exercise of power and the responsibility of defining major objectives to be realized; behind the nonpolitical, we see the implementation (or realization) of these political decisions, which requires scientific knowledge and, consequently, an adequate education. Finally, the term "high office" designates the role filled by a civil servant who, hierarchically, answers directly either to a political decision making body or to another civil servant directly dependent on such a body. To take a concrete example, the Federal Executive Council is a political body. A state secretary directly depends on it; and an assistant secretary is, in turn, directly dependent upon the secretary. According to my definitions, the members of the Executive Council are politicians, but the secretary and his assistants are high civil servants.

Relevant at this point, a special characteristic of the Yugoslavian state apparatus must be noted. In fact, in Yugoslavia, the classical distinction between politicians and high civil servants, according to which a minister is a politician whereas an undersecretary and his immediate associates are high civil servants, is not made. There is, however, a distinction between the Executive Council and the state secretaries. The first is a legislative committee and, consequently, a political body comparable to a classical ministerial cabinet; its members are political figures. The secretaries are responsible for major government services and, accordingly, have to be high civil servants. In the classical system, the minister unites the two positions: member of the government (a political role) and official responsible for a government service (an administrative and, therefore, technical function). This is not so in Yugoslavia where the office of state secretary is more political than administrative or technical. For this reason there is no clear, formal distinction between political and administrative offices and, consequently, between politicians and high civil servants.

Besides, to be taken into account is the fact that, ordinarily, "high civil servant" has a wider meaning than what I have defined. In addition to the government employees already referred to, it includes the directors of important government services other than the state secretaries: members of managerial staffs, councils, and committees, ambassadors, and the like.

From a practical viewpoint, a politician is defined as someone having a "political" profession, whether he holds positions on decision making bodies within the governmental system, is an official in the Party or in other organizations, or is without any definite position. Generally, the politician has no professional (technical) training; or if he has, he does not practice his profession. On the contrary, a high civil servant has a qualified profession, which has necessitated professional training. If he becomes a government employee, he does so precisely in order to follow his profession. Whether doctor, lawyer, or economist, he is at the head of a branch where he uses his education.

What often happens is that persons I have formally described as high civil servants become politicians in practice and, conversely, that some offices which from a theoretical point of view have a mixed composition (both political and technical) are, for the most part, filled by political personalities. As a general rule, correspondence between the theoretical and practical definitions is becoming more complete than just after the Revolution.

Note that, in Yugoslavia, the number of political or high civil service positions occupied by politicians is decreasing because of the development of the system of social and worker "self-management" *(autogestion)*. This is so not only because there is the desire to democratize but also because concrete measures are being taken in order to transform many offices occupied by politicians and high civil servants into collective bodies made up of citizens interested in the function the group is performing. These persons are neither politicians nor civil servants. They are elected for short terms and, what is more important, they continue their own professions during their service. These collective bodies consist of councils, committees, and the like, which replace the former ministers, state secretaries, directors, and other individual officeholders. At the very most, there is an administrator, who is an instrument of technical implementation. Considering him to be a high civil servant is impossible. In any event, his duties are not as important as those of the former officeholder.

2. RECRUITMENT

In practice, how does someone become a politician in Yugoslavia? In a certain sense, the question has no purpose. Yugoslavian development, based on reasons of an ideological and political nature and reinforced by politico-juridicial measures, tends to eliminate "bureaucratization." This also means the elimination of professional politicians and "political workers." This tendency is only another aspect of the attempt to put an end to politics as a distinct calling apart from the daily and professional activities of working people, whether manual or intellectual. This tends toward the elimination of politics considered as a special, alienating, and dominating profession. Entirely democratic with its self-managerial socialism, the ideal society must, at the same time, cause the dwindling away of the state, laws, political parties, and politics itself as a separate activity; and it must lead to the politicization of society as a whole. This necessarily implies the elimination of professional politicians.

Of course, Yugoslavia is still far from this ideal. Foreseeing exactly what the future has in store is very difficult; but within the restricted field which interests us here—the recruitment of politicians—significant changes have taken place. To begin with, the number of professional politicians in the younger generations has actually decreased. Over the past fifteen years, politics has ceased to be one of the most desired professions. Brilliant individuals prefer orienting themselves toward technical rather than political careers, and present political trends favor this tendency.

Remaining from the first period, which favored specialization in political professions, were a number of schools and other more or less official institutions with access to political offices. These schools and institutions no longer exist. The professional politician is now recruited through the political process itself. Youth organizations of the Party (Communist League), unions, or other more or less political organizations are major sources of recruitment for politicians. In these organizations, there exists a certain number of positions requiring more or less professional political work although considerable effort is being made to reduce this number to insignificance. The youths who have done such work later become professional politicians. However, recent observations verify that few young people aspire to political careers. On the contrary, they are acquiring technical training parallel to political work. This does not mean that some of them will not become professional politicians; but the number is decreasing.

As for high civil servants, they are recruited in two ways. For certain positions, political criteria decide selection on condition, of course, that candidates have necessary technical training. In such instances, advancement can be rapid. This is especially true for positions of a more or less mixed nature. But for offices at a relatively lower level (but which are the highest within the organizations where they are found like communes, worker organizations, or social services), a political criterion is also the most important. In both cases, the political factor is so very important that a high civil service office may be confided to someone who, from the technical viewpoint, is less qualified but who has political qualities. The second method of recruitment is principally on the basis of technical qualifications evidenced by university diplomas or previous work. The number thus recruited continues to increase.

As to the form of recruitment for political positions, it takes place through direct election or through appointment by assemblies or other representatives, as happens in other countries. What is distinctive in Yugoslavia is that, for high offices, increasing use is made of appointment by legislatures for governmental positions or of election by the personnel or other representative bodies in accordance with self-managerial principles for directorships in producer organizations. To this degree, political and technical functions are coming closer together.

3. TYPES OF CAREERS

Politicians have different types of careers, chiefly depending upon the moment when they started. If a politician started his career before or during the Revolution, it involved clandestine work in Party organizations. Flight from the police, imprisonment, or emigration mark such a career which often included military duties during and immediately after the revolutionary war. Then returning to civilian life, such a man consecutively held a great number of different positions, more or less political, while progressing from the lowest to the highest. He maintained this level for some time, then, with approaching old age and the appearance of the rotation system, began redescending the hierarchy. If he proved to be incompetent or was not considered safe on the ideological plane, he descended more quickly. This descent generally meant the acquisition of a post which, all the while guaranteeing social prestige, required neither work nor important abilities, especially an ambassadorship, for example.

In 1963, a special institution was created: the Council of the Federation, which has practically no function. Its role defined by the Constitution is to discuss the country's principal problems. The President of the Republic recruits its members by notification, but it has never been convened. Membership in this Council guarantees considerable social and political prestige, and many politicians no longer holding office become members. Then come retirement and, from time to time, a job as representative in some institution of a social nature or some work during important demonstrations. Only a small number among them still hold high positions.

At present, the generation of politicians trained after the Revolution is at the peak of its activity. Whether their careers will have the same possibility for "organic" development as the former generation's is difficult to foresee.

However, the most recent generation, which is just entering political life, has a very different career from the two preceding ones. This generation contains few "pure" professional politicians. They have another profession and are, at the same time, busy with politics. Accordingly, they have followed and are still following another trade, more or less regularly, aside from their political activities. Thus, they are closer to the type of political civil servant who is not a professional politician and who must realize the ideal of democratization of society within self-managerial structures.

As for high civil servants' careers, there is little to be said. Two groups must be distinguished. In one, political reasons at first motivate access to higher offices, and careers are generally rapid. In the other, professional and technical motivations dominate, and careers are often slower and steadier.

4. TRANSFERS

The transferring of politicians into high civil service positions and vice versa is fairly frequent, although no precise figures are available. Generally speaking, the direction of such transfers differs according to the period. The first one, after the Revolution, mostly saw an intensive transfer of political figures into high civil service offices but into ones that are also highly politicized. On the contrary, in the second period, especially during the past ten years, the tendency has been to transfer high civil servants into political positions.

The first period is easily understood. The new government could hardly have confidence in senior civil servants inherited from the old regime. It wanted to replace them with people it could trust. It had very few sufficiently qualified persons at its disposal. Thus, it was forced to choose politicians who were more or less apt for this kind of work. Besides, this process had already begun during the Revolution with the first efforts toward the organization of a revolutionary government and had continued after the seizure of power. Having already proven themselves, these staffs were, to a certain degree, capable of filling these new positions. Naturally, the police and army felt the greatest need. There, new men coming from the Party had to replace nearly all personnel, not only civil servants. These men has been trained either before or during the war. During this period, a correct political ideology was more important for a high government position than was professional and technical training. Hence, top civil servants and their offices were highly politicized. Former senior civil servants were maintained, at best, as counselors.

Of course, these new government officials had a lot of difficulty successfully accomplishing their missions. Certain of them adapted more or less well to their new duties; later, they even acquired the formal qualifications required and made themselves careers as senior civil servants. This happened mostly in the army and police and in the areas of foreign policy and economy. In other fields where former top officials had been maintained in greater numbers and where, besides, new technical staffs were promoted quickly, such cases were less frequent. Some politicians appointed as high civil servants did not feel satisfied by their vocations and considered their new jobs as provisional; they wished to return as fast as possible to their former political duties, a choice turning out well for most of them. In the meantime, new technical staffs trained in Socialism and trusted accordingly acceded to important posts, and the problem was solved.

But there has recently been a new wave of politicians transferring into high civil service positions. This was provoked by the policy of eliminating professional politicians in the fight against bureaucracy.

Many political figures, especially those who have not been entirely successful in their political careers but who have, meanwhile, acquired technical qualifications, have taken over civil service positions in their respective branches. The result is that these positions are much less politicized than before to the degree that the former politicians now occupying them value appearing, as much as possible, like well-informed technicians.

I have said a parallel but inverse movement of high civil servants toward political posts is even stronger. This is the consequence of the combination of several factors: the aging of the former generation of professional politicians; the tendency to fight against bureaucratization by politicians; the endeavor to promote self-management, democratization, and worker participation in the exercise of power; and above all, a very strong trend toward applying scientific principles to politics, avoiding arbitrariness and subjectivity, and basing political decisions on reliable scientific data. Increasingly, men distinguished in their positions as civil servants or as experts—heads of enterprises, university professors, researchers in scientific institutes—have been promoted to places formerly occupied by professional politicians. These "new men" either continue to practice their usual professions while performing temporary public service, or interrupt their professions for the length of their political appointments but return as soon as their terms end.

This means that, although passage from high civil service to political positions remains a reality, there is, in the strict sense, no real transfer from the first category to the second so as to become a professional politician. Only a small number of high civil servants and other experts definitely commit themselves to political careers. The disappearance of professional politicians is so striking that the large majority of legislators no longer belong to this category.

The trend toward rotation, politicization of society, and elimination of professional politicians has even had the effect of causing political offices to lose some of their prestige, so that high civil servants and experts no longer want to serve in them. They think that, by accepting them, they limit their chances for developing technical skills and endanger their professional careers. What happens is that, after the end of their terms, they have difficulty returning to former positions or finding others that suit them. In the eyes of public opinion, the prestige attached to political offices has considerably diminished—a good expert is beginning to be considered of more worth than a politician.

On the other hand, experts and professionals have often greeted the new wave of politicians transferring to high civil service positions with more or less overt reluctance. They view it as undesirable competition.

5. INTERRELATIONS

The relations between politicians and high civil servants in the performance of their duties are of different kinds, depending on a great number of factors. To simplify to the extreme, we can also distinguish here two principal periods which confirm what has already been said: first, the postrevolutionary period of administrative Socialism (or state bureaucracy) and, second, the period of self-managerial Socialism (or democracy).

In general, during the first period, politicians greatly dominated experts and high government employees. Politicians declared themselves competent for deciding not only political matters, which were their proper domain, but also technical questions, which evidently belonged to the areas of competence of experts and high civil servants. Frequently, the politicians decided against the experts' opinions in such matters. Also, very often, some experts or high civil servants did not have the courage to openly voice their opinions when they were contrary to the politicians', thus deluding the latter into thinking that their own judgments were sound.

In the second period, public opinion raised up against such a conception of power. With democratization, public opinion started thinking that one of the most important means for exercising power was trust in science, experts, and scientific studies. This could only reinforce the position of senior civil servants considered as the experts nearest to power and to politicians. Politicians began according much more esteem to the opinions expressed by high civil servants, researchers, and experts in general. On the part of politicians, a certain lack of will in the exercise of power was even noticeable. They were waiting for the experts to settle matters which were clearly political. Thus, the influence of senior civil servants, especially with the backing of experts or of scientific analyses, became predominant. After the arbitrary exercise of power by political personalities, a new danger was beginning to be felt: technocracy. This trend was reinforced, as already pointed out, by the fact that eminent experts, who neither were nor wished to become either political figures in practice or professional politicians, held more and more positions of a mixed, political-technical, nature and even purely political offices.

Naturally, neither one extreme nor the other is desirable. The very fact they existed does not mean the situation was so very bad. On the contrary, most of the time—and during whatever period considered—the relations between politicians in power and high civil servants responsible for the implementation of political decisions were, roughly speaking, what they should have been, with each partner sticking to his own field of competence and loyally cooperating with the other.

6. CONCLUSION

From what has been said concerning the relations between politicians and high civil servants in the performance of their respective duties, we may now reach some conclusions concerning their importance in the state and society. Without a doubt, high civil servants played a lesser role during the first period and assumed more importance during the second. However (if I may hazard this kind of extreme generalization) the overall style of work of Yugoslavian politicians and of their relations with technical counselors and high civil servants is far from that of certain ministers in the Third and Fourth French Republics.

Political figures in Yugoslavia conceive of their duties as the actual exercise of the state's power, and they make their own decisions. Accordingly, even during the second period of Socialism, in spite of certain fears some politicians may have felt about exercising power too directly or too arbitrarily and in spite of their tendency to trust civil servants and experts more than before, real power hardly ever left their hands.

The future is very difficult to foresee. It depends upon the general evolution of the Yugoslavian state and society, also upon progress in self-management. If this system develops and grows even stronger, a progressive reduction of the classical "pure" political factor and, consequently, of the power held by politicians (by professional politicians in the strict sense) is foreseeable at the same time as a strengthening of the role of average citizens participating in self-management, in particular of workers. However, even in such a case, the future of high civil servants is not very clear. Nothing certain can be said about whether their importance will increase all the more. This new tendency opposes hierarchy in general as much as "offices" and "office people," even if they are not bureaucrats. The role of the politician, as well as that of the senior civil servant, will likely be reduced in favor of collective representative bodies made up of workers who will stick to their professions and, especially, in favor of technical and scientific counselors who, from a formal viewpoint, will not be civil servants but will continue working in universities, research institutes, and the like.

RADOMIR LUKIC is professor of sociology at the University of Belgrade and general secretary of the Serbian Academy of Sciences and Arts. He is the author of *Théorie de l'Etat et du Droit*.

14

The Functional Equivalents of
Top Civil Servants in the
Socialist State: The Polish Case

JERZY WIATR

One of the characteristics of the socialist political system is that it lacks a distinction between politicians and top civil servants in the strict sense of the word.[1] This is due to the following tendencies in the development of the socialist polity:

(1) In the early days of the formation of socialist states, high ranking members of the Communist and allied parties, Socialist, Populist, Democratic, and so on, were appointed to top positions in the administration, armed forces, diplomatic service, and economic managerial hierarchies. Originally, they shared these positions with prerevolutionary civil servants whose proportion and influence declined with the passing of time.[2] From the beginning, however, top positions in all these fields were considered basically political. This sort of thinking was reflected in the fact that even when a nonpolitical civil servant held one of these positions, a political deputy with very broad prerogatives usually assisted him.

(2) The expansion of the state administration and the nationalization of large sectors of the economy led to the mass recruitment of new personnel for top and middle level positions of authority. This expansion was undertaken by direct recruitment of politically trusted workers (for instance, twenty thousand had been appointed managers in Polish industry by 1949) and by educating people for professional careers in one of the above listed fields. Neither the first nor the second type of recruit was expected to become a nonpolitical administrator. On the contrary, political involvement was an important requirement. Although writers were sometimes appointed as

ambassadors, or nonpolitical engineers as managers of large enterprises, these exceptions did not affect the overall pattern.

(3) Top administrators, military officers, diplomats, and the like, even if nonpolitical at the time of their appointments, tended to commit themselves politically, if not for personal reasons then because of a desire to be able to participate in key stages of decision making. Consequently, the category of top civil servants in the strict sense of the word was even further reduced in number.

Moreover, the political ideology of the socialist system did not favor the existence of professional civil servants as a separate category. Direction of the state, considered as a powerful instrument of social transformation, stayed in the hands of the Communist Party. No reason whatsoever remained for keeping the politically neutral professional apparatus of the former regime. At the lower levels, nonpolitical personnel have been accepted for carrying out decisions made above; however, at the top, political leaders rather than nonpolitical administrators were required.

These three tendencies mark the universal character of all socialist systems. What R. Lukic refers to as a "special characteristic of the Yugoslavian state apparatus" seems to me to be an attribute common to all socialist states of our age.[3] In short, the socialist state has abolished the civil service as a separate institution (i.e., separate from government) or has not allowed it to develop when it had not existed before the Revolution.

However, this is not the end of the matter. Having said that the socialist political system has abolished the civil service as a separate institution, I must now ask whether it has created a functional equivalent. To put it differently, does the Polish system differentiate between political and nonpolitical functions at top levels of decision making?

1. DEFINITIONS

To reply, I must first of all examine two conceptual questions. First, what can we consider as "top levels" of decision making? Second, how can we differentiate between political and nonpolitical roles in top positions within the government?

An arbitrary decision concerning definition can answer the first question. "Top level" will be defined very broadly so as to include not only the nucleus of senior decision makers, such as members of the Political Bureau, Secretariat of the Central Committee of the Polish United Workers' Party (PUWP), and Presidium of the Council of Ministers, but also: (a) all cabinet ministers, their assistants, and the secretaries-general of the ministries; (b) generals and admirals in the armed forces; (c) ambassadors; (d) chairmen of the presidiums in the voivodships (i.e., provincial and local councils) and heads of provincial administrations; (e) bank presidents, directors on the boards of industries or of other selected economic institutions; (f) presidents or directors of central offices, such as the Statistical or Geological Offices, and their assistants. This relatively large group of top decision makers more or less covers the whole field of functional equivalents to the traditional civil service. The people listed above perform functions that top civil servants perform in the West. The empirical question to investigate is whether and to what extent these top decision makers in the socialist system are politicians.

This brings me to the second conceptual question: What do I have in mind when I distinguish political and nonpolitical roles? First of all, formalistic criteria must be rejected. Membership in the Polish Communist Party (the PUWP) or one of its allied parties such as the United Peasants' Party (UPP) or the Democratic Party (DP), does not by itself prove that a decision maker fills a political role. Most senior decision makers are members of a political party; and party membership is essential for promotion to most of the above listed jobs, albeit not absolutely necessary. Neither does the fact that a person is a legislator prove that he is a politician. Quite a few Polish parliamentarians have distinguished themselves in one or another field of activity, as workers, farmers, university professors, medical doctors, engineers, and the like; and top decision makers can be elected for the same reason. On the other hand, those who do play a political role do not always serve in the legislature.

In order to establish criteria possessing sufficient discriminatory power, I suggest the following two: (a) membership on the central committee of the Communist Party or one of the allied parties; (b) rotation between various top positions of a very different nature. A man who serves as a cabinet minister in charge of one branch of the economy, moves to an ambassadorship, and later becomes chairman of a voivodship is more likely to be a politician than someone who headed the same ministry for ten or fifteen years. Moreover, the second criterion is subordinate to the first. If a person has the same position for a long period of time and serves on the central committee of his party, more likely than not, he is a political rather than a nonpolitical administrator. Also, if a person who does not belong to a central committee frequently changes positions but does not move out of the top decision making category, he likely holds his job by virtue of his being a politician.

Thus, I have constructed an operational definition of nonpolitical decision makers who are the functional equivalents of top civil servants in the West. In addition to this operational definition, I may also try to define politicians and nonpolitical administrators in substantial terms. A top decision maker can be considered a politician if, in addition to directing his sector within the state apparatus, he systematically participates in determining governmental policy. Those whose responsibilities do not include such participation or who participate only sporadically should be considered nonpolitical administrators. By the logic of these definitions, top decision makers line up on a continuum between the poles of purely political and purely administrative. They do not form two pure categories because most of them occupy various places between the poles.

2. ADMINISTRATION AND POLITICIZATION IN THE COUNCIL OF MINISTERS

The composition of the Council of Ministers from the election of the first postwar Diet (the Polish parliament) to early 1971 is given in Table 1.[4] These data suggest two things. First, at two stages of the historical period under consideration, in the mid-fifties and again in the early seventies, the proportion of cabinet ministers who were not Diet members rapidly increased. In each period, the change corresponded to major shifts in PUWP leadership and in governmental policy. Second, the average age of the ministers has remained almost the same since the mid-fifties. This fact points to considerable rotation in office. Concerning the extent of this rotation, I can refer to some additional figures. Most members of the Council left the government during its term, or at least changed portfolios. The numbers who left or who changed positions in each of the six periods are, respectively: 11 and 14 out of 24; 22 and 29 out of 39; 10 and 13 out of 30; 6 and 7 out of 33; 16 and 19 out of 33; 12 and 15 out of 32.

The rotation of cabinet ministers reveals an interesting pattern. Such rotation was particularly strong when the country underwent

TABLE 1

COMPOSITION OF THE COUNCIL OF MINISTERS (First Postwar Diet to 1971)

Diet	Dates	Number of Members of the Council of Ministers	Cabinet Ministers, Members of:				Members of Parliament		Average Age
			Polish United Workers Party	United Peasant Party	Democratic Party	No Party	Number	Percent	
Constituent Diet	Feb. 8, 1947	24^a	12^b	6	3	1	23	96	48.0
	Nov. 19, 1952	45	37	7	1	–	36	80	47.6
First Term	Nov. 21, 1952	39	36	3	–	–	34	87	46.7
	Feb. 19, 1957	34	28	2	2	2	15	44	50.2
Second Term	Feb. 27, 1957	30	23	3	2	2	15	50	50.6
	May 14, 1961	34	28	3	1	2	19	56	52.6
Third Term	May 18, 1961	33	28	3	1	1	18	55	52.2
	June 23, 1965	33	28	3	2	–	17	52	54.0
Fourth Term	June 25, 1965	33	28	3	2	–	17	52	54.3
	June 26, 1969	31	25	3	2	1	13	42	52.8
Fifth Term	June 28, 1969	32	26	3	2	1	13	41	51.7
	Feb. 13, 1971^c	32	27	3	1	1	11	34	51.5

a. The Council included two members of the Labor party, dissolved in 1950.

b. Seven members of the Polish Socialist party and 5 members of the Polish Workers party. The two parties merged in 1948.

c. After changes in the composition of the Council following the political upheaval of December 1970. The Diet of the fifth term dissolved itself in early 1972.

political crises but weak during periods of stabilization. Two critical points mark the terms from 1947 to 1952 and 1952 to 1957: around 1948, the purge of Gomulkaists; and in 1956, the "October changes." Furthermore, the March 1968 student demonstrations effected considerable changes in the composition of the top decision making stratus as did the workers' upheaval in December 1970. On the other hand, general political stability and an extraordinary lack of major domestic problems characterize the periods 1957-1961 and particularly 1961-1965. The rotation of cabinet ministers and other top decision makers in Poland has sprung from political motivation. In this sense, it differs from the "rotation by principle" institutionalized in the Yugoslavian Constitution. The question is not how many top decision makers change jobs but why they do so. "Political" rotation does not exclude long-term specialization in a single sphere of governmental activity, providing, of course, that the person remains within the top decision making category.

Let us now examine changes in the composition of the Council of Ministers from the point of view of party positions held by its members. Of the 24 members of the Council appointed in February 1947, 11 held top posts in their political parties (presidents, vice-presidents, secretaries-general, political bureau members) and 12 others were members of their parties' highest organizations (central committees, general councils, etc.). The only nonparty minister was the Minister of National Defense, Marshal Michal Zymierski. Among the 39 cabinet ministers in 1952, 12 also held party leadership positions, 25 others were members of parliament or a central committee, and only two were members neither of a central committee nor of parliament. In 1957, among the 30 members of the government, only 7 were in top party leadership positions. Among the 33 ministers in 1961, only 6 were top party leaders; in 1965, the number increased to 11. However, in 1969, among the 32 ministers, there were only 7 in top party leadership positions. The increase in 1965 came from changes in the composition of the PUWP's Political Bureau, changes resulting in short-term promotion for some government members. Generally speaking, I may conclude that the proportion of party leaders among members of the government has decreased. What is most visible is the increase in the proportion of ministers who are members neither of a central committee nor of the legislature and who can therefore be considered nonpolitical administrators. In 1969, 10 ministers belonged to this category; they were in charge of economic ministries. In addition, a nonparty expert headed the Ministry of Public Health.

To conclude this part of the analysis, I should like to formulate the following hypothesis. With the passing of time, the Polish cabinet has changed in the direction of increased participation for non-political administrators. However, the decrease in the number of top party leaders holding governmental positions has not meant that nonpolitical administrators are a majority. The largest category among the ministers is composed of people who hold high but not the highest positions in their parties or who serve in parliament. Among these, some may be classified as more, some as less, political; but they do not closely correspond to the concept of nonpolitical administrator.

The picture changes when we look at the problem from a longitudinal perspective. People do not form two closed groups, political and nonpolitical. With very few exceptions, members of government who did not belong to a central committee at the time of their first promotion to the ministerial level were eventually promoted onto such a committee. Also, members of party leadership circles, that is, the political bureaus, were partly recruited from among cabinet members. All this points to the relative nature of the distinction between politicians and nonpolitical decision makers in Poland.

I have based this conclusion on data about cabinet members for whom more information is available than for other categories of high decision makers. But the pattern is a general one. Among ambassadors, generals, local administrative heads, and economic managers, we find that those who, because of professional achievements combined with political activities, move up politically, are also elected to their party's central committee, the Diet, and the like. We also find those who remain basically nonpolitical specialists, even if most of them are party members and do participate in party activities at the lower level. Finally, there is the category of top decision makers who fall below the level of top political leaders but nonetheless occupy high positions. Former members of the PUWP's Political Bureau often serve as ambassadors, ministers, deputy ministers, or directors-general, in which case they are no longer politicians in the strict sense of the word but yet they do not necessarily possess the qualifications indispensable for nonpolitical administrators. With the frontiers between these three groups being so unclear, the political-nonpolitical dichotomy is only an approximation to ideal types.

3. SOCIAL CHARACTERISTICS

An empirical question of considerable interest is how far these top decision makers differ in terms of their social characteristics as related to their political or nonpolitical roles. The data at my disposal do not allow a detailed analysis of differences or similarities. R. Farrell has pointed out differences in formal education and length of service in international relations among senior foreign policy personnel in Polish party and state organs; but he has used a very limited number of cases.[5]

On the basis of nonsystematic observation, I will make three hypotheses. First, the younger the decision makers, the greater the similarities of their educational backgrounds regardless of the nature of their decision making roles. Top decision makers in Poland's younger generation, people in their early forties or late thirties, educated after World War II, have received a university or equivalent education. Among the older generation, there are people who, promoted to responsible positions because of their political past, lack formal university education. This category is disappearing fast.

Second, professional work in the party, rather than party membership alone, is the key factor explaining promotion to the top decision making category. Those who enter this category from outside the professional party apparatus are usually very highly experienced specialists in their fields and could therefore be classified as nonpolitical administrators. However, there are exceptions to this rule. The most obvious is the military where people advance within the services without necessarily becoming nonpolitical administrators.

Third, the homogeneity of the top decision making category, in terms of education, recruitment through party organizations, and to some extent, upward social mobility from a worker-peasant background, tends to reduce the relevance of the distinction between political and nonpolitical roles. To a certain extent, this distinction, perceived as functional specialization between various categories of decision makers, does not call for basis differences in professional perspectives. However, not to be completely excluded is the possibility that, with the passing of time, political and nonpolitical roles will differentiate further.[6]

4. THE FUTURE

The future will probably produce two different tendencies. First, political mobilization and recruitment to positions of responsibility in various fields of political and economic life will produce greater differentiation of skills and professional orientations. This may eventually lead to a sharpening of the political-nonpolitical dichotomy and probably to an increase in the role of nonpolitical specialists. Second, the extension of public participation and of socialist democracy will further politicize decision making. The socialist system, like all political systems of our time, will have to find a workable balance in decision making processes at the top level. Neither total subordination of these processes to the demands of politics nor their complete "technocratization" should serve as a model. As in most governmental problems, the only viable solution will be one based on compromise. Political science may try to anticipate this solution. This calls for systematic research in a field which, till now, has been almost completely neglected.

NOTES

1. The present essay is based on observations and material accumulated during ten years of research on the Polish political system, research conducted by the Institute of Philosophy and Sociology, Polish Academy of Sciences (prior to 1968, by its Department of Political Sociology and later by its Department on the Theory of the Socialist Society); however, no part of this research addressed itself directly to the problem of top civil servants. Jerzy Wiatr and Krzysztof Ostrowski have presented some general findings in "Political Leadership: What Kind of Professionalism?" pp. 140-145 in *Studies in the Polish Political System*, edited by Jerzy Wiatr (Wroclaw: Ossolineum, 1967).

2. In Poland, in 1949 for instance, 18% of all military officers were prewar professionals. On the transformation of the professional military corps in Poland, see Jerzy Wiatr, "Military Professionalism and Transformations of Class Structures in Poland," pp. 229-239 in *Armed Forces and Society*, edited by Jacques van Doorn (Hauge-Paris: Mouton, 1968). Also, Jozef Graczyk, "Social Promotion in the Polish People's Army," pp. 82-93 in *Military Profession and Military Regimes*, edited by Jacques van Doorn (Hague-Paris: Mouton, 1969).

3. Radomir Lukic in chapter 13 of the present volume.

4. All data on Polish ministers are taken from Tadeusz Moldawa, *Composition of the Personnel in the Highest State Organs of People's Poland* (Univ. of Warsaw Press, 1971).

5. R. Barry Farrell, "Top Political Leadership in Eastern Europe," pp. 102-103 in *Political Leadership in Eastern Europe and the Soviet Union*, edited by the same (Chicago, 1970).

6. Repeated warnings against "technocratism" have been voiced by the Polish press and in public discussions. These warnings seem to indicate a genuine concern with the possibility that the differentiation between political and nonpolitical functions may result in the undue

concentration of power in the hands of "experts," thus sacrificing the interests of the masses.

JERZY WIATR, professor of sociology at the University of Warsaw, is past-president of the Polish Association of Political Science and chairman of the Committee on Local Government and Politics, International Political Science Association.